OPPOSITION BEYOND
THE WATER'S EDGE

Recent Titles in
Contributions to the Study of World History

The Playboy King: Carol II of Romania
Paul D. Quinlan

Liberalism and Social Reform: Industrial Growth and Progressiste
Politics in France, 1880–1914
David M. Gordon

British Monarchy, English Church Establishment, and Civil Liberty
John A. Taylor

Prophecy of Berchán: Irish and Scottish High-Kings of the Early
Middle Ages
Benjamin T. Hudson

Assimilation and Acculturation in Seventeenth-Century Europe:
Roussillon and France, 1659–1715
David Stewart

Town Origins and Development in Early England, c. 400–950 A.D.
Daniel G. Russo

The Identity of Geneva: The Christian Commonwealth, 1564–1864
John B. Roney and Martin I. Klauber, editors

Losing a Continent: France's North American Policy, 1753–1763
Frank W. Brecher

"Gone Native" in Polynesia: Captivity Narratives and Experiences
from the South Pacific
I. C. Campbell

The Jacobean Union: A Reconsideration of British Civil Policies
under the Early Stuarts
Andrew D. Nicholls

Ireland's Children: Quality of Life, Stress, and Child
Development in the Famine Era
Thomas E. Jordan

In Search of Woodrow Wilson: Beliefs and Behavior
Robert M. Saunders

Opposition Beyond the Water's Edge

Liberal Internationalists, Pacifists and Containment, 1945–1953

E. Timothy Smith

Contributions to the Study of World History, Number 67

GREENWOOD PRESS
Westport, Connecticut • London

Library of Congress Cataloging-in-Publication Data

Smith, E. Timothy.
    Opposition beyond the water's edge : liberal internationalists,
pacifists and containment, 1945–1953 / E. Timothy Smith.
        p.   cm. — (Contributions to the study of world history, ISSN
0885–9159 ; no. 67)
    Includes bibliographical references and index.
    ISBN 0–313–30777–6 (alk. paper)
    1. Peace movements—United States—History—20th century.
2. Internationalists—United States—History—20th century.
3. Pacifists—United States—History—20th century.   4. United
States—Foreign relations—1945–1953.   I. Title.   II. Series.
JZ5584.U6S63   1999
327.1'72—dc21   98–47748

British Library Cataloguing in Publication Data is available.

Library of Congress Catalog Card Number: 98–47748
ISBN: 0–313–30777–6
ISSN: 0885–9159

First published in 1999

Greenwood Press, 88 Post Road West, Westport, CT 06881
An imprint of Greenwood Publishing Group, Inc.
www.greenwood.com

Printed in the United States of America

The paper used in this book complies with the
Permanent Paper Standard issued by the National
Information Standards Organization (Z39.48–1984).

10 9 8 7 6 5 4 3 2 1

Copyright Acknowledgments

The author and publisher gratefully acknowledge permission for use of the following
material:

Extracts from E. Timothy Smith, "Beyond the Water's Edge," in *The Romance of History:
Essays in Honor of Lawrence S. Kaplan*, edited by Scott L. Bills and E. Timothy Smith (Kent,
OH: Kent State University Press, 1997). With permission of The Kent State University Press.

Every reasonable effort has been made to trace the owners of copyright materials in this
book, but in some instances this has proven impossible. The author and publisher will be
glad to receive information leading to more complete acknowledgments in subsequent
printings of the book and in the meantime extend their apologies for any omissions.

In Memory of Emory C. Smith

CONTENTS

A photo essay follows page 81

ACKNOWLEDGMENTS

The historian is dependent on assistance from many others in research-
ing and writing any book. Among the most important are the librarians
and the archivists who assist in obtaining the materials needed to complete a manuscript. Hugh Ripley and the staff of the Barry University
Library, especially those who have worked in the interlibrary loan department, have my greatest appreciation. The archivists at the Swarthmore College Peace Collection in Swarthmore, Pennsylvania; the
Archives of the Mennonite Church in Goshen, Indiana; the Harry S. Truman Library in Independence, Missouri; the John F. Kennedy Library in
Boston, Massachusetts; the University of Iowa in Iowa City, Iowa; and
the Mary McLeod Bethune Council House in Washington, DC were of
invaluable assistance in gaining access to the materials and photographs
used in this book. In particular, I would like to thank Wendy Chmie-
lewski, curator of the Swarthmore College Peace Collection, Pauline Tes-
terman, audiovisual archivist at the Truman library, and Leonard Gross
and Dennis Stoesz at the Mennonite Archives, for their assistance. One
must have time and financial support to do the necessary research. For
that I would like to thank the Grants, Leaves and Sabbatical Committee
of the Barry University Faculty Senate through which I received a sabbatical and a minigrant that enabled me to do much of the research for
this book.

   Special thanks must be given to friends, colleagues, and scholars who have provided encouragement and assistance in the completion of this manuscript. Scott Bills, Lynne Dunn, Lawrence Kaplan, Ellen Stahl, and Lawrence Wittner read and commented on the manuscript at various stages. Gary, Margaret, and Franny Grizzle and Judi, Jennifer, and Daniel Smith all offered support and encouragement at various times through the completion of this project. Heather Ruland Staines, Elizabeth Meagher, and Diane Burke at Greenwood Press have provided me with excellent advice in the preparation of the manuscript. Kenny Hite at Barry University supplied valuable secretarial assistance.

I wish to thank John Hubbell, director of The Kent State University Press, for permission to use certain previously published materials. Portions of my chapter "Beyond the Water's Edge," from *The Romance of History: Essays in Honor of Lawrence S. Kaplan*, edited by Scott Bills and E. Timothy Smith (1997) have been used in this book with permission of The Kent State University Press. I would also like to acknowledge the University of Iowa Library, the Harry S. Truman Library, the Swarthmore College Peace Collection, the Mary McLeod Bethune Council House National Historic Site, and the Claude Pepper Library, Florida State University Libraries in Tallahassee, Florida, for their permissions to use the photographs reprinted in this book.

I dedicate this book to the memory of my father, Emory C. Smith, who was a dedicated pacifist, a conscientious objector to war, and eulogized as a lover of peace.

ABBREVIATIONS

AAUN	American Association for the United Nations
ADA	Americans for Democratic Action
AFSC	American Friends Service Committee
APC	American Peace Crusade
AVC	American Veterans' Committee
AWP	American Women for Peace
CAA	Council on African Affairs
CAW	Congress of American Women
CIO	Congress of Industrial Organizations
CPA	Committee for Peaceful Alternatives
ERP	European Recovery Program
FCNL	Friends Committee on National Legislation
FOR	Fellowship of Reconciliation
LWV	League of Women Voters
MDAP	Mutual Defense Assistance Program
NAACP	National Association for the Advancement of Colored People
NAT	North Atlantic Treaty
NATO	North Atlantic Treaty Organization
NCPW	National Council for Prevention of War

NSC	National Security Council
PCA	Progressive Citizens of America
PWWC	Post War World Council
SDS	Students for a Democratic Society
UMT	Universal Military Training
UN	United Nations
UWF	United World Federalists
WILPF	Women's International League for Peace and Freedom
WRL	War Resisters League

INTRODUCTION

With the announcement of the Truman Doctrine in March 1947, U.S. foreign policy actively aimed at stopping any expansion by the Soviet Union. Assuming that the Soviet Union sought the establishment of a communist world order, American leadership rallied public opinion behind a confrontational policy toward the Soviets. Until the development of opposition to the Vietnam War, this policy met with little dissent from the public, from within the government, or from within the Democratic or Republican parties. Despite the fact that "playing politics with foreign policy is an American game as old as the Republic," the view that politics stopped "at the water's edge" became an article of faith in the post–World War II era.[1] Republican Sen. Arthur H. Vandenberg of Michigan, noted for his cooperation in foreign policy with the Democratic administration of Harry S. Truman, was fond of referring to the water's edge as a place where politics stopped. In the postwar era, his name, more than any other, was associated with the emergence of a bipartisan foreign policy. The senator felt that there should be a two-party collaboration "in order to achieve a nonpartisan approach to foreign policy." Vandenberg insisted that bipartisanship meant "that argumentation look to national security rather than to partisan advantage." The president agreed with the nonpartisan approach. In accepting the Democratic nomination for president on July 15, 1948, Truman said that the "foreign policy should be the policy of the whole Nation and not the policy of one party or the other. Partisanship should stop at the water's edge."[2]

Although facilitated by bipartisanship, the foreign policy that emerged in the late 1940s transcended two-party cooperation because it survived subsequent fierce partisan battles and was accepted by those with little or no concern about partisan politics. What developed was a consensus on how the United States should approach the world, and the Soviet Union in particular. Ole R. Holsti and James N. Rosenau define consensus as "a broad agreement on some basic principles that define the nation's proper orientation toward the world."[3] Viewing the Soviet Union as a threat to a stable and prosperous world order, the United States initiated a policy of containment of the Soviet Union and communism in general. The United States then sought a broad popular consensus for that policy.

This containment policy assumed an active American role in the world; it was an internationalist rather than an isolationist policy. Containment, which came to include economic and military assistance, anti-Soviet alliances, covert actions, and wars in Asia, had the overwhelming support of the American people. Although there were disputes between Democrats and Republicans, these were usually limited to "tactics and nuances." The basic assumptions were seldom questioned and real alternatives were almost never advocated.[4] As Thomas McCormick wrote, American leaders were "startlingly successful" in achieving a long-term consensus that was accepted "from top to bottom" of American society.[5] In March 1945, a Gallup Poll revealed that 55 percent of the American public believed that Russia could be trusted to cooperate with the United States at the end of the war. By February 1949, the attitude had changed. When asked if the Russian government sincerely desired peace, 72 percent of Americans said it did not.[6] U.S. politicians rewarded supporters and nullified potential adversaries by "co-optation of the right and suppression of the left."[7] Anyone who challenged those assumptions risked being accused of indifference to national security in a period of international tension—or worse still, accused of being a communist.[8]

Historians have argued that the Cold War consensus remained substantially unchallenged until the mid-1950s when opposition to nuclear testing created a "ban the bomb" peace movement, which expanded into an anti–Vietnam War movement in the 1960s. Until the late 1980s, the objective of containment of the Russians guided Washington's foreign policy. Nonetheless, there were critics of the consensus from the beginning. The dominant and traditional view of these critics argues that they were "unrealistic, misguided, wrong . . . duped and disloyal." It has been commonly accepted as well that they apologized for and excused Joseph Stalin's brutal foreign policy.[9] Political figures who emerged to criticize the containment consensus, or who simply raised fundamental doubts about it, were often discredited, usually losing their elective offices and political credibility.[10] The end of the Cold War has not substantially altered those views, and, in fact, with the apparent popular consensus that the United States won the Cold War, the critics appear even less credible. Containment, it appears, had worked.

Nonetheless, there were vocal critics of the containment policy who, despite the fact that they were out of step with the popular consensus and a small minority, continued to voice their opinions. Many of the points presented by these individuals and groups were maintained and expanded upon by the stronger and more active peace movements of the mid-1950s and 1960s. Some of their ideas and arguments also contributed to the development of the historiographic revision of the causes of the Cold War.

The peace movement that emerged from the end of World War II consisted of a broad range of generally middle-class reformers, including various internationalists who had great hopes for the success of the United Nations (UN), world federalists who hoped for the development of world government, atomic scientists concerned about the spread of atomic weapons, and religious and radical pacifists and feminists who sought the end of war.[11] However, as the Cold War unfolded, and as U.S. foreign policy developed into the containment consensus, many of these groups abandoned opposition, believing that Washington had no choice but to pursue active containment. By the late 1940s, the peace movement was limited to pacifist groups, some feminist groups, and a small group of liberal internationalists. In this book, the term "liberal internationalist" will be used to mean groups and individuals who supported an active U.S. foreign policy, but differed from proconsensus internationalists over whether the United States should continue to cooperate with the Soviets in the postwar world. The term "feminist" refers to groups advocating women's rights, such as the Women's International League for Peace and Freedom (WILPF) which, in their constitution, pledged support for peace movements, internationalism, and freedom for women.[12]

This book examines how individuals and groups involved in the opposition to containment developed comprehensive analyses of world politics and proposed solutions to the conflicts of the era that are still worthy of consideration. However, what united them was not just the desire for peace. After all, most Americans claimed peace as their goal. What they shared was a belief that reconciliation with the Russians was possible without sacrificing the national interest. They believed that U.S. misconceptions were aggravating Soviet-American friction and feared the militarization of the Cold War. They sought a diplomatic solution to the conflict between the two powers.[13] However, there were significant differences among the groups. Liberal internationalists tended to be gradual reformists, supporters of U.S. entry into World War II, believers in independent nation states cooperating voluntarily through international organizations, and defenders of enlightened capitalism. The pacifist groups, although not in complete agreement even among themselves, saw peace as a transnational process based on individual and group cooperation, and they tended to be more receptive to socialist analyses.[14]

Most of these critics were political independents or outsiders, although several of the best known were political figures. However, the politicians were mavericks unpopular with the party leadership. The dissenters mostly remained outside official circles and only rarely were heard or seriously given consideration.[15] Frequently, they were viewed as supporting isolationism, a bad word in the post–World War II world. Although it would depend on how one defined isolationism, they tended to be more anti-imperialist than isolationist. They advocated a disengagement from empire rather than from international relationships. They tended also to place less reliance on the military, distrusting military alliances.[16] However, their support for the United Nations and an active role for the United States in that organization was nearly universal.

The purpose of this book is to explore an often ignored and frequently marginalized time in the history of the American peace movement.[17] With the powerful consensus dominating American politics and culture, it was very difficult, and at times impossible, for the critics of that consensus to be heard. What has been viewed as the postwar nadir for the peace movement is nonetheless an important era for the peace advocates. The ideas they kept alive survived and reemerged into the public debate in the next two decades. In spite of the current and dominant view of the success of containment, the points they raised deserve a reexamination. Even if the conflict with the Soviet Union was inevitable, need it have been so severe, destructive, and militarized? Was the massive arms build up ultimately necessary? The critics thought not.

While examining the emergence of the containment policy and its critics, this book concentrates on the liberal internationalists and various pacifist groups, although other groups will also be considered. The focus is on those whose ideas continued to have an impact and were revived with the revitalization of the peace movement in the mid-1950s. Although their critiques of U.S. foreign policy begin with the gradual development of hostility between the Russian and American governments in 1945–46, the main focus of the book is on the reaction of various groups and individuals to the key elements of containment as developed by the Truman administration between 1947 and 1950: the Truman Doctrine, the Marshall Plan, the North Atlantic Treaty (NAT) and rearmament of Western Europe, and the Korean War. Although in the case of each of these policies there were disagreements among the critics as to the need for and the consequences of those policies, over a period of five years the reaction to these initiatives and actions demonstrated a consistency among the key opposition individuals and groups. The opposition eventually centered on several key beliefs. These included strengthening the economic foundation of the world, negotiating a settlement with the Soviet Union, developing the UN into an effective organization, reducing armaments worldwide, emphasizing the importance of the colonial and former colonial areas, and opposing the militarization of American policy and society. Despite their failures in the 1940s, over time these concepts did help to reduce Cold War tensions.

With the end of the Cold War, the UN has come to play a more active role in world affairs. Although the proposals discussed in the early Cold War by containment's critics may have not been viable at that time, much of the opposition to the policy focused on a greater role for the UN, which is certainly worthy of reconsideration in today's post–Cold War world. The planning and creation of the UN stands as an example of how groups, individuals, and nations sought to find solutions to human conflict. After the war, however, many of these ideas were ignored as the United States set out to deal with the Soviets with a policy in which the UN became a means of confrontation and containment rather than an organization seeking cooperative solutions. Thus, potentially viable strategies for the resolution of world conflicts remained only lost opportunities.

NOTES

1. Norman Graebner, *The New Isolationism: A Study in Politics and Foreign Policy since 1950* (New York: Ronald Press Co., 1956), 3; Carl Van Meter Crabb Jr., *Bipartisan Foreign Policy, Myth or Reality?* (White Plains, NY: Row, Peterson and Co., 1957), 156.

2. Arthur H. Vandenberg Jr., ed., *The Private Papers of Senator Vandenberg* (Boston: Houghton Mifflin Co., 1953), 112–13; Graebner, *The New Isolationism*, 15; *Public Papers of the Presidents of the United States*: Harry S. Truman, 1948 (Washington, DC: GPO, 1964), 407.

3. Ole R. Holsti and James N. Rosenau, *American Leadership in World Affairs: Vietnam and the Breakdown of Consensus* (Boston: Allen and Unwin, 1984), 218.

4. Richard Falk, "Lifting the Curse of Bipartisanship," *World Policy Journal* 1 (winter 1986): 127.

5. Thomas J. McCormick, *America's Half-Century: United States Foreign Policy in the Cold War* (Baltimore: Johns Hopkins University Press, 1989), 10.

6. George Gallup, *The Gallup Poll: Public Opinion 1935–1971*, 2 vols. (New York: Random House), 1:492; 2:792.

7. McCormick, *America's Half-Century*, 10.

8. Crabb, *Bipartisan Foreign Policy*, 156.

9. Thomas G. Paterson, "Introduction: American Critics of the Cold War and

Their Alternatives," in Thomas G. Paterson, ed., *Cold War Critics: Alternatives to American Foreign Policy in the Truman Years* (Chicago: Quadrangle Books, 1971), 4.

10. Falk, "Lifting the Curse of Bipartisanship," 127.

11. Charles DeBenedetti, "The American Peace Movement and the National Security State, 1941–1971," *World Affairs* 141 (1978): 118–19.

12. For more on the use of the term "liberal internationalist," see chapter 1. For definitions of "feminism," see Harriet Hyman Alonso, *Peace as a Women's Issue: A History of the U.S. Movement for World Peace and Women's Rights* (Syracuse, NY: Syracuse University Press, 1993), 83, 5.

13. Paterson, "Introduction: American Critics," 4–5.

14. Charles DeBenedetti, *Peace Reform in American History* (Bloomington: Indiana University Press, 1980), 106.

15. Paterson, "Introduction: American Critics," 9.

16. Ibid.

17. Charles DeBenedetti, "American Peace Activism, 1945–1985," in Charles Chatfield and Peter van den Dungen, eds., *Peace Movements and Political Cultures* (Knoxville: University of Tennessee Press, 1988), 225. DeBenedetti argues "After failing to build a new world through the United Nations, peace activists did not reassemble in a visible way until 1955."

1

POSTWAR PACIFISM, INTERNATIONALISM, AND CONSENSUS

Since colonial times, there has been a strong belief in the United States of its exceptionalism—that it was a new, unique nation. The image of that special position, of the "city on the hill," has had a strong impact on the American psyche. One manifestation of this belief was the concept of isolationism in foreign policy. Usually portrayed as noninvolvement or nonentanglement with European affairs, for some isolationism was the dominant theme in American foreign policy until the late 1940s when the Cold War lured the United States out of its isolation into a military and political alliance with Europe to contain the Soviet Union. However, the issue of American isolationism has been under dispute by diplomatic historians, some who argue that the United States was never an isolationist power.

ISOLATIONISM AND INTERNATIONALISM

Part of the problem with the concept of isolation in American foreign policy is the way it has been defined. A definition of isolation is difficult because various historians use the word differently. The most narrow definition limits it to the concept of the absence of political or military commitments with Europe. Technically, then, the United States was isolated from 1800 to 1949 as it had no alliances with any European power.[1] However, the term has had more widespread uses and definitions, sometimes simply to mean a disinterested noninvolvement with the world. In particular, the 1930s, during which time the United States did little to stop the spread of fascism, has been used as the typical example of an isolationist America. The result was a negative connotation that carried into the postwar world. The critics of isolationism have incorrectly interpreted it as a friendliness toward fascism, or a condoning of it, despite the fact that many of the "isolationists" were among the earliest critics of fascism.[2]

One view of isolationism argues that nonentanglement facilitates a unilateral foreign policy. By restricting its overseas activities, especially in Europe, the United States could follow an independent, unilateral course by minding its own business. The belief that the United States could fulfill its basic aims by unilateral action has been one of the key themes of isolationism. Kenneth Thompson argues that the core idea of isolationism is the concept of a "national reserve" or a regular abstention from certain types of political relationships. Because of geographic detachment, the need for alliances was remote. This antipathy gradually resulted in a resistance to all sources of entanglement.[3]

Whether defined as avoidance of entanglements with Europe or as the belief in unilateralism, isolationism as a powerful American political belief ended with Pearl Harbor. After the war, the majority of Americans came to support an activist foreign policy that viewed an ongoing U.S. role in the world as a necessity; they came to support membership in the UN and then in the North Atlantic Treaty Organization (NATO) and other alliances as the best means to maintain world peace against the threat of a powerful, expansionist Soviet Union.

Isolationism of the 1930s survived the war, but its advocates shrunk, and the isolationist opposition to American foreign policy was very narrow. Some of its ideas continued into the postwar world and were shared by nonisolationists, too. The isolationism of the 1930s had a wide variety of viewpoints, which were often contradictory and usually involved differing methods of implementation. These isolationists had a profound abhorrence of war and militarism, supported nonintervention in other nations' affairs, and favored unilateralism.[4]

Many of these concepts were shared by various opponents of the Truman foreign policy. However, during the first decade of the Cold War, isolationism was significantly altered. The postwar isolationists focused on several main points. They were alert to the usurpations of congressional war-making powers, rejected U.S. imperialism, disliked U.S. unwitting support for reactionary regimes, feared that Cold War policies would result in indiscriminate aid, believed that the administration was using war scares to secure appropriations, warned against overcommitment, believed that the Soviet Union posed no military threat to Europe, and feared the creation of a garrison state.[5]

Most critics of the Truman Cold War policies agreed with the isolationists on those points, and often critics of the containment policy were all lumped together as isolationist or, at least, neoisolationist. However, Cold War isolationism should not be confused as the only form of opposition to U.S. foreign policy, nor should all the noncommunist opponents of U.S. foreign policy be called isolationist. The focus of this study, the pacifists and the various peace advocates that will be labeled liberal internationalists, were not isolationists. Many had advocated U.S. intervention in World War II, and were more anti-imperialist than anti-interventionist. They were among the strongest supporters of the UN and U.S. participation in the UN.

Justus Doenecke provides a critique of postwar isolationism which can be used to differentiate the isolationist from the pacifist/internationalist peace advocates who emerged as critics of containment. Postwar isolationists, he writes, promoted Asia first, ignoring their own warnings against globalism. Their alternatives took on a more and more unilateral cast, coming to see air power as the answer to American defense needs. The isolationists were among the strongest supporters of General Douglas MacArthur in his struggles with President Truman over military strategy in the Korean War. Many became obsessed with conspiracy theories, such as those associated with the Japanese attack on Pearl Harbor, the Yalta conference, and the belief in the significant danger of internal communist subversion. They believed that foreign aid would only result in domestic and foreign disintegration. Doenecke asserts that the result was that the isolationists had no policy, and even asserts that they would have allowed the fall of Europe to the Soviet Union. He notes that although postwar isolationism could still be defined in terms of aloofness from Europe, its focus moved away from withdrawal from the world's battles and "more and more upon the most hazardous of commitments on the Asian continent."[6]

On each one of these issues, the pacifist/internationalist critics differed with the isolationists. Rather than no policy at all, the pacifists and the liberal internationalists had policies and visions of the world that were alternatives to the containment policy. Although they did not have one single viewpoint, and certainly many of these alternatives can be seen as unrealistic, their view was not isolationist, unless one's definition of isolation is limited to avoidance of military and political alliances with Europe, both which they opposed. In the postwar era, the term "isolationist" describes a conservative movement that primarily feared communist penetration from within the United States and then became obsessed with Asia.

Alexander DeConde argues that when Henry Wallace, one of the leading critics of Truman's foreign policy, spoke as an internationalist and believer in peace, "he really spoke as a reformer-isolationist." He asserts that Wallace attacked the Cold War policy of Truman "with the tradi-tional economic interpretation of the liberal isolationist."[7] However, for the purposes of this book, "postwar isolationism" refers to the conser-vative, anticommunist critics of containment. Instead of isolationist, the pacifists, and especially the left/liberal internationalist critics and peace advocates, are portrayed as fitting into the internationalist category. As Dorothy Detzer of the WILPF wrote in 1945, "I have always felt . . . that Balance of Power and isolationism . . . have to be destroyed together."[8] Sen. Glen Taylor of Idaho, in the 1949 debate over the North Atlantic Alliance, spoke of the various uses and misuses of the term isolationism in the Cold War. He noted that a few years earlier the word isolationist had been built up as a bad word and had ceased to be a complementary term. He continued,

I, myself, think isolationism is very bad—that we all must live together in this shrinking world. But . . . seeking to bypass, undermine, and destroy the United Nations is not internationalism. . . . And opposition to alliances of a military na-ture, or any arrangements outside the United Nations, which tend to weaken that organization certainly is not isolationism. The term has become a little con-fused. We now find those who were rank isolationists a few years ago to be among the most vocal in denouncing defenders of the United Nations as "iso-lationists."[9]

Although the pacifist and liberal internationalist opposition was criti-cal of the way the UN was constructed, once it was in place most sup-ported it as a progressive development and hoped it could be used to reconstruct a peaceful world.[10] In their support for the UN, both groups can be viewed as internationalist, supporting international organizations and a partial subordination of state sovereignty to such organizations. Although the term "internationalism" has gone through various changes in meaning, according to Robert Kleidman it has retained as a principle focus "the belief that violence between nations can be reduced or elim-inated through greater international cooperation and interdependence and peaceful resolution of disputes."[11] Internationalists tend to view world peace and cooperation as a vital U.S. interest and believe that with global interdependence a reality, the United States should be a moral and humanitarian leader.[12]

The definition of internationalism can also be difficult. One useful ap-proach, developed by Sandra Herman, divides internationalists into two types. The political internationalists (or institutionalists) favored the de-velopment of legal machinery for the peaceful settlement of international disputes. They believed that international organizations could "civilize the natural aggressiveness of men." A second group, the community internationalists, argued instead that such formal arrangements could not prevent war. They believed that what was needed was the development of "a sense of international community" achieved through various international programs, such as arms control and regulation of the food supply. Such programs, the community internationalists believed, "would undermine contentious nationalism."[13]

Various postwar peace advocates were divided between these two types of internationalists. Pacifists leaned toward the position of the community internationalists, supporting various programs designed to undermine nationalism. These pacifists were joined by some liberal internationalists who supported various goals of the community internationalists, including disarmament and the limitation of national sovereignty, but who were also political internationalists placing great faith in the UN as a means to maintain the peace.

The majority of postwar internationalists were political or institutional internationalists. They supported the development of the UN as a means to maintain the peace. However, this group was ultimately split by the foreign policy of the Truman administration. A few joined with the liberal internationalists who argued that Truman pursued a unilateralist foreign policy and abandoned the UN. The majority of internationalists came to see the UN as one means, combined with others, including military alliances, to achieve a stable, orderly world for the expansion of U.S. power and influence abroad and to contain the Soviet Union, which was seen as the main threat to U.S. interests. It was this latter group that came to dominate U.S. postwar foreign policy. As a result, the community internationalists had very little, if any, impact on public opinion in the Cold War era.[14] Nonetheless, they struggled to get their point of view across and provided a different vision of the world, one that was less divided and less militarized than the one that was rapidly developing in the late 1940s.

POSTWAR PACIFISM

As it emerged from the Second World War, the American peace movement primarily included two groups: the pacifists and the liberal internationalists. Organized pacifists in the postwar era consistently refused to approve any militarization of the foreign policy of the United States. Pacifism is a belief, often but not always associated with religious and philosophical movements, that refuses to sanction war or violence. While rejecting collective security because of its reliance on force, pacifists are seriously committed to international cooperation.

Pacifists in the twentieth century fundamentally have been internationalists. In their efforts to create an antiwar public, they were committed to internationalism. Pacifists were convinced that war was useless, and they believed that the United States should avoid the power struggles of Europe and Asia and not participate in the economic exploitation of Latin America. Pacifists have tended to be the most radical of all peace advocates, supporting or directing a variety of peace programs. They promoted internationalist attitudes and have traditionally sought to influence the government to curb militarism and participate in world organizations. Although in the 1930s pacifists tended to be viewed as isolationist, pacifists were isolationist in that they wanted to stay out of war. They had combined that desire with calls for international cooperation and "brought the sanction of internationalism to the concept of strict neutrality."[15]

The organized pacifist movement, however, consisted of several different groupings with often conflicting approaches in the expression of their pacifist beliefs. The leading secular pacifist groups active in the postwar era included the War Resisters League (WRL), the WILPF, and the National Council for Prevention of War (NCPW). The WRL, established in 1924 and dedicated to an absolute opposition to war, was the most radical of these pacifist organizations. The American section of the WILPF was founded in 1920 and, although not an absolute pacifist organization, was dedicated to establishing peace and freedom, and human rights, on a worldwide level. To the WILPF, peace was more than the absence of war; it was associated with cooperation for the common good.[16] The NCPW was established in 1921 to serve as a clearinghouse for the American peace movement. Although it reached its peak strength in the 1930s, and in the public mind was associated with the isolationism of that decade, it continued to function into the Cold War era. Each of these groups remained active in the late 1940s, presenting their views before Congress and the American public.

Religious pacifism in the United States was centered in church-related organizations, ranging "from Catholic to Unitarian, from Jewish to peace sectarian."[17] However, one significant interdenominational organization that played a major role in the presentation of religious-based pacifist ideas in the United States was the Fellowship of Reconciliation (FOR). The FOR, led by the dynamic A. J. Muste, was founded in 1915 to apply Christian principles and nonviolent change to social issues. Opposed to totalitarianism, the FOR believed that the United States could best stop communism by creating a model of economic and racial justice at home.[18] In addition to the FOR, included among the active religious pacifist groups are the historic peace churches—the Church of the Brethren, the Mennonites, and the Society of Friends (Quakers)—who frequently made their opinions known on Capitol Hill. Other church groups also had pacifist organizations (such as the Catholic Worker Movement and Catholic Association for International Peace) that frequently presented a pro-peace position before the Congress and the public.

Of all the individual pacifists, the best known in the postwar era was

A. J. Muste. Muste became the executive director of the FOR in 1940, after serving in the ministry of the Dutch Reformed Church and then working for a period of time as a labor organizer. With the onset of the Cold War, Muste renewed his efforts to fight militarism and war. He took strong stands against the emergence of the U.S.–Soviet rivalry and each nation's perception of the other as the enemy. Muste saw enemies, but they were "militarism, expansionism, nationalism, and colonialism." He felt that the Cold War political rivalry was insane and inhumane and that nations needed to renounce the deadly game of power politics, unilaterally divest themselves of their military arsenals, and launch a global crusade to end poverty and suffering.[19]

Muste's ideas often went against the accepted ideas of his allies, and most Americans considered his goals unreachable and utopian. But Muste believed strongly in his ideals and struggled for their achievement until his death in 1967. In May 1950, he noted that peace-minded people generally agreed on a program that included universal disarmament, negotiation of U.S.–Soviet differences, large-scale efforts for economic rehabilitation, and steps in the direction of world government. He noted, however, that this "conventional program" failed to take into account the fact that "we no longer have democratic process in dealing with the issue of war and peace." He warned that unless a great change occurred, "public officials are where they are to do just what they are doing. Sham battles will go on, but foreign policy will be 'bi-partisan' and big decisions secret." He also said that the conventional approach failed to take into account the extent and depth of the changes required in the economic order. He criticized progressives and socialists, saying they "are woefully wrong" if they "think radical economic improvement can be had without ending war and the power-struggle," as are peace workers who think "that war can be eliminated while practically all else, including American 'business as usual,' remains as is." Consistently critical of the Soviets, he also warned that the conventional peace approach underestimated the "tremendous dynamism of Russian expansionism . . . and the genuine and deep-seated evil in the totalitarian philosophy and practice." He warned that if Harry Truman and Soviet leader Joseph Stalin agreed to coexistence without drastic changes, it "could hardly mean anything except a time based on a division of spheres of influence."[20]

His program was based on his strong religious beliefs: preach a repentance from the sin of war, an individual renunciation of war and acceptance of a nonviolent way of life, a renunciation of war by nations through unilateral disarmament, and the use of national energies and resources for the service of mankind to bring about profound economic and social changes. Muste acknowledged that this would require a spiritual rebirth in the individual and a commitment not just at the national level, but on the local level in churches and communities. It would mean a pacifist crusade to bring churches and members to an unconditional break with war. To Muste, there was no just war. Instead, a peace army should be created to challenge Russia and to engage in a nonviolent struggle for social justice.[21]

Frederick Libby, head of the NCPW, was another leading spokesperson for the pacifist movement. An ordained Congregationalist minister, Libby, because of his opposition to U.S. involvement in World War II, was associated with the isolationists of the 1930s. However, he always sought to make a differentiation between the isolationists and pacifists. The America First Committee, which sought to keep the United States out of World War II, was unacceptable to Libby. He stated that he could not join the committee because it called for an "impregnable defense." He also was critical because its members did not share his attitude toward war. The America First Committee disbanded when the United States entered the war, and, in fact, its members joined in promoting the war.[22] Nonetheless, Libby's biographer noted that it was unfortunate that much of what he worked for was obscured by his rigid position in the 1930s. His advocacy of neutralism caused pacifists to be judged "within the confines of rigid moral guidelines even though their thinking was influenced as much by the political climate as by morality." Libby retained his antiwar views into the Cold War era. Although he believed that the Soviet Union aimed at world conquest, he felt that Washington should not prepare for war with Moscow and should abandon conscription. However, he did support postwar economic programs that aimed at rebuilding war-torn Europe.[23]

In the Cold War era, the peace churches maintained their historic opposition to all war. Although the Mennonite opposition to war goes back to the founding of the church in the 1500s, the twentieth century brought new challenges and caused them to "give fresh expression" to their pacifism. In a statement adopted by the Mennonite General Conference in 1937, the church reaffirmed its belief that "As followers of Christ . . . we believe His Gospel to be a Gospel of Peace, requiring us as His disciples to be at peace with all men . . . even toward our enemies, and to renounce the use of force and violence in all forms." The statement firmly declared that "war is altogether contrary to the teaching and spirit of Christ . . . that therefore war is sin." The Mennonite Central Committee, at a November 1950 study conference in Winona Lake, Indiana, reasserted their firm antiwar position. The committee stated that "We cannot compromise with war in any form. . . . We cannot . . . participate in military service in any form." Although the Mennonites recognized that in a world filled with good and evil there is a necessary place for the use of force by the state in restraint of evil, "the Christian cannot be the executor of this force. . . . [F]orce can never create righteousness . . . it can at best only restrain the evil in varying degrees."[24]

In a similar statement in 1935, the Church of the Brethren Annual Conference declared " 'We believe that all war is sin; that it is wrong for Christians to support or to engage in it; and that war is incompatible with the spirit, example and teachings of Jesus.' " This was reaffirmed in a 1948 Resolution on Peace that stated, "we reaffirm our conviction that all war is sinful and that all attempts to promote and prepare for war are inimical to peace and antagonistic to Christ's way."[25]

The Quakers expressed similar views, stating that war was contrary to the will of God and the Christian should refuse arms and seek peace. In a 1951 statement, the Quakers stated that "Friends do not believe that war preparation to meet the threat of aggression can be justified on the principle of deterrence. The idea that men can be frightened out of their evil ways is not the teachings of the Gospel."[26]

The implementation of these beliefs varied. By World War II, the Church of the Brethren had shifted from a nonactivist, nonresistant pacifism toward modern pacifism of political reform and abolition of war. The Mennonites' social action was more limited by their belief that the Christian express "faith by nonconformity to the world in life and conduct and should refuse any forms of coercion to achieve justice." The Quakers were led in activism by the American Friends Service Committee (AFSC), founded during World War I, which set an example of constructive pacifism.[27] More often than not, however, the position of the leadership and church organizations did not mean universal support among the membership of the peace churches. Nonetheless, church activists did attempt to make known their opposition to much of the emerging containment policies in the halls of government.

In defending the practicality of pacifist ideas that were often dismissed as unrealistic, John Swomley Jr., a FOR leader from 1940 to 1960, noted that the term "utopian" has been applied to many proposals throughout history, including world disarmament ideas espoused by pacifists. There appeared to be no connection between their ideas and reality, no practical step-by-step method of moving from the present to the desirable goal. However, he argued that political idealism and utopianism "cannot be dismissed out of hand." There was a place for them in focusing attention on real problems, and "their advocates are effective critics of existing foreign policy." In contrast, "realists" create more problems than idealists "because they concentrate too much on military power as the answer to difficult or complex situations."[28]

Nonetheless, how to accomplish those "utopian" goals in the Cold War was much debated within the pacifist community. In overwhelming numbers, Americans were not pacifists. One analyst felt that the failure of pacifism in the 1930s resulted from the belief that an insightful minority could make the world "be good" by outlawing war through some technique of minority control.[29] In an attempt to confront that problem in the postwar era, several WRL leaders wrote to Muste asking, "[I]n view of the lack of identity of the American public with the pacifist minority . . . what can pacifists expect to accomplish and what should be our goals?" They answered that question themselves, writing that the goal was easy, and they called for an all-out campaign against war and for disarmament. But, "if it cannot [be done], let us face the inadequacy of the pacifist minority to influence the entire course of American policy." Despite that pessimistic point of view, they stated that, "Of course we must continue to cry out with all our might for the *whole* of what is needed. . . . We must keep trying, even if immediate success is not in sight." They hoped that they could use all the issues raised by power politics "to urge our policy and oppose warmaking measures. . . . [W]e will not win out. But we will make our voices heard and sometime . . . we may have decisive influence."[30] Thus, American pacifists were realistic enough to know that they had little influence, but they were determined that their point of view be heard.

THE LIBERAL INTERNATIONALISTS

In the interwar years, American internationalists remained active despite the failure of the United States to join the League of Nations. In the 1920s and 1930s, they advocated a more active role for the United States in world affairs and called for the United States to assume a greater role in maintaining global order. The advocates of internationalism in the 1920s and 1930s faced a majority of Americans who remained opposed to U.S. membership in the League. Although they supported the League, most internationalists never challenged American nationalism, tending instead to favor the internationalization of American institutions and values.[31]

The support for American sovereignty was one difference between the internationalists and the pacifists in the 1930s. There were others. In that decade, pacifists and isolationists hoped to use the neutrality legislation to tie the hands of Franklin Roosevelt's administration to prevent the president from taking action that would involve the United States in war. Internationalists also sought to avoid war, but believed that the United States should take no action that would hinder the efforts of the League of Nations to impose sanctions against aggressors.[32]

During the war, and then with the onset of the Cold War, many internationalists favored collective security, believing that force was necessary to maintain the peace. Thus, many supported the Truman administration's foreign policy aimed at stopping Soviet expansion. Pacifists rejected that view, asserting that collective security and force would threaten peace rather than ensure it.[33] As Lawrence Kaplan has pointed out in his analysis of the debate over American participation in the NAT, the critics who emerged to oppose the Truman policies were old isolationists or "new internationalists who looked to the UN Charter for guidance in foreign policy." What the two groups had in common was a dislike for entangling alliances or engagement in the balance of power.[34] By the 1949 NAT debates, these "new internationalists" had disassociated themselves from the politics of the Truman administration, tending to see Truman's policy as a threat to the UN and no longer based on internationalism but on unilateralism and interventionism on a global basis.[35] It was these liberal internationalists who joined with the pacifists to criticize much of the Truman Cold War foreign policy.

During World War II, the liberal internationals joined with others in the belief that the easing of economic rivalries and the establishment of a strong international association would help maintain the peace. In the postwar era, they believed in democratic humanism, exemplified by the Universal Declaration of Human Rights; they supported independence for former colonies; and they came to oppose the spread of communism because of its undemocratic nature. To the internationalists, the UN represented their desire to create a viable international community.[36] Once the UN unity began to break apart, the liberals retained hope for the institution and tended to blame U.S. policy for some of the problems of the organization. The Cold War internationalists, those who supported the Truman administration, placed greater reliance on unilateral U.S. actions, such as assistance to Greece and Turkey and the Marshall Plan. Liberal internationalists argued that such programs, undertaken outside of the UN, weakened that organization just when it should have been strengthened.

Just as the pacifists were divided in their views and in their tactics, so were the liberal internationalists. Some opposed nearly all the foreign policy initiatives of the Truman administration. Although some supported particular policies with great enthusiasm, others reluctantly lent support to certain policies. Not nearly as organized as the pacifists, the liberal internationalists were more influential. That influence was based on the fact that many were individuals who spoke or wrote from influential positions, including from within Congress and the Truman administration itself.

One of the early liberal critics was Freda Kirchwey, publisher of *The Nation*. Through 1947, she rejected the view that the Soviet Union was an expansionist nation that threatened the United States. She warned that the western democracies would attempt to salvage as much of the old order as possible. Although Kirchwey became more critical of the Russians after a 1946 trip to Europe, she continued to worry about the expanding U.S. commitment to prevent the spread of communism.[37]

By far the most significant critic of Truman's foreign policy was Henry A. Wallace. As a former vice president, and as the commerce secretary in the Truman administration until he was fired in September 1946 for his opposition to Truman's policies, Wallace spoke from a position of authority. He had a large personal following, including many former Roosevelt supporters who remained convinced that Wallace, not Truman, was the heir apparent to the late president. Until his failed 1948 presidential challenge, Wallace was the leading critic of containment in the United States. Although he remained critical of the Truman foreign policy until the outbreak of the Korean War in 1950, his influence rapidly declined after the 1948 election campaign failure.

Wallace's opposition to U.S. Cold War policies had its roots in World War II, during which time he urged responsible American leadership and the establishment of a strong UN. He became the leading spokesman for closer ties between the Americans and Russians. Wallace's views of the Soviet Union, according to one historian, were "excessively charitable." However, "he was not blind to some of the more unsavory aspects of Soviet society," and he disliked American communists. Wallace held that the goal of a democracy for the "common man" could provide "a basis for mutual understanding." At the end of the war, Wallace continued to speak for many although the number of his supporters steadily diminished. Some continued to echo his opposition to the Truman Doctrine, but not his opposition to the Marshall Plan. By the fall of 1947, Wallace was becoming increasingly isolated in his dissent and spoke only for a small band of supporters.[38]

One of the keys to Wallace's objections was the failure of the United States to work through the UN. The former vice president continued to envision a significant role for that organization in ensuring world peace and in encouraging commerce. However, critics point out that his call for a strong UN ignored its weaknesses.[39] Wallace was critical of both aid to Greece and Turkey in 1947 and the Marshall Plan of 1948 primarily because those programs, run unilaterally by the United States, circumvented the UN. But Wallace's concerns started earlier, soon after the end of the war, when he became convinced that the president was predisposed against the Russians. On the other hand, Wallace believed that there were no irreconcilable differences between the United States and the Soviet Union.[40] This conflict led to Wallace's exit from the administration and, in 1948, to his presidential campaign against Truman. In the process, the internationalists divided between the Cold War internationalists, who supported Truman's containment policy, and the liberal and leftist internationalists, who opposed many of its aspects.

A third important figure who differed with the consensus Cold War policy that developed in the late 1940s was Sen. Glen Taylor of Idaho. Unlike fellow senator Claude Pepper of Florida, who opposed some of the Truman policies but also supported many, Taylor's opposition was based on a different view of the Russians, which led him to oppose most of Truman's policies and to run with Wallace as the vice presidential candidate of the Progressive Party in 1948. Taylor disagreed with the necessity of containment, which he believed was a smokescreen for American business to economically dominate world postwar reconstruction. Many of Taylor's contemporaries dismissed him as a clown or a communist dupe, but he was neither. Taylor was a ham actor, a hillbilly musician, and an egotistical opportunist, but also a dedicated liberal and humanitarian. He viewed colonialism and imperialism as the main threat to world peace, and he hoped that international organizations could bring an end to dangerous economic competition between nations.[41] Taylor made his devotion to the UN clear on many occasions. In April 1949, he noted that he was

elected to the United States Senate upon my promise to the voters of Idaho that I would support an organization to maintain peace in the world. As it turned out, that organization was the United Nations. I have determined . . . to oppose everything that seems to me to have the effect of weakening the United Nations. . . . I refuse to accept something which I feel is hurting the United Nations, even though it may accomplish something good.[42]

Outside of the government, the best-known critic was James P. Warburg, a former government official in the Roosevelt administration and a member of a leading northeastern banking family. Warburg was also a friend of Dean Acheson, secretary of state from 1949 to 1953, writing him in 1948 that they should "get drunk together," and reminding him that there was "an all night pub at 34 East 70th Street."[43] Warburg's role in the postwar era was one of a "dissident and gadfly" whose friends in government, including Acheson, backed away from him. Through the 1950s, he was a "lonely soldier of lost causes" as he argued for an alternative foreign policy.[44]

Warburg's alternative policy centered on the economic recovery of Western Europe. He argued that the Russians did not intend to conquer Western Europe with military force. Instead, he viewed the primary threat to be political subversion which could best be countered by economic recovery, which military efforts such as the NAT disrupted and weakened.[45] Although he often expressed his own views, he also became active in the United World Federalists (UWF).

The UWF was founded in February 1947 at Ashville, North Carolina. It was a combination of three pro–world government organizations.

World government advocates viewed the nation-state as crucially important, but also felt it was becoming obsolete. Initially, they favored a strengthening of the powers of the UN. At the very beginning of the Cold War, the world federalists were inclined to view both the United States and the Soviet Union as responsible for the rivalry, feeling that both were reacting in a "natural, predictable manner" within the nation-state system. However, as the Cold War deepened, the UWF, without losing sight of their long-term objective of world government, adapted to the increasing American nationalism caused by the Cold War and eventually became active cold warriors themselves in the 1950s. Thus, the world federalists were not in the mainstream of the peace movement. Very few world federalists were pacifists, and "most feared that pursuit of peace as an end in itself might encourage aggression and war."[46]

Finally, one other example of a liberal internationalism, and the diversity of opinion within this grouping, is Norman Thomas. Although a socialist and at times an advocate of pacifism, Thomas gave reluctant support to some Truman administration programs, but was nonetheless a consistent critic of the policies. Thomas's overwhelming postwar purpose was to avoid a World War III in which Russia would be the enemy. Despite his "loathing" of Stalin, he believed it more important that the public be made to understand that war was obsolete.[47] As a leading member of the Socialist Party, and their frequent candidate for president, and as the leading spokesman for the Post War World Council (PWWC), which was founded during World War II to establish a just and durable peace and to end war and poverty, Thomas made his opinions known in government circles.[48] Although he was a critic of the Truman Doctrine, he lent reluctant support to the NAT as a means to stop the Soviet Union. However, his greatest contribution to the postwar peace movement was in his antiwar and anticolonial advocacy.

Another group of internationalists were those who primarily focused on colonial issues. Included in this group were civil rights activists and leading African Americans who supported decolonization efforts, especially in Africa. During World War II, a broad left and liberal alliance of black anticolonial activists had argued that their struggles in the United States were linked to the struggles of African and Asian people for their independence.[49] As the Cold War began and intensified, many African Americans felt that U.S. policy supported European states who were the colonial powers in Africa and Asia. These included the French Empire in Indochina and North Africa, British colonies in Malaya, Belgian colonies in the Congo, and the African colonies of Portugal. Black critics of American policy saw in U.S. support for these Europeans the seeds of U.S. involvement in colonial wars and a possibility, in the Cold War context, of American-Soviet confrontations in the developing world.[50]

Opposition to colonialism was quite strong in the African American community. In addition, blacks held fewer Cold War attitudes than whites, and proportionately fewer blacks than whites supported programs such as the Truman Doctrine and the Marshall Plan.[51] Thus, the leading African American organization, the National Association for the Advancement of Colored People (NAACP), voiced strong opposition to imperialism. During World War II and into the early Cold War, Walter White of the NAACP expressed opposition to imperialism, arguing that the restoration of the colonial system would lead to World War III. In July 1944, the NAACP adopted a resolution urging the abolition of imperialism. NAACP activist W.E.B. Du Bois even attempted to petition the UN to gain civil rights for blacks in the United States. In the early stages of the Cold War, Walter White viewed Winston Churchill's 1946 Iron Curtain speech as an effort to ensure the continuation of imperialism.

Cold War pressures eventually led the NAACP, by 1947, to shift toward support of the containment policy. After 1947, the achievement of equality at home was emphasized as providing a major weapon in the arsenal against international communism. Acceptance for black demands for equality was won "at the expense of direct sponsorship of anti-colonialism abroad." The Cold War was the key factor in the collapse of black protest against colonialism and U.S. cooperation with the colonial powers. U.S. policy makers believed that the creation of a strong Western Europe, including alliances with colonial powers, was more important than overhauling the African colonial structure.[52]

As the NAACP joined the consensus, the only other significant African American organization active in opposition to the Cold War policies was the small, left-leaning Council on African Affairs (CAA). Associated with the talented Paul Robeson, the CAA was founded in 1936 to provide Americans with information on Africa. Eventually, Du Bois became its leading spokesman. The CAA aimed in organizing to win mass American support for African anticolonial struggles. The CAA tended toward pro-Soviet positions and believed that a strong Russian role in Africa "would stimulate a healthy competition among the great powers" and would thus offer each side the ability to show that it had the greatest commitment to indigenous African interests.[53] However, the CAA had little influence because of the Communist Party connections of Du Bois and other members.

The liberal internationalists included those noted above and others who will be encountered later. The greatest weakness they faced was the division that came to the internationalist movement and that culminated in the Wallace candidacy in 1948, and its overwhelming failure. The result was that some supported the emerging Cold War consensus, eventually leaving only a minority, who, along with the pacifists, remained the only critics of consensus in the nation, except for the Communist

Party. Those who continued their criticism were ignored and became increasingly ineffectual, or worse, they became targets for the Red-baiting of the late 1940s and 1950s.

THE INTERNATIONALIST SPLIT AND THE COLD WAR CONSENSUS

During the 1930s American liberals were united by the New Deal and the opposition to fascism. Although the pacifists were drawn closer to the isolationists in their opposition to the drift toward war, most liberals supported the Roosevelt administration and joined other international-ists in support for collective security and eventually intervention in World War II. During the war, the liberals worked with the noncom-munist left, and even the communists, to fight the war. But the alliance, just like the larger one between the United States and the Soviet Union, did not survive the end of the war. Many liberals eventually abandoned this united front of the 1930s. The New Deal and the fight against the fascist powers could not hold them together. Differences concerning Soviet-American relations overpowered the heritage of Franklin Roose-velt.[54]

The immediate postwar years found the American liberals divided and in retreat in face of a conservative resurgence. The political left remained a large and powerful force, which included the Congress of Industrial Organizations (CIO) trade unions and spokesmen, such as Secretary of Commerce Henry Wallace and other New Dealers with access to the government. However, soon the emergence of anticommunist policies would destroy this left and remold liberalism into something very dif-ferent in tone from the old liberalism of the 1930s.[55]

To American liberals, the purpose of foreign policy was to seek a re-alization of "freedom, justice and human dignity." Out of the war they sought to create a new order "characterized by peace, cooperation, de-mocracy, and stability." Liberal hopes for the postwar world were based, initially, on a continuation of the antifascist alliance, which would allow for the United States to develop programs of democratization and eco-nomic development on an international level.[56]

The organization created to carry out such ideals was the UN. The hopes that it could guarantee the peace were shattered by the onset of the Cold War. The Truman administration viewed a series of actions taken by the Russians at the end of the war as threats to U.S. political, economic, and security goals. The veto power in the UN prevented Washington from using that institution to thwart Soviet ambitions, which resulted in the decision to take a more unilateral approach with the Truman Doctrine and the launching of the containment policy.

Beginning with the use of the atomic bomb on Hiroshima, there were critics of Truman's policies. There was a growing disillusionment particularly among liberals with the development of hostility between the United States and the Soviet Union. This disillusionment rose to the surface on September 12, 1946, with Henry Wallace's speech at Madison Square Garden in New York City. The speech, which Wallace felt had been given full approval by President Truman, was an attack on Truman's foreign policy. He criticized the United States for making Great Britain the key to its policy and advocated cooperation with the Soviet Union, emphasizing that it could only be achieved when the Russians understood that the United States was not aiming to save the British Empire.[57] The Wallace speech led to his forced resignation from the cabinet, primarily because of the objections of Secretary of State James Byrnes. The Wallace plea for greater Soviet-American cooperation was not the direction that the administration was moving by late 1946.

The widening division led to the formation of two liberal organizations. The Americans for Democratic Action (ADA), which was founded in January 1947, and the Progressive Citizens of America (PCA), which was founded in December 1946 and led by Wallace, disagreed particularly on the issue of relations with the Soviet Union. The ADA emphasized the totalitarian and expansive nature of the Russian regime, whereas the PCA viewed the Soviet Union as a continuing ally in the struggle against fascism. Most liberals abandoned the idea that fascism was the only threat to peace and freedom, abandoned their sentimental attachment to the Soviet Union, and supported the ADA view. By 1947, some liberals were no longer willing to support any group that accepted communist membership.[58] The split widened beyond repair with the 1947 Truman Doctrine. The Truman request for assistance to Greece and Turkey in stopping Soviet expansionism antagonized liberals who continued to see a need for cooperation with the Soviets and who acknowledged the Russian right to a protective sphere of influence in Eastern Europe.[59]

Ultimately, this split led to the formation of the Progressive Party and the 1948 presidential campaign by Wallace and Taylor. The struggle within the U.S. noncommunist left reached its peak during the campaign, revolving around the issue of U.S. policy toward Russia. What was at stake was the leadership of American liberalism. The result was a massive defeat for the forces favoring a continuation of the popular front and cooperation with the Soviets. The new Cold War liberalism that emerged was less idealistic, but was also more conservative. The liberalism of the Cold War was centrist and clearly delineated from traditional leftist politics and what remained of the political left.[60] To Wallace, liberalism demanded an opposition to all the talk that war was inevitable. He felt that liberals should seek out the causes of war and eliminate them without "perverting science and wasting human energies and natural resources in preparation for conflict."[61] The Wallace candidacy, however, came under attack by liberals for the role of the Communist Party in the PCA and Progressive Party. Although evidence points to the fact that the communists were not crucial in the founding of the party, once formed the party reflected general leftist assumptions, including support for civil rights for African Americans and negotiations to settle Soviet-American differences.

Nonetheless, anticommunism played a significant role in the Wallace defeat, and Truman's reelection was interpreted at the time as a victory for the ADA and its emerging center coalition. With the Wallace left and Republican right defeated, "the future seemed to belong to the adherents of the new Cold-War liberalism."[62] This coalition was given the name the "vital center" in 1949 by Arthur M. Schlesinger Jr. The term "vital center" became shorthand for the liberal anticommunism that emerged by the late 1940s.[63]

The election of 1948 "solidified the bipartisan consensus and discredited the liberal critique of the Cold War. When it was over the meaning of the words 'liberal' and 'internationalist' in American politics had shifted." Cold War liberals, who were a crucial part of the bipartisan consensus supporting the containment policies of the Truman administration, supported enlarged military spending and a strong presidency that would work for domestic reform and international stability. The consensus liberals no longer identified with the left in criticism of the social order, but instead stressed the virtues of American political and economic institutions.[64] By 1948, Americans had to decide whether one could embrace liberalism while criticizing American foreign policy.[65]

The bipartisan coalition that emerged by 1947–48 enabled the Truman administration to carry out the containment policy. In the conduct of foreign policy, Secretary of State Dean Acheson noted that bipartisanship was the ideal for the executive branch:

[Y]ou cannot run this damned country any other way except by fixing the whole organization so it doesn't work the way it is supposed to work. Now the way to do that is to say politics stops at the seaboard—and anyone who denies that postulate is a son-of-a-bitch and a crook and not a true patriot. Now if people will swallow that, then you're off to the races.[66]

At least, Congress swallowed. The Senate votes for the major proposals of the containment policy were solidly favorable:

Aid to Greece and Turkey, 67–23

European Recovery Program, 69–17

Vandenberg Resolution, 64–4

North Atlantic Treaty, 82–13[67]

The consensus on economic and military leadership, although fostered by governmental publicity, was supported by the mass media, universities, and economic and religious organizations. It moved into the public realm and resulted in the labeling of sincere, devoted pacifists and liberal internationalists as sons-of-bitches, crooks, and, more often, communists.[68] The ultimate result was the emergence of McCarthyism and efforts to suppress dissent within the United States.

DISSENT AND THE COMMUNIST ISSUE

One of the most difficult problems faced by opponents of containment in the postwar era was the attempt, over and over again throughout the entire Cold War era, to link them with communists or communism. This was done on all levels of American culture and had damaging results on universities, popular culture, and even on foreign policy itself. One example of this attempt to link the opposition with communism came in March 1948 during the Senate debate on the European Recovery Program (ERP). Sen. Wayne Morse of Oregon attacked Sen. Taylor's loyalty. Morse was careful to state, "I sincerely and honestly do not think that the Senator from Idaho is a Communist." However, he went on to essentially accuse Taylor of communist sympathies, stating, "But I do wish to say, just as sincerely and honestly, that he has presented to the Senate a speech which follows . . . the present Communist line in America." In response, Taylor was forced to reply, in what becames a familiar recitation during the Cold War, that he had not "praised the foreign policy of Russia or anything Russia has done." He indicated with sarcasm that "anyone who did not agree to this bipartisan coalition on foreign policy had to be following the Communist Party line, because the Communist disagreed with it. I happen to differ with it, so therefore I am following the Communist Party line."[69]

By the late 1940s, anticommunist rhetoric became common in American politics. The radical elements of the labor movement and much of the New Deal were pushed out of the political arena. Advocates of civil rights, peace, disarmament, and other reforms had to "prove" that they were not acting as fronts or dupes of communism. As Richard Fried wrote, "To be leftist was to be suspect." This tendency to see peace seeking as subversive grew rapidly after 1949 with the Russian acquisition of the atomic bomb, the communist triumph in China, deepening tensions in Europe, and then the Korean War in 1950. Peace advocates were forced on the defensive, and many groups disintegrated. By the early 1950s, the movement was limited to a hard core of the faithful.[70]

Most foreign policy critics and peace activists steered clear of communists and Soviet-sponsored peace initiatives. However, the association of communism with peace activists was a frequent issue. At the May

1950 Mid-Century Conference for Peace held in Chicago, the issue of cooperation with the communists in a united front for peace was a significant issue. The conference itself was a united front effort, and all attempts to include a plank that rejected totalitarianism were defeated. Throughout the conference, which included the participation of church groups, labor representatives, Progressive Party members, and some communists, there was a distinct effort to keep the platform broad so that the communists could participate. Ultimately, a committee of pacifist representatives did get the conference to approve a statement that the American people had a special responsibility to change the policies of the U.S. government that continued the Cold War and that the "Russian people have the same responsibility in regard to their own government." They also got a second addition which asserted that the conference was "united in devotion to democratic principles and methods." One observer noted that the limited extent of communist participation indicated that it was clearly the intent of the party not to try to pack the conference or to capture it, but to find a platform and organization that it could work with without being labeled.[71]

Despite examples of such cooperation, peace activists were leery of joining communists in many endeavors. However, their support for civil liberties led them not to join the domestic attack on communists. Muste noted that his concern for the attempts to suppress free speech for communists "does not grow out of any sympathy for the Communist point of view." He wrote that communism is a form of totalitarianism and "to abolish it as a way of life and as a political dictatorship is therefore necessary and urgent purpose of believers in democracy." However, repressive measures, he argued, cost too much and divert attention away from other problems of society. Thus, peace activists attempted to walk two fine lines: They condemned Soviet totalitarianism while encouraging great-power conciliation, and they defended communist political activism while avoiding collaboration in leftist coalitions.[72]

CONCLUSION

The end of World War II and the creation of the UN led many to hope that the United States, in cooperation with the Soviet Union, could bring about a lasting peace. The breakdown of that coalition led to the destruction of the left-liberal alliance that had formed in the New Deal era and had hopes for an ongoing international role for the United States in cooperation with the Russians. The failure of the pacifists to be heard, the failure of the Wallace campaign in 1948, the fear of Soviet motivations in Europe, and the increasing anticommunism in America made criticism of American foreign policy increasingly suspect. By the early 1950s, the movement had been seriously crippled; however, it did survive and revive in the later 1950s. More significant were the issues that they raised. These issues, including disarmament, colonialism, the role of the UN, and the militarization of American foreign policy on a worldwide basis, were valid and laid the foundations for a more active and successful criticism of U.S. policy in the 1960s.

Dissent emerged at the very beginning. Despite the later, more favorable view of the UN, criticisms of that organization's weaknesses from the pacifists and internationalists were present at the beginning of its existence. Through 1945–46, criticism of the Truman foreign policy began to mount as the administration started to take a more and more critical view of Soviet actions in Europe and the Near East. The result was that by March 1947—the time of the Truman Doctrine—there were growing numbers of critics of the administration's policy.

NOTES

1. For this point of view, see the writings of Lawrence S. Kaplan, including his *NATO and the United States: The Enduring Alliance* (Boston: Twayne Publishers, 1988), 1.

2. Thomas G. Paterson, *Meeting the Communist Threat: Truman to Reagan* (New York: Oxford University Press, 1984), 220.

3. Thomas G. Paterson, *On Every Front: The Making of the Cold War* (New York: W. W. Norton, 1979), 118; Justus D. Doenecke, "The Strange Career of American Isolationism, 1944–1954," *Peace and Change* 3 (summer/fall 1975): 79; Kenneth W. Thompson, "Isolation and Collective Security: The Uses and Limits of Two Theories of International Relations," in Alexander DeConde, ed., *Isolation and Security: Ideas and Interests in Twentieth-Century American Foreign Polity* (Durham, NC: Duke University Press, 1957), 165. A recent interpretation of unilateralism and isolationism can be found in Walter A. McDougall, *Promised Land, Crusader State: The American Encounter with the World since 1776* (New York: Houghton Mifflin Co., 1997).

4. Manfred Jonas, *Isolation in America 1935–1941* (Chicago: Imprint Publications, 1990), 6; Paterson, *Meeting the Communist Threat*, 215.

5. Justus D. Doenecke, *Not to the Swift: The Old Isolationists in the Cold War Era* (Lewisburg, PA: Bucknell University Press, 1979), 10; Doenecke, "The Strange Career of American Isolationism," 79–80.

6. Doenecke, "The Strange Career of American Isolationism," 80–81; Doenecke, *Not to the Swift*, 10. Also see Selig Alder, *The Isolationist Impulse: Its Twentieth-Century Reaction* (New York: Abelard-Schuman, 1957).

7. Alexander DeConde, "On Twentieth-Century Isolationism," in Alexander DeConde, ed., *Isolation and Security: Ideas and Interests in Twentieth-Century American Foreign Policy* (Durham, NC: Duke University Press, 1957), 27–28.

8. Detzer, "Report of the National Secretary," October 1945, WILPF, Reel 130.12, Series A, Swarthmore College Peace Collection, Swarthmore, PA. Hereafter referred to as SCPC.

9. Glen Taylor, July 20, 1949, *Congressional Record*, 81st Cong., 1st sess., Vol. 95, pt. 7:9783.

10. See chapter 2 for the initial views of the pacifists and liberal internationalists toward the United Nations.

11. Robert Kleidman, *Organizing for Peace: Neutrality, the Test Ban, and the Freeze* (Syracuse, NY: Syracuse University Press, 1993), 7. See also Warren F. Kuehl, "Internationalism," in Alexander DeConde, ed., *Encyclopedia of American Foreign Policy* (New York: Charles Scribner's Sons, 1978), II:443–54.

12. Warren F. Kuehl and Lynne K. Dunn, *Keeping the Covenant: American Internationalists and the League of Nations, 1920–1939* (Kent, OH: Kent State University Press, 1997), xvi–xvii.

13. Robert Divine and Sandra Herman, "Internationalism as a Current in the Peace Movement: A Symposium," in Charles Chatfield, ed., *Peace Movements in America* (New York: Schocken Books, 1973), 172.

14. Ibid., 179–80. Divine portrays the division between the institutionalists as a split between what he called "realistic" internationalists, "those who accepted the necessity for a continued role for a new international organization—and 'idealistic' internationalists, who called for various forms of world government."

15. For a definition, see Robert D. Accinelli, "Militant Internationalists: The League of Nations Association, the Peace Movement, and U.S. Foreign Policy, 1934–38," *Diplomatic History* 4 (winter 1980): 19; Charles Chatfield, *For Peace and Justice: Pacifism in America 1914–1941* (Boston: Beacon Press, 1971), 5, 100, 286.

16. "Principles of the WILPF, U.S. Section," n.d., Reel 130.4, DG 43, SCPC.

17. Chatfield, *For Peace and Justice*, 130.

18. DeBenedetti, *Peace Reform in American History*, 153.

19. Jo Ann Robinson, "A. J. Muste: Prophet in the Wilderness of the Modern World," in Charles DeBenedetti, ed., *Peace Heroes in Twentieth-Century America* (Bloomington: Indiana University Press, 1986), 153, 158–59.

20. A. J. Muste, "Pacifist Strategy," May 1950, NCPW, Box 414, Conference on Church and War file, SCPC.

21. Ibid.

22. Libby to Mary Cornelia Ogburn, July 22, 1950, DG 23, NCPW, Reel 41.255, SCPC.

23. George Peter Marabell, *Frederick Libby and the American Peace Movement, 1921–1941* (New York: Arno Press, 1982), 248–49, 240–41.

24. "A Statement of Position Adopted by the Mennonite General Conference in 1937," in Guy Franklin Hershberger, *War, Peace, and Nonresistance* (Scottdale, PA: Herald Press, 1944), 374; Report on the Mennonite Central Committee Study Conference, November 9–12, 1950, Mennonite Central Committee, CDG-A, SCPC, 20; Mennonite General Conference, "A Declaration of Christian Faith and Commitment with Respect to Peace, War, and Nonresistance," August 23, 1951, Goshen, IN, Mennonites, CDG-A, SCPC.

25. Rufus D. Bowman, *The Church of the Brethren and War, 1708–1941* (Elgin, IL: Brethren Publishing House, 1944), 241; 1948 Annual Conference Resolution on Peace, *Messenger*, 140 (March 1991): cover.

26. "Quaker Statement on Basis of Witness of Historic Peace Churches," March 16, 1951, Mennonite Central Committee Peace Section, x-7-5, Box 6, Historic Peace Churches Continuation Committee 1950–51 file, Archives of the Mennonite Church, Goshen, IN. Hereafter cited as Mennonite Archives.

27. Chatfield, *For Peace and Justice*, 131, 51. On the role of the AFSC in the Cold

War, see H. Larry Ingle, "The American Friends Service Committee, 1947–49: The Cold War's Effect," *Peace and Change* 23 (January 1998): 27–48.

28. John M. Swomley Jr., *American Empire: The Political Ethics of Twentieth Century Conquest* (New York: Macmillan, 1970), 14–15.

29. John Howard Yoder, "The Unique Role of the Historic Peace Churches," *Brethren Life and Thought* 14 (summer 1969): 147.

30. Bret Andersen, Abraham Kaufman, and Frances Ross Ransom (WRL) to A. J. Muste, June 3, 1947, DG 46, War Resisters League, Box 26, Atlantic Pact file, SCPC. Emphasis in original.

31. Harold Josephson, "The Search for Lasting Peace: Internationalism and American Foreign Policy, 1920–1950," in Charles Chatfield and Peter van den Dugen, eds., *Peace Movements and Political Cultures* (Knoxville: University of Tennessee Press, 1988), 205, 208–9.

32. Ibid., 212.

33. Ibid., 215–16. See also Kleidman, *Organizing for Peace*, 19–20.

34. Lawrence S. Kaplan, "Collective Security and the Case of NATO," in Joseph Smith, ed., *The Origins of NATO*, Exeter Studies in History, no. 28 (Exeter, UK: University of Exeter Press, 1990), 97.

35. Josephson, "The Search for a Lasting Peace," 205, 215.

36. Kleidman, *Organizing for Peace*, 21; Warren F. Kuehl, "Concepts of Internationalism in History," *Peace and Change* 11, no. 2 (1986): 6. See also Steven Charles Goldman, "The Conservative Critique of Containment: An Isolationist Alternative to Cold War Diplomacy" (Ph.D. diss., Johns Hopkins University, 1974), 45.

37. Margaret Morley, "Freda Kirchwey: Cold War Critic," in Lloyd C. Gardner, ed., *Redefining the Past: Essays in Diplomatic History in Honor of William Appleman Williams* (Corvalles: Oregon State University Press, 1986), 159–60, 167.

38. J. Samuel Walker Jr., *Henry A. Wallace and American Foreign Policy*, Contributions in American History, no. 50 (Westport, CT: Greenwood Press, 1976), 88–89, 177.

39. Ibid., 119, 199–200.

40. Ibid., 121.

41. F. Ross Peterson, *Prophet without Honor: Glen H. Taylor and the Fight for American Liberalism* (Lexington: University of Kentucky Press, 1974), 149, x, 78.

42. Taylor, April 8, 1949, *Congressional Record*, 81st Cong., 1st sess., Vol. 95, pt. 3:4141.

43. Warburg to Acheson, February 6, 1948, James Warburg Papers, Box 13, Acheson file, John F. Kennedy Library, Boston, MA. Hereafter referred to as the Warburg Papers.

44. Ron Chernow, *The Warburgs: The Twentieth-Century Odyssey of a Remarkable Jewish Family* (New York: Random House, 1993), 580, 582.

45. Warburg, "The Atlantic Defense Pact and the Proposal to Rearm Western Europe," 10–11, James Warburg, CDG-A, SCPC.

46. Wesley T. Wooley, *Alternatives to Anarchy: American Supranationalism since World War II* (Bloomington: Indiana University Press, 1988), 21–22, 35, 53, 71, 70.

47. W. A. Swanberg, *Norman Thomas: The Last Idealist* (New York: Charles Scribner's Sons, 1976), 293.

48. "Constitution of the Post War World Council," PWWC, DG 62, Reel 90.1, SCPC.

49. Penny M. Von Eschen, "Challenging Cold War Habits: African Americans, Race, and Foreign Policy," *Diplomatic History* 20 (fall 1996): 629–30.

50. Mark Soloman, "Black Critics of Colonialism and the Cold War," in Paterson, ed., *Cold War Critics*, 214–16, 222. See also Brenda Gayle Plummer, *Rising Wind: Black Americans and U.S. Foreign Affairs, 1935–1960* (Chapel Hill: University of North Carolina Press, 1996), 176.

51. See Alfred O. Hero Jr., "American Negroes and U.S. Foreign Policy: 1937–1967," *Journal of Conflict Resolution* 13, no. 2 (1969): 224.

52. Gerald Horne, *Black and Red: W.E.B. Du Bois and the Afro-American Response to the Cold War, 1944–1963* (Albany: State University of New York Press, 1986), 2, 277, 20, 22–24; James L. Roark, "American Black Leaders: The Response to Colonialism and the Cold War," *African Historical Studies* 4 (1971): 264, 267; Carol Anderson, "From Hope to Disillusion: African Americans, the United Nations, and the Struggle for Human Rights, 1944–1947," *Diplomatic History* 20 (fall 1996): 561; Helen Laville and Scott Lucas, "The American Way: Edith Sampson, the NAACP, and African American Identity in the Cold War," *Diplomatic History* 20 (fall 1996): 580; Soloman, "Black Critics of Colonialism and the Cold War," 212.

53. Anderson, "From Hope to Disillusion," 539; Soloman, "Black Critics of Colonialism and the Cold War," 207–8, 213.

54. Mary Sperling McAuliffe, *Crisis on the Left: Cold War Politics and American Liberals 1947–1954* (Amherst: University of Massachusetts Press, 1978), 1–2; Alonzo L. Hamby, *Beyond the New Deal: Harry S. Truman and American Liberalism* (New York: Columbia University Press, 1973), vii.

55. McAuliffe, *Crisis on the Left*, 2.

56. Hamby, *Beyond the New Deal*, 13, 87.

57. *New York Times*, September 13, 1946, 4. For a discussion of Truman's approval of this speech, see Graham White and John Maze, *Henry A. Wallace: His Search for a New World Order* (Chapel Hill: University of North Carolina Press, 1995), 224–30.

58. McAuliffe, *Crisis on the Left*, 7, 5; Alonzo L. Hamby, "Henry A. Wallace, the Liberals, and Soviet-American Relations," *Review of Politics* 30 (April 1968): 156.

59. McAuliffe, *Crisis on the Left*, 23.

60. Ibid., 38, 146–47.

61. Henry Wallace, "Liberalism," March 1948, Wallace Papers, Reel 44, University of Iowa, Iowa City, IA.

62. McAuliffe, *Crisis on the Left*, 38–39, 47.

63. John Ehrman, *The Rise of Neoconservatism: Intellectuals and Foreign Affairs 1945–1994* (New Haven, CT: Yale University Press, 1995), 2.

64. Richard Barnet, *The Rockets' Red Glare: When America Goes to War, the Presidents and the People* (New York: Simon and Schuster, 1990), 281; DeBenedetti, *Peace Reform in American History*, 154–55, McAuliffe, *Crisis on the Left*, 63.

65. Allen Yarnell, *Democrats and Progressives: The 1948 Presidential Election as a Test of Postwar Liberalism* (Berkeley: University of California Press, 1974), 87.

66. Acheson quoted in Thomas Paterson, *On Every Front*, 135.

67. Ibid.

68. Ralph B. Levering, *The Public and American Foreign Policy, 1918–1978* (New York: William Morrow and Co., 1978), 106.

69. Morse, March 12, 1948, *Congressional Record*, 80th Cong., 2nd sess., Vol. 94, pt. 2:2684; Taylor, *Congressional Record*, 80th Cong., 2nd sess., Vol. 94, pt. 2:2684.

70. M. J. Heale, *American Anticommunism: Combating the Enemy Within, 1830–1970* (Baltimore, MD: Johns Hopkins University Press, 1990), 123; Richard M. Fried, *Nightmare in Red: The McCarthy Era in Perspective* (New York: Oxford University Press, 1990), 87; Charles DeBenedetti, ed., "Introduction," *Peace Heroes in Twentieth-Century America* (Bloomington: Indiana University Press, 1986), 12.

71. DeBenedetti, "Introduction," *Peace Heroes*, 11; Herman Will Jr., "Report on Mid-Century Conference For Peace," June 5, 1950, Committee For Peaceful Alternatives, CDG-A, SCPC. For more on the conference and the issue of communists see chapter 5.

72. DeBenedetti, "Introduction," *Peace Heroes*, 11; A. J. Muste, "Communism and Civil Liberties," in Nat Hentoff, ed., *The Essays of A. J. Muste* (New York: Bobbs-Merrill Co., Inc., 1967), 323, 326.

2

THE EARLY OPPOSITION

The end of World War II brought both good and bad news for those who sought a lasting world peace. In the process of negotiating a postwar settlement, all the major powers, including the United States, had agreed to create an international organization that they hoped could maintain the peace through the continued cooperation of the major powers. On the other hand, the war in the Pacific came to a sudden end with the introduction of atomic warfare. This new force would change the way many viewed the world and the danger of war forever. Perhaps, as many hoped, the new UN would be able to control this awesome force.

Despite the atomic danger, the atmosphere of the immediate postwar era was a supportive one for an American peace movement. Advocates of world government and nonviolent revolutionaries within the internationalist and pacifist ranks took the lead in organizing antiwar campaigns. There was, for a short time, a climate of hope.[1] The FOR, in a statement issued celebrating the end of the war in Europe, reflected this optimism: "[W]e must now as a people turn our thoughts and energies to the making of peace. We need . . . to cultivate the mentality and spirit of peacemaking." However, the statement also warned that there could be peace only if the mentality of war-making ended and if the world came together again.[2]

Despite the hope that World War II had strengthened antiwar tendencies by demonstrating the consequences of war as a solution to international problems, World War II may have weakened the antiwar movement, especially the pacifist wing. The war had stripped pacifist groups of many supporters, and the movement's inability to stop the aggression of the fascist powers had shattered its confidence. The result was that pacifism was discredited to many people, and pacifists found themselves isolated from broader social and political currents within the United States.[3] By 1946, many peace activists found themselves in opposition to many of the Truman administration's policies, especially the policy toward the Soviet Union.

THE BOMB AND THE UNITED NATIONS

The massive destruction of World War II, culminating with the atomic attacks on Hiroshima and Nagasaki, Japan, made it evident that war needed to be avoided as a solution to international differences. With the advent of atomic weapons, the concern about war was greater, and the control of atomic weapons became a major issue for peace activists in the postwar era.[4] The threat posed by these weapons was recognized from the very beginning of the nuclear age. Although Americans overwhelmingly supported the use of the bomb, there were also critics. The critical voices, however, were isolated and ranged in expression "from troubled uneasiness to anguished dismay."[5]

One of the leading organizations, on both a local and national level, speaking out critically on the use and dangers of the atomic bomb was the American Section of the WILPF. Gladys Greene, the president of the California branch, wired President Harry Truman on August 6, 1945, stating the organization's horror at the indiscriminate destruction and pleading that the "hideous disgrace" not be repeated. Later, Dorothy Detzer, the organization's national executive secretary, wrote that the WILPF recognized that the bombing of Hiroshima changed society, and contended that "it was monstrous that man's genius should have been prostituted once again to the service of Death." She argued that no government is wise or good enough to hoard the secret of atomic energy and that the bomb should be "in the keeping of the United Nations."[6] The leadership of the FOR urged its membership to express its moral outrage against the resort to atomic bombing and call on government officials to pledge not to use the weapon again. Political commentator Dwight Macdonald called the dropping of the bomb on a civilian population an act that signaled America's "decline to barbarism."[7]

Those who felt indignation over the dropping of the bomb saw it also as an opportunity to organize opposition to war. A. J. Muste, executive secretary of the FOR, wrote Detzer that pacifists should lose no time in seeing what could be done "to get a movement for the abolition of war going, using the atomic bomb as a springboard."[8]

Where World War II may have weakened the pacifist movement, it politicized the scientific community, especially on the issue of atomic weapons. In 1944, atomic scientists, led by Danish physicist Niels Bohr, called on Washington to initiate a more cooperative atomic policy, including the sharing of information with the Russians. He hoped that such a sign of solidarity would be a step toward investing in the UN as a multilateral means of controlling atomic weaponry.[9] But gradually, even the scientific community, which worried about the use of the power they had done so much to unleash, shifted from activism toward an acquiescence to Cold War policies and further development of atomic weapons.[10]

As the Cold War emerged, the issue of sharing the "secrets" of the bomb with other states, especially the Soviet Union, led to a consensus opinion in the United States that the bomb itself would guarantee the peace.[11] Most peace activists opposed the continuation of the American monopoly on atomic weapons. However, Muste felt that sharing it with the Russians alone was not enough. Expressing one of the concerns of the postwar peace movement, the domination of the world by the great powers, Muste feared that big power control of the bomb would enhance the "arbitrary power they hold over others" and provided no guarantee that "they may not some time fall out with each other and resort to atomic warfare." Instead, he supported the internationalization of its control and development.[12] Muste and many others hoped that the UN could serve to control these new weapons. However, the WRL was not so sure that the UN was the answer. They opposed both the attempt of the United States to monopolize the weapon and handing the bomb over to the UN because of its domination by the Big Three. Instead the WRL called for a multilateral treaty renouncing the manufacture and employment of atomic energy for destructive purposes.[13]

It was in the UN that many in the peace movement, both pacifists and internationalists, placed their greatest hopes. That is not to say that there were not serious reservations about the organization from the very beginning. Despite the refusal of the United States to join the League of Nations after World War I, internationalists had remained actively supportive of U.S. membership in that international body.

After the beginning of World War II, internationalists organized in the pursuit of various concepts, ranging from a new league to a world federation to a new balance of power where the big powers policed the world.[14] Bipartisan support was carefully cultivated for an international organization. In the September 1943 Mackinac Island Declaration, the Republican Party pledged to support U.S. participation in a postwar organization to attain permanent peace. This declaration allowed the Democratic administration of President Franklin Roosevelt to work with the Republican opposition to attain a commonly shared goal, avoiding past partisanship.[15] In September 1943, the House of Representatives passed the Fulbright Resolution, introduced by J. William Fulbright of Arkansas, supporting an international agency to maintain the peace. The U.S. Senate followed the House lead in November with the Connally Resolution, proposed by Tom Connally of Texas. This support for an international organization laid the foundations for the bipartisan Cold War foreign policy in the postwar years.

With bipartisan support in Congress, the Roosevelt administration proceeded with negotiations creating the UN. By October 1944 at the Dumbarton Oaks conference, Russia, Britain, the United States, and China tentatively agreed on a charter for the UN Organization, establishing a type of collective security system to maintain the peace. More agreements followed at the Yalta conference in early 1945; the process culminated in the April 1945 San Francisco conference which formally established the UN Organization.

A majority of Americans accepted U.S. membership in the UN. Most involved in the peace movement, whether pacifist or internationalist, supported American participation in the new organization. Groups that tended toward isolationism prior to U.S. entry into World War II came to view the UN as a first step toward the maintenance of peace. Some individuals and groups, however, felt that the UN contained serious weaknesses that needed to be corrected for the organization to succeed. These criticisms, presented by many organizations that would eventually oppose the consensus Cold War policy of the Truman administration, were centered on various ideas that formed the basis of much of their later critique of the containment policy.

Frederick Libby, executive secretary for the NCPW, criticized the UN Charter for its reliance on the use of force to maintain the peace. He stated that the UN rejected the concept that war should be limited to the smallest areas, because, with UN collective security, Libby believed that all wars would become world wars. Looking ahead to what he saw as the greatest danger, Libby argued that the Charter did nothing to prevent war among the Big Three powers. He told the Senate Committee on Foreign Relations that the gravest danger was war among the great powers. In addition, the Charter also appeared to be "a military alliance of three rival imperialist powers." Reflecting his opposition to entanglement, Libby told the senators that "[c]ooperation without entanglements would be my slogan."[16]

Libby's fellow pacifists had similar problems with the Charter. The FOR's A. J. Muste noted that the emphasis on the use of force to prevent the resort to force is "chimerical." He felt that the attempt to build a rigid structure, which would be very difficult to alter, produced a false security. The FOR felt that the UN was "an effort to maintain an order imposed on the world by the might of victors in war and is bound to fail."[17] The WILPF agreed that it amounted to the domination of the world by the most heavily armed powers. The more radical pacifist organization, the WRL, argued that it did nothing to deal with the causes of war. The UN did little to incorporate the more transnational ideas of the pacifists.[18] Despite these criticisms, each of these organizations, once established, supported the UN and sought to strengthen it against what they viewed as a growing, aggressive unilateralism by the United States.

Although internationalists would soon divide over the issues of the Cold War, on the issue of the UN there was general support for the organization, but again, not without reservations. One such critical supporter was Norman Thomas, leader of the Socialist Party and of the PWWC. During World War II he had shed an earlier reputation as an "isolationist" and cooperated with many liberal internationalists.[19] Thomas agreed with much of the pacifist critique of the UN. He stated that it was "an alliance of strong powers, and no alliance of the strong in history has ever lasted long after the particular war or threat of war which brought it into existence is over." Thomas noted the power of the Big Five and warned that no peace could be guaranteed by an organization "which perpetuates the dangerous myth of equality of absolute national sovereignty at the same time that it leaves all real power in the hands of five great nations." Nonetheless, Thomas supported ratification not because he believed it an adequate basis for lasting peace but because he felt that "the United States will be in a better position to lead in the establishment of such a basis if it should ratify the Charter and in good faith use its constructive provisions."[20]

Various other liberal internationalists, especially religious groups, were optimistic about the organization. Charles Boss Jr., the executive secretary of the Commission on World Peace of the Methodist Church, noted that the Charter was not the solution to the problems of war but was the constitution for "a new world order, an international instrument for the facing and solving of problems." The Executive Committee of the Federal Council of Churches of Christ in America felt that the UN offered humanity "an important means for the achievement of a just and durable peace."[21]

One other category of critical supporters were the anticolonialists. Within this group, African American leadership played a significant role. Between 1943 and 1947, American black leaders raised strong protests against European colonialism and against U.S. foreign policy which they believed supported that colonialism. The establishment of the UN created an atmosphere of hope among anticolonialists. U.S. African American leaders were disappointed though that the charter did not call for an immediate end to colonies. However, they remained hopeful that the organization would be a leading force in a quick transition to independence.[22]

The leftist CAA was disappointed at what it saw as the easy willingness of the United States to accommodate the positions of the European colonial powers.[23] The spokesman, at that time, for the more widely known NAACP was W.E.B. Du Bois. Du Bois indicated his support for the Charter, but with certain reservations. He favored the inclusion of a statement on racial equality and on colonies. He warned that the colonial system was undemocratic, socially dangerous, and a main cause of wars. Nonetheless, in a statement to the Senate Foreign Relations Committee, Du Bois indicated that he believed that the UN "is a step and a far step toward peace and justice."[24] On the other hand, Howard University Professor Rayford Logan, an NAACP consultant, called the UN Charter a "tragic joke," saying that the UN "signatories had already violated the terms of the charter by denying democracy to their subjects."[25]

Once the UN was established, the NAACP attempted to use it to support human rights for African Americans. In 1947, the organization backed Du Bois's "An Appeal to the World" to get the UN to put that issue on its agenda. Supported first by India and later by the Soviet Union, the petition failed, and the UN effectively consigned the appeal to oblivion. The connection with the Soviet Union caused the NAACP to start what one historian called "a slow and steady retreat from the issues of human rights and decolonization."[26]

For some, such as the WILPF's Mildred Olmsted, the fact that the United States was willing to join the UN was cause for postwar optimism. Although she, too, was concerned that the Big Five held on to too much power, Olmsted felt that the organization was a step in the right direction. Throughout the latter 1940s, the WILPF emphasized the importance of the UN as a significant force in achieving diplomatic cooperation and the end of violence in foreign affairs. The organization supported the peaceful settlement of international disputes, complete universal disarmament, universal UN membership, respect for worth and dignity of the individual, self-determination for all peoples, and the use of specialized agencies to achieve world reconstruction.[27]

Despite high hopes for the UN, the emerging conflict between the United States and the Soviet Union over the political and economic reconstruction of Europe led quickly to a breakdown of big power cooperation in the UN. The issue of Soviet withdrawal from war-occupied Iran brought an early confrontation between the big powers. The issue of regulation of atomic weapons brought more disagreement. Within the Truman administration, there were discussions about how the United States would give up its atomic monopoly to an international authority. Ultimately, the view was that the United States should be free to continue building and testing atomic bombs until any plan became fully operational. Meanwhile the Russian position, elaborated by Andre Gromyko, the Soviet representative to the UN, was that a world moratorium on the production and use of atomic weapons had to precede an agreement on international control.[28] Hopes that atomic energy could be controlled effectively by the UN finally collapsed with the conflicts over the U.S. Baruch Plan in 1946.

Meanwhile, activists worried about atomic power were concerned with continued U.S. production of atomic weapons. The PWWC stated its "indignation" over reports that the United States "is continuing the manufacture of atomic bombs." They stated that there was no excuse for such actions, because it "incites universal suspicion of our sincerity in seeking renunciation of the use of atomic energy for war." The PWWC argued that continued production "goes far toward justifying the almost pathological concern of the Soviet Government for its security."[29]

By 1947, both Protestant and Catholic groups had addressed the moral issues raised by the development of atomic warfare. Both condemned the concept of total war and the deliberate terror bombing of civilians, along with the complete destruction of Hiroshima and Nagasaki. However, they hesitated to issue a categorical condemnation of the bomb as an instrument of war. One who did not hesitate was A. J. Muste. In his 1947 *Not By Might*, Muste condemned Hiroshima as a crime, just as Dachau was a crime. Hiroshima, he wrote, breached the final barriers separating warfare from mass murder. Atomic warfare, he wrote, was "sin of the most hideous kind."[30]

Pacifists remained sharp critics of the bomb and its continued production and development. This opposition continued through the postwar period as they came to emphasize various programs for disarmament or reduction of atomic stockpiles. As time passed, however, the critics had considerably less appeal to Americans. Although concern remained, especially after the Russians developed their own bomb in 1949, there was a growing apathy about it, and the emphasis on the atomic threat helped to create the Cold War consensus and civil defense movements.[31] There were also other issues. Although the opposition to the Cold War policies of Truman did not fully develop until 1947, critics were raising concerns about the implications of various American actions. In addition to the development and testing of atomic weapons, policies that came under scrutiny included the Truman proposal for universal military training (UMT), continuation of the selective service, and the U.S. role in deteriorating Soviet-American relations.

UNIVERSAL MILITARY TRAINING AND CONSCRIPTION

Unlike previous wars in American history, the United States did not demobilize a large portion of its armed forces after World War II. Although some demobilization did take place, for a variety of political and economic reasons the U.S. military remained large. To maintain that size in the immediate postwar years, the Truman administration discussed a number of ideas to meet manpower requirements. Most Americans (70 percent according to a Gallup Poll taken in January 1945) favored requiring every able-bodied young man to serve one year in the military. Only 25 percent opposed the one-year idea. The same question asked in May received the same percentage of support.[32] The new Truman administration favored the implementation of a UMT program. In October 1945, President Truman stated that for years to come, U.S. efforts for a just and lasting peace depended on the strength of those who are determined to maintain that peace. He stated, "We can ensure such a peace only so long as we remain strong." To accomplish that goal, short of a large standing army, Truman favored "a comparatively small regular Army, Navy and Air Force, supported by well-trained citizens, who in time of emergency could be quickly mobilized." General George Marshall, the chief of staff, also felt that UMT had to be the fundamental basis of peace. He believed that UMT would "have a far reaching effect in obtaining a satisfactory international agreement for the terms of peace."[33] However, almost universally, pacifists and liberal internationalists opposed both a continuation of the wartime draft and the establishment of a program of UMT.

During the war, pacifists began to express their concerns about the continuation of some form of mandatory military service when the war ended. Muste's view was that there was a difference between wartime and peacetime drafts, but with the issue of a permanent conscription, there could be no compromise. Speaking before the House Select Committee on Post War Military Policy, Mary Farquharson of the WILPF noted that the drive to continue conscription would lead to a radical departure from traditional U.S. policy. She noted that without question the reason behind a push for conscription was its "alleged guarantee of security." But she argued that it was "self-defeating." Farquharson stated, "Not a single country has been saved from the ravages of war because of its military machine. No matter what the motives are in building up military power, its very presence affects relationships with all other countries . . . as well as changing the thinking of its own citizens." She called for an international convention for the abolition of conscription as the first step in changing patterns and easing the "crushing burdens of armaments." The PWWC, in a September 1945 public letter to Truman, stated that conscription in the atomic age "will be enormously wasteful and completely useless except for indoctrinating our young men in a military point of view which, as European experience . . . has proven, is equally dangerous to democracy and peace." Socialist leader Norman Thomas wrote to President Roosevelt in January 1945 that he favored a worldwide move to end the draft, because no nation could endure the costs of universal conscription and noted the link between the draft and militarism and imperialism.[34]

The peace churches, after working with the Selective Service System to create alternatives to military service for pacifists during World War II, looked forward to an end of the draft at war's end. In a statement on UMT at their 1945 Annual Conference, the Church of the Brethren expressed their opposition to the continuation of conscription. The church noted that it was "compelled by virtue of religious conviction to register . . . opposition to the plan." They noted that it reversed U.S. traditions and sought "to establish conformity and obedience rather than independent leadership." The Brethren warned that "[h]istory shows that universal military conscription is usually a first step away from Christianity and democracy in the direction of tyranny." They also objected because of international politics, stating "that fear, suspicion and military rivalry among the nations of the world are one of the large contributors to war." To the Church of the Brethren, conscription stood in direct contradiction to the Atlantic Charter, the Dumbarton Oaks declaration, and the objectives of the San Francisco conference. Dr. Warren D. Bowman, pastor of the Washington, DC Church of the Brethren, told the House Committee on Post War Military Policy that the church believed "that universal military training is in the final analysis preparation to wage war."[35]

Although not known as one of the historic peace churches, the Methodist Church also expressed its opposition to peacetime conscription. Its Commission on World Peace adopted a strong statement in opposition to compulsory military training and called for a universal abolition of conscription through the UN. The pacifist Catholic Worker Movement also actively opposed conscription, working for the first time with other pacifist groups, including the FOR and the WRL. When the peacetime draft was proposed in 1948, they continued their tradition of advocating noncooperation and offering to support men prosecuted for draft resistance.[36]

Nonetheless, one of Truman's first acts as president was to sign a one-year extension of the draft. Of course at that time the United States was still at war. The debate over a peacetime draft continued into 1946. The draft was set to expire in May 1946, but the War Department stated that occupation duties required that troops stay in service. In January 1946, Truman stated that he wanted a UMT program, but would settle for a renewal of the draft because the armed services could not rely on volunteers. As the Cold War developed, the administration began to tie the draft to the threat from Russia, and again in May 1946, the draft was extended, first for six weeks, then again until March 31, 1947. Through the end of 1946 and into 1947, the War Department tried to move toward an all-volunteer system while Truman continued to push his UMT plan. On March 3, 1947, Truman recommended the end of the draft, replacing the Selective Service with the Office of Selective Service Records as a caretaker operation. He hoped that the end of the draft would help gain the passage of a UMT program.[37]

Despite arguments for its continuation, after 1947 the draft was allowed to expire. To help build up support for his UMT idea, Truman had appointed an advisory commission on UMT in December 1946. After study, the commission called for the military training of every qualified male for a minimum of six months. However, hopes for the establishment of such a program stalled in the Senate. With his plans for a UMT delayed, and with the all-volunteer plan failing, Truman, in his 1948 State of the Union address, called for a renewal of the peacetime draft and for a UMT. In June 1948, the Selective Service Act of 1948 was signed into law, but the UMT was buried. The Selective Service was extended again in 1950 and then made a permanent act in 1951. In the 1951 act, the Congress accepted the principle of UMT, passing the Universal Military Training and Service Act in June. However, this UMT section would go into effect only when the president through executive order, or the Congress by concurrent resolution, reduced or eliminated the requirement for two-year service. In essence, the UMT was "stillborn." The result was that Congress enacted legislation that continued a reliance on selective service.[38]

Truman explained his proposals for the draft and UMT in a March 1948 speech. He stated that as long as communism threatened the existence of democracy, the United States must remain strong enough to support those countries of Europe which were threatened by communism. The president explained his belief that a strong military was a means of preventing war; he argued that "a sound military system is necessary in time of peace if we are to remain at peace" and that universal training is a feasible way to build up the civilian components of the U.S. armed forces that would be required in emergencies.[39]

Hearings on the renewal proposals began in March 1948. Secretary of State George Marshall presented the administration's point of view on the need for a draft and a UMT program before the Senate Committee on Armed Services. Referring to ERP, he stated that the rapid march of events made it clear that the future safety of those areas could not be dependent solely on the slow process of reconstruction. He stated that the United States "must show . . . the nations of the world that the United States intends to be strong and to hold that strength ready to keep the European world both at peace and free." He argued that "[d]iplomatic action, without the backing of military strength in the present world can lead only to appeasement."[40]

Secretary of Defense James Forrestal echoed Marshall's testimony and countered some of the critics' arguments. He said that more men needed to be trained to meet the threat of war. The existence of atomic weapons did not, according to Forrestal, make armies unnecessary, but instead made necessary the training of large numbers of men to handle them. Because future wars will be indiscriminate and universal in their targets and effects, "training also has to be universal."[41]

Both pacifists and liberal internationalists testified before the committee in opposition to the administration's conscription and UMT proposals. If the testimony in opposition is representative, there was much broader opposition to conscription than any other Cold War policy. The opposition went beyond just the pacifists and liberals and included a variety of religious groups.

The most obvious critics were the peace churches whose members would face difficulties with any mandatory draft or military training. Calvert N. Ellis, moderator of the Church of the Brethren, told the committee that the UMT plan cut across the church's historic faith and thus by virtue of their religious conviction they had to register their opposition. Going beyond simply the church's religious opposition, Ellis stated that the church believed "that some aspects of our foreign policy have been ill-advised and may already have taken us far down the road to war." Quoting from the Church of the Brethren's June 1947 Annual Conference statement, Ellis said that "war with Russia is avoidable, and that all attempts to maneuver our people into that suspicion, fear and hatred of Russia . . . are a disservice to the basis of peace." Speaking for the Mennonite Central Committee, Don E. Smucker stated that "[c]onscription for war we consider un-Christian." Smucker argued that "further extension of the power of the state over lives of men through military training is not desirable." Dr. Henry J. Cadbury, speaking for the Friends Committee on National Legislation (FCNL), argued that history went against the administration's argument that conscription was needed to prevent war through deterrence. Cadbury noted that "[n]early all wars have been preceded by precisely some act intended to be a preventive show of force."[42]

Pacifist organizations also spoke before the Committee on Armed Services. Charles W. Iglehart, chair of the national council of the FOR, asked the committee to look behind the proposals to where the real danger lay. He cited two dangers. The first was that the UMT was just as much a conscription as a selective service, as it would involve the compulsory induction of civilians into a military force. With so many young men coming into the hands of military authorities, "one can see something gathering on the horizon which has never been contemplated in the American tradition." The second danger was that the training should not be considered as much a real preparation for fighting as a period of indoctrination in "militant nationalism." Instead, Iglehart called for the abolition of all national military establishments. Speaking for the NCPW, Frederick Libby told the committee that it was a fundamental error to base U.S. foreign policy on the "fallacious military theory that Russians will recognize nothing but force." Libby stated that it was not in the military, but the economic field that U.S. success in promoting peace would be found. Edward Richards of the WRL argued that the draft was wrong "because it demands the surrender of the individual conscience to the dictates of the state." Mrs. Robert W. Rea of the WILPF opposed conscription and UMT because it would be a drastic departure from American tradition and because it "would be a step in the direction of war." Rea issued a warning that such a proposal for permanent military indoctrination of American boys "would undermine our faith in peace."[43]

In addition to their religious opposition to war, the pacifists tended to emphasize a fear that conscription was a step toward war because such aggressive deterrence would not work. Both the religious pacifists and the WRL expressed their opposition to governmental compulsion that came with a draft or UMT. A third theme, raised by several individuals in their testimony, was the belief that universal training would contribute to a militant nationalism or a militaristic society. These themes, particularly the fear of militarism and the belief that American actions were not deterrents but steps toward war, became common themes among opponents of Truman's foreign policy.

In addition to the pacifist groups, religious and secular, many other church groups spoke out against conscription and the idea of a UMT. Sidney A. Temple Jr. of the Episcopal Pacifist Fellowship told the Armed Services Committee that there was a "feeling" in the church, not just among the pacifists, that conscription was a denial of Americanism and would be perceived by others as threatening. Dr. Donald B. Cloward, representing the Northern Baptist Council on Christian Social Progress, stated that selective service and UMT would make the United States into the world's police department. He noted though that it "does not mean that we are isolationist. On the contrary, we have consistently called for the founding of the United Nations and urged its strengthening." What Cloward opposed was unilateral international action. Representing the Methodists, Charles Boss Jr. expressed fear that UMT would result in the loss of freedom and liberty and would lead the United States to be "tempted to seek the goal of dominant military power rather than a restrained partnership with a broken and bleeding world." Instead of UMT, Boss hoped that the United States could take the lead in a UN plan for reduction of forces and armaments around the world. Rev. Haber F. Klemme of the Evangelical and Reformed Church, in expressing the Church's opposition to UMT, warned that "conscription in peacetime opens the way to the militarization of our country." Rev. Paul Payne of the Presbyterian Church, Walter Sikes of the Disciples of Christ, and Merrill E. Bush of the Unitarian Commission on World Order also expressed their churches' opposition.[44]

Several religious-based organizations also testified. Dr. W. H. Jernagin, the director of the Washington bureau of the National Fraternal Council of Negro Churches of America, opposed UMT as a way of maintaining the peace. Jernagin also questioned the claim that UMT would defend democracy "when we understand that Jim Crow is the official policy of our Government with respect to the armed services." Walter W. Van Kirk, representing the Federal Council of the Churches of Christ in America, stated that the organization "believes that the existing crisis in international affairs is primarily social and economic in character, and as such can best be met by measures designed to promote economic recovery and social stability on a global scale." Robert Tesdell of the United Christian Youth Movement, representing forty denominations and interdenominational councils, told the committee that among youth, opposition to UMT is so universal that they have directed their attention and energies to discussing ways of combating all forms of militarism, including compulsory military training.[45]

In addition to the pacifist and religious opposition, many liberal internationalists spoke out in opposition of UMT and conscription. The leading liberal internationalist in opposition was Henry Wallace, who was to challenge Truman's policies as the presidential candidate of the Progressive Party in 1948. Wallace placed his opposition to UMT in the context of the Truman Doctrine and the Marshall Plan (see chapter 3). He argued that this was the third stage, the application of military force. He warned that the UMT and the draft would reduce the entire society to gears in the American war machine. This sentiment was echoed by Seymour Linfield, the veterans' director of the national Wallace for President Committee. Linfield stated the UMT "would place American youth in a military straitjacket, mold their minds to military thinking" and was "a major step toward the total mobilization of America for war." In a rare moment of agreement, especially in 1948, Don Willner of the Students for Democratic Action, affiliated with the ADA, noted that organization's opposition to UMT because it had no military value. He stated that "[m]ilitarization may be necessary as a temporary emergency condition, but it was unjustifiable as a permanent part of American life."[46]

Within the Senate, one of the most outspoken critics of the draft was Wallace's 1948 running mate, Glen Taylor. Sen. Taylor's opposition to the draft resulted in part from his dislike of the military establishment. According to the senator, a large standing army could not be trusted, because with a huge army just waiting, some general will want to use it. In addition, Taylor opposed the draft because he believed it a clear break with U.S. traditions, feared it would lead to the creation of a huge military complex that would keep the economy geared to the military, felt that with atomic bombs it was unnecessary, disliked the racial discrimination in the military, and believed its continuation would be an admission that foreign policy had failed and the United States was re-arming. Truman's March 1948 call for a renewal of the draft and a UMT program led Taylor to criticize the diplomatic course of the Truman administration. He contended that the Truman policy was losing friends for the United States, especially among the newly emerging nations in Africa and Asia. To Taylor, a decision to draft an army was an act of aggression. Twenty-two years later, Taylor still contended that if the nation had not resorted to a draft in 1948, and had not remilitarized, " 'the coldest days of the cold war would have been more temperate.' "[47]

Various leaders of the noncommunist left spoke out against UMT. Norman Thomas, speaking for the PWWC, argued that UMT would weaken the United States, because it would take men away from where they were economically essential. He warned that peacetime conscription would reduce hope for universal disarmament by creating the economic and psychological interests that armaments and armies always build up. Speaking for the Socialist Party, Howard Penley argued that UMT was a step toward war and would fail to stop the spread of communism. He believed that UMT was part of a military answer to what he saw as "basically a political problem." Arthur Schutzer of the American Labor Party of New York echoed many of those same themes and warned that peacetime conscription would "fasten the grip of the National Security Council upon the American Government as a superagency of military domination." A. Philip Randolph, representing the Committee Against Jim Crow in Military Service and Training, told the senate committee that blacks were in "no mood to shoulder a gun for democracy abroad so long as they are denied democracy here at home." He warned that the draft would be met with civil disobedience. As passed, the new draft law banned discrimination, not segregation. Truman had to end that on his own.[48]

Other groups, many formed specifically to oppose the peacetime conscription, spoke out in opposition to the administration's proposals. Rev. Rodney Shaw of the Chicago Committee to Oppose Peacetime Conscription noted many of the same points cited by others above. Shaw offered some reasoned alternatives while noting that UMT was a poor preparation for defense. He told the committee:

With a navy greater than all other navies put together, with the atomic bomb, with unequalled industrial productivity, and a great air force, we have enough might to gain for ourselves a respectful bearing. What we need is a constructive program for building peace, which is morally right, and not imperialist, and which we are prepared to back with our economic power.[49]

Rev. John Darr Jr., the chair of the National Youth Assembly Against Military Training, noted that Truman argued that UMT was needed because of international crises. Darr speculated that this crisis atmosphere was created to "silence the voices of those opposing militarization of America." He charged that the crisis was not an international one, but an American crisis arising from the "bankruptcy" of bipartisan foreign policy. He continued, "It appears that the United States is so weak in moral power that it must employ economic warfare and military might to impose its policies on the world." Both Dr. Henry Crane, a Methodist minister representing the Michigan Council Against Conscription, and Alonzo Myers, representing the National Council Against Conscription, emphasized use of the UN to maintain peace. Myers said that if U.S. leaders would work as hard to strengthen the UN as they were working to "bamboozle the country and Congress into adopting UMT," the outlook for peace would be brighter. Crane stated that the chief impediment to the fulfillment of conditions for the development of the UN was "the military mind that never really gives reason and conscience a fair chance to compete on equal terms with military force as a preventive power."[50]

Despite the broad nature of the opposition, broader than in any other foreign policy initiative, the Truman administration was able to gain congressional approval for conscription in 1948. The idea of a peacetime draft was one policy that convinced many individuals and groups that the United States was drifting toward war with the Soviet Union. Throughout 1946 and 1947, prior to the announcement of the Truman Doctrine, many expressed concern about the U.S. role in growing Soviet-American hostility. Many of the significant criticisms of the containment policy emerged during the debate on the draft.

FROM DISARMAMENT TO CONTAINMENT

From the beginning of the postwar era, opponents of the Truman foreign policy had a different view of how the United States should act in the world. The most unfailing of these opponents was A. J. Muste. He called for the United States to renounce war, demonstrate that it meant business by disarming unilaterally, and then take the money that would be spent on arms and take food, healing, and economic rehabilitation to needy peoples. Aware that it looked too idealistic, Muste defiantly wrote that "it is the only program that furnishes real hope of abolishing war in our time."[51] Muste and other pacifists focused on unilateral disarmament as the answer to the problem of war. Others varied in the approach, unilateral or multilateral, but disarmament was one of the key alternatives proposed by peace advocates in the postwar era.

The WRL also looked to disarmament as a solution. To its members, "[t]he first essential for ending war is the determination of people not to rely on armed violence for securing the thing they value." The organization noted that the war of nerves with the Nazis prior to World War

II proved that appeasement is of no value when people are taught that their ultimate reliance must be on armed resistance. WRL did not favor "a similar sort of appeasement where Russia is concerned." Instead, they favored an effort to persuade all nations to abandon large-scale militarism. A conference of various religious peace activists held in Atlantic City in December 1945 called for universal atomic disarmament through a multilateral treaty. Frederick Libby, in his 1946 annual report to the NCPW, stated that their basic goals were to achieve the establishment of a progressive world organization, the worldwide reduction of armaments by international agreement, and to carry out a worldwide education for peace.[52]

Another leading advocate of disarmament was Norman Thomas. As a supporter of universal disarmament, Thomas went to great lengths to define what he meant. To be effective, any disarmament had to control atomic energy, reduce arms and armies in all countries to a level necessary "for the preservation of international order," universally abolish peacetime conscription, demilitarize narrow waterways, and rapidly and orderly liquidate all imperialism (both the colonial and spheres of influence type). Thomas and the PWWC believed that hopes for a sound beginning for peace "would be a successful drive for universal national disarmament under international supervision and international arrangements for security."[53]

The theme of disarmament often conflicted with Truman administration policies, which steadily moved toward a militarization of U.S. policy. As various groups and individuals criticized the continuation of atomic weapons development and the large U.S. arsenal, many of the critics remained hopeful that the UN could reduce conflict and control arms. Most believed, like the Methodists in 1948, that despite its imperfections, including the Security Council veto, the UN "provides techniques for peaceful settlement of disputes . . . [and] the General Assembly provides a valuable sounding board for the moral judgment of the world."[54]

During 1946, U.S. policy was influenced more by the ideas of George Kennan, who was the *chargé d'affaires* in the U.S. Embassy in Moscow, than by the advocates of disarmament. On February 22, 1946, he sent a "Long Telegram" to the Department of State reflecting on "The Sources of Soviet Conduct," as it was later called in a July 1947 *Foreign Affairs* article. In the telegram, and later in the article, Kennan provided an explanation for Soviet behavior under Joseph Stalin, blaming the Soviets for the emerging Cold War and suggesting that Russia should be contained and no longer negotiated or compromised with. By the end of 1946, at the suggestion of his special counsel Clark Clifford, Truman began to implement Kennan's suggestions which came to be known as the containment policy.[55]

By the end of 1946, critics felt that U.S. policy toward the Soviet Union was headed in the wrong direction, away from cooperation, toward confrontation. James S. Warburg emerged as one of the critics of the more militant approach toward the Russians. He felt that the whole structure of peace constructed by Roosevelt rested on continuing friendly cooperation among the members of the victorious coalition, including the Soviets. To Warburg, the key was an agreement on Germany. If an agreement could be reached on Germany, Warburg believed, "the mounting East-West tension might still abate." Warburg believed that the Soviet Union was not a military threat to the West and refused to accept as credible the idea that the Russians were intent on world domination or even European hegemony based on force.[56]

The most notable critic by the fall of 1946 was Henry Wallace. It was his September 1946 speech in Madison Square Garden that led to his removal from the cabinet. Throughout 1946, he sought to maintain U.S. cooperation with the Soviets. On March 15, 1946, he wrote Truman that "much of the recent Soviet behavior which has caused us concern has been the result of their dire economic needs and of their disturbed sense of security." He told the president that the United States could "disabuse the Soviet mind and strengthen the faith of the Soviets in our sincere devotion to the cause of peace by proving to them that we want to trade with them and to cement our economic relations with them."[57]

As U.S.–Soviet relations deteriorated, Wallace again wrote Truman on July 23. He told the president that he was disturbed by the trend in international affairs since the end of the war and that he was especially troubled by the growing feeling in the United States that another war was coming "and that the only way that we can head it off is to arm ourselves to the teeth." He pointed out to Truman that, to the rest of the world, American actions since World War II must be of some concern. He noted that the United States had continued to fund the War and Navy Departments at $13 billion, carried out the atomic tests in the Bikini Islands, continued the production of bombs, produced B-29s and B-36s, and attempted to secure bases spread over half the globe from which the other half of the globe could be bombed. He wrote that to all other nations, it must look as if "we were only paying lip service to peace at the conference table." He argued that instead the United States should judge Soviet needs for security against the background of what the United States and Britain had insisted upon as essential. Returning to his March theme, Wallace stated, "[W]e should discuss with the Russians in a friendly way their long-range economic problems and the future of our cooperation in matters of trade."[58]

For Wallace, certain limited concessions to the Russians, such as security and trade, could be used to reestablish the wartime alliance. The July letter, released in September, combined with the New York speech, ended his cabinet career. Although moderate, and hardly pro-Soviet, the speech and letter called for a drastic shift in U.S. foreign policy.[59]

After leaving the cabinet, Wallace continued his criticism of the Truman policy, leading him into the 1948 political challenge to Truman. He broadened his criticism in a letter to Secretary of State George Marshall in January 1947. Wallace presented the United States as a status quo power in a changing world. In almost every country, he wrote, "men and women are desperately trying to alter the old order . . . because the old order has brought upon them poverty, disaster and war." While the Russians have been allowed to parade themselves to the colonial world as the only enemy of imperialism, the United States has been on the defensive, erecting "Maginot Lines of the spirit." He told the secretary that what was needed was "a mobile offensive . . . an affirmation of the revolutionary tradition" of the United States.[60]

At the same time, Sen. Taylor also emerged as a leading critic of what was developing into the containment policy. Taylor believed that to avoid future wars "it was necessary to eliminate economic competition among nations." He believed that the main enemy of world peace was imperialism and colonialism. He hoped that international organizations "could be instrumental in bringing an end to such economic rivalry."[61]

By the end of 1946, the relationship with the Soviets dominated pacifist concerns, too. The FOR hoped that discussions with the Soviets could continue. Fearing that the administration's policy was bound to lead to war, they called for a campaign for disarmament and abolition of conscription through international agreement. At the Atlantic City Conference for Peaceworkers, pacifists agreed that part of their job was to destroy the image of Russia as the bogeyman. Although recognizing Russian expansionism as a serious concern, the group, noting U.S. military bases and the attitude toward the bomb, stated, "[W]e must see that U.S. policies are at least parallel, if not actually provocative." Instead of armed diplomacy and competing imperialism that would lead to war in their view, the conferees called for the adoption of a policy of "aggressive good will."[62]

Despite these criticisms, some heard by government officials, some not, the Truman administration moved toward the implementation of containment of the Soviet Union. With the announcement of the Truman Doctrine, the United States committed itself to a policy that, as it unfolded, came to mean confrontation with the Soviets, an alliance with European nations, and, ultimately, a war in Korea.

NOTES

1. Lawrence S. Wittner, *Rebels against War: The American Peace Movement, 1941–1960* (New York: Columbia University Press, 1969), 151.

2. National Executive Committee of the Fellowship of Reconciliation, "V-E Day Statement," May 8, 1945, FOR, 3 Minutes and Reports, 1942–49, DG 13, SCPC.

3. Lawrence S. Wittner, *One World or None: A History of the World Nuclear Disarmament Movement through 1953*, vol. 1: *The Struggle against the Bomb* (Palo Alto, CA: Stanford University Press, 1993), 43.

4. For a detailed study of the efforts to control and eliminate atomic weapons, see Wittner, *One World or None*.

5. Wittner, *One World or None*, 1:56; Paul Boyer, *By the Bomb's Early Light: American Thought and Culture at the Dawn of the Atomic Age* (New York: Pantheon Books, 1985), 196.

6. Gladys Greene to Truman, August 6, 1945, WILPF, DG 43, Reel 130.75, SCPC; Dorothy Detzer, "Tentative Statement on the Atomic Bomb," October 1945[?], WILPF, DG 43, Series A, 4, Reel 130.36, SCPC.

7. Wittner, *One World or None*, 1:56; Macdonald quoted from *politics* in Robert Jay Lifton and Greg Mitchell, *Hiroshima in America: Fifty Years of Denial* (New York: G. P. Putnam, 1995), 37.

8. Muste to Detzer, August 29, 1945, WILPF, Reel 130.75, SCPC.

9. DeBenedetti, *Peace Reform in American History*, 144.

10. Wittner, *One World or None*, 1:43; Boyer, *By the Bomb's Early Light*, 342.

11. Wittner, *Rebels against War*, 168.

12. Muste to Henry Wallace, September 26, 1945, WILPF, Reel 130.75, SCPC.

13. Executive Committee of the WRL, "The Atomic Bomb," February 11, 1946, WRL, DG 40, Series A, Box 2, SCPC.

14. Robert A. Divine, *Second Chance: The Triumph of Internationalism in America during World War II* (New York: Atheneum, 1967), 34, 62, 144.

15. Crabb, *Bipartisan Foreign Policy*, 50–51.

16. Frederick Libby, July 12, 1945, U.S. Senate, Committee on Foreign Relations, *The Charter of the United Nations, Hearings before the Committee on Foreign Relations*, 79th Cong., 1st sess., 395–98. Hereafter referred to as *UN Hearings*.

17. A. J. Muste, "Dumbarton Oaks Will Not Do," n.d., A. J. Muste Papers, DG 50, Reel 89.4, SCPC; "Statement of the Executive Committee of the Fellowship of Reconciliation on Proposals for International Organization," May 9, 1945, Fellowship of Reconciliation Papers, DG 13, Minutes and Reports 1942–49, SCPC.

18. Charles Chatfield, *The American Peace Movement: Ideals and Activism* (New York: Twayne Publishers, 1992), 91.

19. Charles Chatfield, "Norman Thomas: Harmony of Word and Deed," in DeBenedetti, ed., *Peace Heroes in Twentieth-Century America* (Bloomington: Indiana University Press, 1986), 111.

20. Norman Thomas, "A Socialist Looks at the United Nations," Syracuse University Press Series no. 2, DG CDG-A, Norman Thomas file, SCPC, 6–14; Norman Thomas, "Statement on Ratification of San Francisco Charter to the Senate Foreign Relations Committee," n.d., DG 62, PWWC, Reel 90.7, SCPC.

21. Boss to Sen. Tom Connally, July 12, 1945, *UN Hearings*, 695; "Statement Adopted by the Executive Committee of the Federal Council of Churches of Christ in America," June 26, 1945, *UN Hearings*, 698.

22. Roark, "American Black Leaders: The Response to Colonialism and the Cold War," 253; Thomas J. Noer, *Cold War and Black Liberation: The United States*

and White Rule in Africa, 1948–1968 (Columbia: University of Missouri Press, 1985), 16–17.

23. Hollis R. Lynch, *Black American Radicals and the Liberation of Africa: The Council on African Affairs, 1937–1955* (Ithaca, NY: Cornell University African Studies and Research Center, 1978), 29.

24. Statement of W.E.B. Du Bois, July 10, 1945, *UN Hearings*, 393, 391.

25. Plummer, *Rising Wind*, 149.

26. Ibid., 178–81; Anderson, "From Hope to Disillusion," 561–63.

27. Margaret Hope Bacon, *One Woman's Passion for Peace and Freedom: The Life of Mildred Scott Olmsted* (Syracuse, NY: Syracuse University Press, 1993), 238–39; Alonso, *Peace as a Women's Issue*, 162–63.

28. Boyer, *By the Bomb's Early Light*, 54, 56.

29. Statement by the PWWC Board of Governors on the Atomic Bomb, December 19, 1945, PWWC, Reel 90.1, SCPC.

30. Boyer, *By the Bomb's Early Light*, 229, 219.

31. Wittner, *One World or None*, 71; Boyer, *By the Bomb's Early Light*, 341.

32. Gallup, *The Gallup Poll: Public Opinion 1935–1971*, 1: 483, 501.

33. Truman, October 23, 1945, and Marshall, June 1945, quoted in John O'Sullivan and Alan Mechler, eds., *The Draft and Its Enemies: A Documentary History* (Urbana: University of Illinois Press, 1974), 197, 199, 192, 193.

34. Muste to Paul Comly French, June 1, 1943, National Service Board for Religious Objectors (NSBRO) collection, A20, A. J. Muste file, SCPC; Mary Farquharson, June 13, 1945, testimony before the House Select Committee on Post War Military Policy, WILPF, DG 43, Series A, 4 Reel 130.36, SCPC; PWWC public letter to the president, September 6, 1945, PWWC collection, DG 62, Reel 90.7, SCPC; George Q. Flynn, *The Draft, 1940–1973* (Lawrence: University Press of Kansas, 1993), 88.

35. "A Statement on Universal Military Training," Church of the Brethren Annual Conference, 1945, CDG-A, Church of the Brethren Reports, SCPC; BCPS Bulletin, June 22, 1945, Vol. I, no. 20, NSBRO collection, A12, Brethren Service Commission Publications, SCPC.

36. Charles Boss Jr., "Commission on World Peace of the Methodist Church," January 31, 1946, NSBRO, A-27, SCPC; Patricia McNeal, *Harder than War: Catholic Peacemaking in Twentieth-Century America* (New Brunswick, NJ: Rutgers University Press, 1992), 75; Nancy L. Roberts, *Dorothy Day and the Catholic Worker* (Albany: State University of New York Press, 1984), 139.

37. Flynn, *The Draft*, 93–97.

38. O'Sullivan and Mechler, eds., *The Draft and Its Enemies*, 162–63; Flynn, *The Draft*, 101–2, 108, 124.

39. Truman, March 17, 1948, quoted in O'Sullivan and Mechler, eds., *The Draft and Its Enemies*, 265–66.

40. Marshall, March 17, 1948, U.S. Congress, Senate, *Universal Military Training, Hearings before the Committee on Armed Services*, 80th Cong., 2nd sess., 4. Hereafter cited as *UMT*.

41. Forrestal, March 18, 1948, *UMT*, 33–34.

42. Calvert N. Ellis, March 31, 1948, *UMT*, 750–51; Don E. Smucker, March 31, 1948, *UMT*, 757–58; Henry J. Cadbury, March 30, 1948, *UMT*, 591.

43. Charles W. Iglehart, March 29, 1948, *UMT*, 480–81, 485; Fredrick Libby,

March 23, 1948, *UMT*, 195; Edward Richards, March 31, 1948, *UMT*, 821; Mrs. Robert Rea, March 31, 1948, *UMT*, 721.

44. Temple, March 23, 1948, *UMT*, 124; Cloward, March 30, 1948, *UMT*, 530–31; Boss, March 30, 1948, *UMT*, 523–25; Klemme, March 30, 1948, *UMT*, 506–7; Payne, March 30, 1948, *UMT*, 615; Sikes, March 31, 1948, *UMT*, 763–65; Bush, March 31, 1948, *UMT*, 707.

45. Van Kirk, March 30, 1948, *UMT*, 513–14; Jernagin, March 30, 1948, *UMT*, 620–21; Tesdell, March 23, 1948, *UMT*, 213–14.

46. Wallace, March 30, 1948, *UMT*, 62–63; Linfield, March 24, 1948, *UMT*, 246, 253; Willner, March 24, 1948, *UMT*, 229, 233.

47. F. Ross Peterson, "Fighting the Drive toward War: Glen H. Taylor, the 1948 Progressives, and the Draft," *Pacific Northwest Quarterly* (January 1970): 42–45.

48. Thomas, "Testimony against the UMT before the House Military Affairs Committee," July 11, 1947, PWWC, DG 62, Reel 90.7, SCPC; Penley, March 29, 1948, *UMT*, 475, 477; Schutzer, March 23, 1948, *UMT*, 175, 178; Randolph, March 31, 1948, *UMT*, 687; Flynn, *The Draft*, 103.

49. Shaw, March 24, 1948, *UMT*, 319.

50. Darr, March 24, 1948, *UMT*, 310, 303; Myers, March 30, 1948, *UMT*, 502; Crane, March 24, 1948, *UMT*, 296.

51. A. J. Muste, "A Personal Memo on Pacifist Strategy in the Atomic Age," July 1946, FOR, DG 13, Series F, Releases 1946–47, SCPC.

52. "Proposed Statement by Executive Committee of the WRL," WRL, DG 40 Series A, Box 2, October 7, 1946, SCPC; "Record of Proceedings," Atlantic City Conference for Peaceworkers, December 4–7, 1945, IX-7-2, Mennonite Central Committee Peace Section, 1946 Atlantic City Conference file, Mennonite Archives; "Annual Report by F. J. Libby," November 9, 1946, NCPW, Reel 41.17, SCPC.

53. Thomas, "What Do We Mean by Universal Disarmament?" October 15, 1946, NCPW, Reel 41.285, SCPC; Thomas to Jesse Cavileer, October 7, 1946, PWWC, DG-62, Reel 90.1, SCPC.

54. "The Methodist Church on War and Peace," adopted by the General Conference of the Methodist Church, May 7, 1948, CDG-A, Box 1, Methodist Commission on World Peace, Commission on the World, SCPC.

55. For Kennan and the Long Telegram, see Walter LaFeber, *The American Age: United States Foreign Policy at Home and Abroad since 1750* (New York: W. W. Norton and Co., 1989), 449–52. For Kennan's own views, see George F. Kennan, *Memoirs, 1925–1950* (Boston: Little, Brown and Co., 1967), chapters 11 and 15.

56. James P. Warburg, *The Long Road Home: The Autobiography of a Maverick* (New York: Doubleday and Co., 1964), 225; William C. Berman, "James Paul Warburg: An Establishment Maverick Challenges Truman's Policy Toward Germany," in Paterson, ed., *Cold War Critics*, 55–56.

57. Wallace to Truman, March 15, 1946, Wallace Papers, Reel 39, University of Iowa, Iowa City, IA.

58. Wallace to Truman, July 23, 1946, Wallace Papers, Reel 41.

59. Hamby, *Beyond the New Deal*, 127, 131.

60. Wallace to Marshall, January 13, 1947, Wallace Papers, Reel 42.

61. Peterson, *Prophet without Honor*, 78.

62. FOR on International Relations, September 24, 1946, FOR, SCPC; Record of Proceedings, Atlantic City Conference for Peaceworkers, December 4–7, 1945, IX-7-2, Mennonite Central Committee Peace Section, 1946 Atlantic City Conference file, Mennonite Archives.

3

OPPOSITION TO THE TRUMAN DOCTRINE AND THE MARSHALL PLAN

Although the Truman administration began to implement the containment policy toward the Soviet Union as early as 1946, it took a specific problem for Truman to formally and publicly announce the policy. A civil war in Greece and apparent Soviet pressure on Turkey concerning use of the Straits led to the March 12, 1947 speech in which the Truman Doctrine and the containment policy were announced. In 1946, Secretary of State James Byrnes moved toward a firm approach in dealing with the Soviet Union. In adopting this stance, the United States no longer relied on negotiating differences with the Russians but came to oppose any extension of Soviet influence. Used initially to pressure the Russians out of Iran in 1946, containment was in place in Europe by 1947, and Truman used the March speech to gain congressional approval of funding for the policy.[1]

The war in Greece and the concern about Turkey led to numerous administration warnings about the spread of communism out of Greece into Western Europe. Washington's decision to play an active role in the political and military affairs of Greece, Turkey, and then all of Europe came as a result of the inability of the British to maintain their dominant position in the Mediterranean region. Unable to continue bearing the financial burden of fighting the rebellion in Greece, London asked the United States for assistance. Truman then asked Congress to appropriate $400 million for Greece and Turkey. In his speech requesting the funding,

Truman announced his Doctrine: "I believe that it must be the policy of the United States to support free peoples who are resisting attempted subjugation by armed minorities or outside pressure."[2] Although Truman used universal terms, most historians agree that the Truman Doctrine, in 1947, was aimed at Soviet actions in Europe. However, over the next five years the implementation of the policy was expanded to cover most of the world outside of the Soviet sphere in Eastern Europe.

The efforts of the United States to stop the perceived Soviet thrust into Greece sparked a great deal of opposition and, more than any other issue, marked a dividing point in postwar policies between those who supported the consensus and those who were critical of U.S. policy. The critics cited several key ideas in explaining their objections to aid to Greece and Turkey: the failure to use the UN to provide the assistance would weaken that institution; the use of military rather than economic assistance could lead to war by provoking the Soviet Union; the policy was in apparent continuity with British imperialism; and the assistance would be to dictatorial regimes in Greece and Turkey that were known for their oppression and corruption. In addition, Carl Van Meter Crabb Jr. noted that the opposition protested that the program would establish a precedent for other more costly ones.[3]

The concern for the UN took the Truman administration by surprise. No one in the administration had raised the objection that the aid program would bypass the UN. What Lawrence Kaplan and Morrell Heald called a "flourishing of a variation of the old isolationism" emerged in objection to the program. This "variation" believed that the new collective security system would keep America free of alliances.[4] However, the critics were not just the old isolationists. Liberal internationalists and pacifists who had great hopes for a new world based on cooperation and disarmament saw the bypassing of the UN as a step not just away from the UN, but toward another war. In fact, the concern about the UN was quite widespread. A Gallup Poll, taken on April 13, 1947, indicated that 63 percent of those surveyed believed that the program of aid to Greece and Turkey should be turned over to the UN.[5]

Warren Austin, the U.S. ambassador at the UN, attempted to deflect the criticism by arguing that the program fit the principles of the UN. Sen. Arthur Vandenberg, Republican chair of the Senate Foreign Relations Committee, then tacked onto the bill's preamble an explicit link for the program to the UN, explaining that the United States was acting only because the UN was not in a position to help. With the assistance of the ranking Democrat, Sen. Tom Connally, Vandenberg wrote into the bill an innocuous provision that authorized the Security Council or the General Assembly to terminate U.S. assistance whenever UN action made such assistance unnecessary.[6]

The assistance to Greece and Turkey did not assure officials in the Truman administration that Europe was secure. American officials abroad were warning about the dangers of economic collapse. James Dunn, U.S. ambassador to Italy, told Secretary of State George Marshall that if democratic government were to survive in Italy there would have to be efforts to achieve maximum employment and production. He warned that the political situation had reached a point of a delicate balance where the struggle between the communist and democratic forces might be decided by the extent to which outside aid would support democratic elements.[7] Despite ongoing U.S. assistance to Western Europe then, the economic situation was grave. The United States responded with the ERP, popularly known as the Marshall Plan after Secretary Marshall who proposed it in a commencement address at Harvard University on June 5, 1947. It was clear that the program went far beyond economic reconstruction, and was intended to stabilize the economies of Western Europe as part of the containment policy. The fact that anticommunism was linked to economic containment helped create the bipartisan consensus that was necessary to carry out the administration's policy.[8]

Coming so close to the Truman Doctrine, and also avoiding the UN, the Marshall Plan did not gain universal support. The ERP did, however, get more support among the pacifists and liberal internationalists than any other significant Truman foreign policy initiative. There were opponents, however, especially those who feared that by circumventing the UN the program threatened the viability of that international organization.

THE TRUMAN DOCTRINE AND AID TO GREECE AND TURKEY

The Truman administration's decision to go before Congress and request assistance for Greece and Turkey was carefully planned to gain as much bipartisan support as possible. Assistant Secretary of State Dean Acheson met with congressional leaders, including Sen. Vandenberg, on February 27, 1947, to explain the administration's decision to support the British request. Acheson told the delegation that the request had little to do with the British empire but instead with the containment of communism. One version of that meeting reported that Vandenberg, while promising his support, told Acheson to have Truman scare the hell out of the American people to get support for the program.[9]

Despite the effort to gain bipartisan congressional support, the response to Truman's March 12 speech was not enthusiastic. Applause in the house chamber was "notably restrained," and some legislators soon voiced opposition. Public opinion, too, was not enthused. A Gallup Poll showed only 56 percent support, whereas a Roper poll indicated 51.9 percent of Americans supported the aid program.[10]

In presentations before the House Committee on Foreign Affairs and the Senate Committee on Foreign Relations, Acheson explained the administration's rationale for the assistance. The Greeks needed money to import food, clothing, and fuel; to organize and equip their army; for reconstruction; and to provide for U.S. technical assistance. The Turks needed funding for economic development. To Acheson, there were only two choices: grant the aid, or not. There was no possibility, as far as the administration was concerned, to put the responsibility for aid on another country or on the UN. Acheson did recognize a UN role, saying that the Greeks had placed before the UN Security Council the issue of armed bands entering their nation from neighboring states. He admitted that this was "a United Nations problem and one with which the United Nations is dealing." But what was needed more immediately was money for supplies, and the UN did not have adequate resources to assist the Greeks. He noted that in the future the UN might be able to respond to such needs, but at this point the UN is not "in position to extend help of the kind that is required."[11]

As for Turkey, Acheson stated that Soviet pressures on Turkey concerning access to the Straits had caused Turkey to believe that a considerable portion of their military establishment should be kept mobilized, which strained their economic resources and led to other problems for the Turks. The purpose of assistance for the Turks would be to prevent further deterioration of the internal situation.[12]

In his presentations before Congress, Acheson attempted to answer two of what became the main criticisms of the assistance program. Rep. Mike Mansfield of Montana asked Acheson if such a program might lead to war. Acheson responded by saying he did not see how it could because it was designed to strengthen the forces of democracy and freedom by strengthening the economies of those two countries. Before the Senate Foreign Relations Committee, Acheson gave a similar statement, noting that rather than leading to war it would have the opposite effect by providing opportunity for democratic development.[13] How this would assist democratic development in a Greek government that was a repressive dictatorship was not explained to the committees.

A second issue addressed was the role, or lack of one, for the UN in the program. Acheson told the Senate committee that the UN was not designed for and could not at that time shoulder all the burdens of the world. It had a well-defined role that, perhaps, could later be extended, but not now. Acheson explained that by membership in the UN the United States or any other nation did not absolve "itself of responsibility for fostering through its own action the same objectives as the charter sets for the United Nations." In fact, he argued that what the United States was doing was to "support the basic structure on which the United Nations" was built, preventing aggression against its members.[14]

Within the Congress, one of the more vocal critics of the assistance program, Sen. Claude Pepper of Florida, challenged Acheson on his views. During Acheson's testimony, Pepper asked the assistant secretary tough and probing questions. On the issue of the UN, Pepper questioned supporting an army of a nation directly threatened without the UN Security Council being called into consultation or without the UN wrestling with the problem first.[15]

Another of the senator's concerns related to the British role in the Mediterranean region. Pepper stated that he understood why, given their historic position there, the British might be concerned about another great power getting a foothold in the area. He asked Acheson if that was also the basis for the U.S. interest. Acheson said that the United States had a different interest, which was "to support the continuation of the constitutional regimes in these countries." However, Acheson's rhetoric covered the effort to keep the Middle East and its oil reserves in the Western orbit, which tinged the United States with imperialism.[16]

Pepper also questioned the deepening responsibilities the United States might take on, wondering what impact this would have on the self-determination of the states involved. He asked Acheson whether once the United States put up all the money and furnished them with all the assistance, "will [we] be determining the policies of the Government?" Acheson indicated that some conditions would be set for the use of the money, so that the money the United States put in the country "will be usefully employed." But the objective, according to Acheson, would be for the Greeks to help themselves to the full extent of their ability in restoring the economic foundations of life.[17]

Pepper's questioning of Acheson indicated his skeptical approach toward aid to Greece and Turkey. He was joined by others within the Congress. The left-liberals who stressed the necessity of cooperation with the Soviets were especially antagonized by Truman's proposal. They viewed the doctrine as aggressive and provocative in an area where they felt that the Soviets should have a protective sphere of influence. They also objected to the intervention in Greece on behalf of a monarchy and the remnants of British imperialism, and the unilateral transformation of a localized conflict into a global one. Eventually, Pepper and Glen Taylor introduced a resolution opposing military assistance to Turkey and calling for economic assistance to Greece through the UN. Both feared that unilateral action would weaken the UN and destroy any hope for a reconciliation with the Soviet Union.[18]

The debate over aid to Greece and Turkey had a significant political impact outside of Congress. The program of assistance decisively split the old coalition of liberal internationalists into consensus, Cold War liberals who supported the program and the liberal and leftist internationalists who opposed that consensus. The leftist PCA, led by Henry Wallace, denounced the doctrine as leading to war and hoped that the opposition to it could lead to a revival of the old popular front. Meanwhile, the ADA aligned itself closely with Truman's foreign policy and supported the program, although with some reservations. Anticommunist liberals separated from the more radical liberals who favored closer cooperation with the Russians.[19]

Although the focus of this work is the liberal and pacifist opposition, it is important to note that the Truman Doctrine, which to many was a significant departure in U.S. policy with a military commitment to Europe in peacetime, also received criticism from other, more conservative quarters. The writer and columnist Walter Lippmann was a moderate critic of the Cold War who felt that containment needed to be reconsidered. The conservative Republican Sen. Robert Taft of Ohio objected to many of the Cold War policies of the Truman administration, fearing that they would limit U.S. freedom of choice abroad and involve the United States in war. In particular, he objected to the overcommitment of American military and economic power abroad.[20] Former conservative New York Congressman Hamilton Fish warned the House Committee on Foreign Affairs that the Truman doctrine "is . . . a dangerous departure from our traditional foreign policy and in effect sabotages the Monroe Doctrine." Although he supported the relief, Fish opposed the military aspects because he felt that it would lead directly to war, and he was "against war with Soviet Russia or any other country until . . . the issue becomes drawn and the Congress and the American people decide to declare war."[21]

The issue drew so much attention that even the nonpartisan League of Women Voters (LWV) felt compelled to state their position. Anna Lord Strauss, the president of the organization, told the House Committee that they had received so many letters and telegrams that the LWV decided that they had to bring it to the attention of the committee. Strauss said that an overwhelming majority of the letters argued that if aid is to be given by the United States to Greece and Turkey, the administration of such aid "should be carried on under the supervision of the United Nations."[22]

One of the leading individuals behind the formation of the UN, Clark Eichelberger, speaking for the American Association for the United Nations (AAUN), gave the aid package lukewarm approval. He said that the AAUN "regretfully" recognized that in this emergency it was necessary to accept the Greek request for aid. Eichelberger indicated that he believed that the American people would overwhelmingly support it, provided that it was done with a full explanation to the UN.[23] The amendments added by Vandenberg placated their concerns. Ultimately, the objections were overcome, and the majority of Americans did support the assistance programs and the policy of containment. Truman had the majority of Americans behind him; however, there were those who stood at the water's edge and continued to object loudly to the administration's policies.

THE LEFT-LIBERAL OPPOSITION TO THE TRUMAN DOCTRINE

The most obvious place to look for the public opposition to the Truman Doctrine and the aid to Greece and Turkey is in the House and Senate hearings on the program. In addition, individuals and organizations issued public statements and wrote letters to other activists explaining their opposition. This opposition can be divided into several categories: liberal government and public figures, noncommunist leftist groups, liberal internationalists, religious groups, religious and secular pacifists, and anti-imperialists.

The critics of the policy centered their opposition in four main areas. First, they feared that the unilateral aid would damage the UN. Second, they felt that the policy was a military provocation toward the Soviet Union and could lead to war. Third, they believed that the United States, in aiding these states in an area of historic importance to Britain, was involving itself in actions supportive of imperialism. Finally, the critics disapproved of the fact that the policy would support undemocratic governments.

Almost universally, liberal critics feared the weakening of the UN. The leading public figure who was critical of the Doctrine was Henry Wallace, then the editor of the *New Republic*. Only recently removed from the Truman cabinet for his opposition to the administration's foreign policy—not yet the defeated pariah of late 1948—Wallace's opposition was significant. Although the Truman Doctrine was the antithesis of Wallace's vision of the world, he acknowledged that Greece needed assistance. In fact, in August 1946 as commerce secretary, he had proposed a loan for Greece but was opposed by the State and Treasury Departments because of Greek instability and corruption. Wallace objected to the bypassing of the UN. Instead, he favored an alternative to the assistance. He proposed that Washington underwrite a $150 billion spending program over ten years to be administered by the UN to restore wartorn areas and raise world living standards.[24]

There were also strong critics who remained in the government. In Congress, Sen. Claude Pepper and Sen. Glen Taylor strongly opposed the administration's policy and led the fight against it. As noted above, during the hearings Pepper had forcefully questioned the proposals. In his memoirs, Pepper wrote that his opposition to the Truman Doctrine "was rooted in my conviction that the United Nations had to succeed and that it could not if one of the major signatories undercut it." That is just what he feared the doctrine would do. He wrote that he was convinced that "the Truman Doctrine would strangle the UN in its cradle, fuel United States–Soviet antagonisms, and leave the world without an effective instrument for settling disagreements among nations." His concern was partially based on the fears raised by UN Secretary General Trygve Lie in a meeting with Pepper. The secretary general told Pepper that he was alarmed by such unilateral action and that one more action like the Truman Doctrine and the UN would be dead. One historian argued that one of Pepper's "most consistent and telling critiques" of U.S. Cold War policies was that the administration professed support for international organizations but was acting unilaterally.[25]

Once it was clear that the assistance program would pass, Pepper pushed an amendment that stated that if the UN adopted a resolution that U.S. troops be recalled from Greece and Turkey, the United States would honor that resolution. Included as part of the aid package, Pepper believed that it spared the UN a "complete humiliation." Looking back forty years later, Pepper believed he was wrong in 1947, that both the Truman Doctrine and the Marshall Plan were "stunning successes" and his opposition was "wrongheaded."[26] Nonetheless, his concerns at the time were legitimate and reflected the concerns of many others.

What worried Glen Taylor the most was the future of the UN. A believer in the necessity of world government, he worked for a more powerful UN. In July 1947, he cosponsored a resolution that undertook to make the UN capable of enacting, interpreting, and enforcing world law. He did so to combat the argument used by the administration that the UN was too weak to deal with the Greek-Turkish situation.[27]

Although there were other critics in the Congress, and the government in general, most of the opposition came from the outside. The best known of those critics was James Warburg. After a 1947 European trip, James Warburg pushed an American mission to the world that was devoted to the promotion of American ideals and ideas. In the process, he wrote books and delivered many speeches devoted to his opposition to the Cold War mentality of the majority of Americans and his belief in the need to regenerate Germany as a bastion of Western civilization. His efforts culminated with the winning of the Gandhi Peace Prize in 1962.[28]

Although Warburg believed that there was good reason to give aid to Greece and Turkey, he felt that the successful UN intervention in Iran demonstrated that the UN could be used to render such aid instead of unilateral actions by the United States. He also believed that there was no valid reason for the United States to appoint itself as a global anti-communist policeman and to fulfill such a commitment was beyond the power of the United States alone. In a letter to Acheson, Warburg spelled out his concerns. Although he supported a "planned program of economic reconstruction," Warburg was concerned about a vague ideological or political crusade implemented by dollars. He told Acheson that he saw two dangers in the course the administration was taking. A domestic danger was that the

Truman Doctrine . . . has brought out in this country all the latent fear and hate of the U.S.S.R. and won for the support of our new foreign policy a dangerous mixture of unreconstructed and partially reconstruction isolationists, unreconstructed and partially reconstructed tories, puzzled and reluctant liberals and progressives. . . . The danger is . . . that the people who supported the first step for the wrong reasons may run away with and prevent the rest of the program.[29]

In testimony before the House and Senate committees considering the aid program for Greece and Turkey, many lesser known witnesses testified in opposition to the program. They included a large number of individuals, some representing groups, some speaking for themselves, fitting into the profile of the liberal internationalist. That is, their opposition centered on their support for and concern about the U.N. In the process, they also raised other concerns about the nature of the Truman Doctrine. These individuals and groups ranged from the middle of the political spectrum to the noncommunist left.

Among those testifying before Congress, the desire to see the UN work was clearly the dominant issue. Samuel Guy Inman, a professor at Ohio Wesleyan University, summed up this feeling in his comments to the House Committee on Foreign Affairs: If the United States bypassed the UN in the very beginning, then the United States would never live down the accusation that it killed that organization through unilateral action. Russell Smith of the National Farmers Educational and Cooperative Union of America told the same committee that, if bypassed, the UN would be receiving a seriously damaging blow from its most powerful member. Mabel Vernon, representing the Peoples' Mandate Committee for Inter-American Peace and Cooperation, asked the House committee if the United States shall "act alone to handle any situation affecting its national security as it sees fit or shall it deal with every threat to peace through the power of the United Nations which was created for this specific purpose?"[30]

Martin Popper, the executive secretary of the leftist National Lawyers Guild, argued that the proposed unilateral action by the United States violated the UN Charter. Citing articles 34 and 39 of the UN Charter, he told both the Senate and House committees that responsibility for maintaining the peace was vested in the UN and cannot be assumed by an individual member. The UN Charter, he stated, was adopted to prevent nations from acting unilaterally. Popper noted that not only would it violate the charter, it would set a precedent that would nullify the charter. In response to the argument that the emergency nature of the situation made U.S. action justifiable, Popper stated that whether the situation were an emergency itself "is a question to be determined by the Security Council and not unilaterally by an individual member."[31]

The newly formed Progressive Citizens of America was represented before the Senate committee by Frank Kingdom, cochair of the organization. Making their position clear on the importance of the UN, he stated that

[n]o amount of semantics can disguise that fact that the President's proposals in Greece and Turkey rock the very foundations of the United Nations, . . . substitute unilateral action for the conference table, put relief on a political basis, and pledge our support to any regime, no matter how undemocratic as long as it is anti-Communist.[32]

Various other leftists spoke before the congressional committees, stating the main themes of the critics. Arthur Schutzer of the American Labor Party criticized the failure to take the issue to the UN Security Council and, although the American Labor Party supported relief for Greece, they "opposed the use of American money to assist in arming and training the military forces of the present Greek and Turkish Governments." Harry Fleischman, the national secretary of the Socialist Party, argued that the United States could not "achieve the objectives of halting Russian expansion and preserving the peace" if it acted unilaterally, further weakening the feeble structure of international organization. William Gausmann, a Washington representative of the Socialist Party, noted that although the party agreed with Truman's objective of halting Soviet expansion, "the extension of American imperialism" was not the answer. He said the U.S. objective should be "a just and lasting peace, not an improved strategic position for war with Russia."[33]

Although the UN was the primary concern for the liberal internationalists, some like Gausmann did touch on the other critical themes. Several of the internationalist critics charged that the Truman Doctrine was a provocation toward the Soviets and could lead to war.

As an alternative to Truman's program, Pepper and Taylor introduced a joint resolution on aid to Greece. Their proposal eliminated Turkey, excluded military aid, and called for the aid to be administrated by the UN. Pepper told the National Peace Conference that he believed that the United States "should not support foreign soldiers as part of a global policy of power politics which can only lead to war." This reflected the senator's view that the Truman policy might lead the country into World War III.[34]

In addition to their fear for potential damage to the UN, Corliss Lamont and Henry Pratt Fairchild of the National Council of American-Soviet Friendship, Inc., pointed out the aggressive nature of the program as a reason for their organization's opposition. The National Council passed a statement in opposition that was signed by 255 churchmen. The statement argued that the legislation divided the world into two armed camps and served notice to the world that the United States alone will "determine the way of life to be maintained in any country in which . . . we take an interest." The chair of that organization, Rev. William H. Melish, told the Senate committee in blunt terms that the doctrine was "a tacit declaration of political and economic war upon the Soviet Union."[35]

Within the PWWC, there was strong opposition to the military features of the Truman Doctrine. Testifying before the Senate committee, Broads Mitchell, a member of the Council's board of directors, argued that without changes, the Truman program would open the door to war. He noted, like most other critics, that the UN should be used to internationalize the assistance. The PWWC's main concern though was the military aspect of the program. They favored loans to Greece and Turkey for relief with the condition that the two states use them to further democracy. This, Mitchell argued, would eliminate the Soviet claim that their country was a victim of encirclement.[36]

At this early point in the Cold War, liberal internationalists did not express great concern about the connections the program may have with imperialism. Sen. Pepper had raised questions about it during the Acheson testimony, but the liberals were concerned more with the undemocratic nature of the Greek government and the implications this may have for future U.S. foreign policy initiatives.

In his speeches, Wallace challenged much of the Truman program. He wondered how "support given to the undemocratic Governments of Greece and Turkey [could] aid the cause of freedom?" Instead of a limited program of aid to Greece and Turkey, Wallace called for "an all-out worldwide reconstruction program for peace." "This," he said, "is America's opportunity." In attacking the Truman Doctrine, Wallace said that the world cried out "not for an American crusade in the name of hatred and fear of communism, but for a world crusade in the name of the brotherhood of man." The former vice president also felt that political instability in Greece could be ended by bringing the leftists into a coalition government. This, he felt, could also eliminate repression. Viewing Truman's program as " 'ill-conceived and self-defeating,' " Wallace proposed technical assistance instead of military aid. He felt that by supporting corrupt and undemocratic regimes, the United States would become " 'the most hated nation in the world.' "[37]

During the debates on the aid package, Sen. Taylor also expressed concerns about the nature of the program and its objectives. He believed that the administration was throwing reason out the window when the word "communism" was mentioned and that the Truman Doctrine would cause the United States to become involved in a worldwide witch hunt. He feared prophetically that the United States would determine its allies by how loudly they claimed to fight communism. It was the Truman Doctrine that brought about Taylor's final break with the Truman administration.[38]

Warburg, too, saw other problems with the assistance program. In his May 9, 1947 letter to Acheson, he indicated his belief that Washington was compromising itself in the eyes of the "forward-looking forces" of the world. He warned that "[t]o the extent that we make the wrong friends now we may find it impossible to make the right ones later." In fact, he noted that the danger abroad was "very much of the same nature as the danger here."[39] As the containment policy unfolded, Warburg increasingly expressed his concerns with the nature of the programs.

Others also raised concerns about the nature of the Greek government. Charles G. Bolte, the national chair of the American Veterans' Committee (AVC), told the House committee that the United States could not stop the spread of communist ideology by bolstering "a corrupt and reactionary regime." Neither could the Red Army, he said, be stopped by giving American military assistance to Greece. The AVC National Planning Committee passed a resolution stating their belief that "communism can only be defeated by removal of those conditions of poverty which make communism possible."[40]

THE RELIGIOUS, PACIFIST, AND ANTI-IMPERIALIST OPPOSITION

Various religious and pacifist groups also opposed the Truman Doctrine, and particularly military aid to Greece and Turkey. Their opposition reflected their belief in the need for assistance to help war-torn Europe and in the need to strengthen the UN. By and large the majority of Catholics, Protestants, and Jews approved the U.S. assistance to Greece.[41] Nevertheless, there were various religious organizations, outside of the peace churches and pacifist organizations, who spoke out against the assistance program and echoed most of the arguments of the liberal internationalists. Although they, too, expressed a concern about the UN, the pacifist groups argued strongly against the military assistance to be provided to Greece and Turkey.

In testimony before the House and Senate committees, representatives from several Protestant denominations rejected the Truman plan for aid to Greece and Turkey. Walter Sikes, the national director of peace for the Disciples of Christ Churches, stated that "the proposal is unilateral action of precisely the kind the United Nations is designed to stop." Instead, he called for an economic reconstruction effort for all Europe. Donald Cloward, the executive secretary of the Council on Christian Social Progress for the Northern Baptist Convention, also questioned U.S. motives and expressed support for the UN. He said, "[l]et us not take unto ourselves the task of policing the world.... Let us turn rather to the international organization we have worked so hard to help create."[42]

Although the WILPF had other problems with the Truman program, the primary reason for its opposition was the bypassing of the UN. The WILPF spokesperson before both the House and Senate committees considering aid to Greece and Turkey was Katharine Lee Marshall, the organization's legislative secretary. Marshall told the committees that if the UN was ever to become the instrument for peace, no major power should be allowed to skirt the councils of the UN, and when no UN structure existed to handle a problem, one should be created. According to Marshall, the case of Turkey should be turned over to the UN. She said, "I think it is ... evident that there is not the question of time involved in the Turkish situation."[43] At its annual meeting in April 1947, the WILPF passed a resolution in opposition to the Truman policy toward Greece and Turkey. The resolution expressed concern because the problem was not placed before the UN prior to Truman's call for unilateral U.S. action. The league would support legislation that endorsed regular UN consultation on U.S. aid and U.S. efforts to secure UN assumption of the responsibility for assistance to Greece at the earliest possible date.[44] Although certainly the WILPF was not responsible alone for the Vandenberg amendment, which would require the United States to terminate its program when the UN took over, it was one of the few times that opposition to a Truman policy contributed to administration and congressional changes in foreign policy.

Most of the religious and pacifist opposition to the Truman Doctrine centered on concerns about the potential for war. The *Christian Century*, a liberal nondenominational journal, spoke out strongly against the administration's policy. In their March 26, 1947 editorial, the editors wrote that "Congress should reply with an absolute NO! [sic] to President Truman's request," and stated that Truman had taken the road to war. Particularly opposed to Truman's bypassing of the UN, the editors stated that the president's argument that the UN cannot deal with this situation "is simply not true." The Truman policy, they argued, reflected a militaristic ideology that aimed at establishing a Pax Americana.[45]

By far, the Methodists were the most active in their opposition. The New York East Annual Conference of the Methodist Church issued a statement calling for the rejection of the Truman proposals "to underwrite monarchy, and tyranny in Greece and Turkey." Alson Smith of the Methodist Federation for Social Action testified before the House committee. Smith concluded that if the UN was not strong enough to carry out nonmilitary assistance, then "we should put all our energies into strengthening the United Nations." Charles Boss Jr., the secretary of the Methodist Commission on World Peace, was one of the most active critics of the Truman foreign policy. He testified before both congressional committees and noted that Truman's proposals have aroused the United States into a discussion of U.S. policy. He indicated an American "determination to participate in world affairs, and not retreat to a policy of isolationism." However, he stated that although the commission opposed the use of funds for the purpose of political war against the Russians in Greece and Turkey, they did support appropriations for genuine relief under UN supervision. In a broad critique of the administration's emerging containment policy, Boss testified that he believed that the United States could not develop a world leadership role on the basis of an international policy seeking to establish an American imperialism, dominating the world with a monopoly of the atomic bomb, and giving away military aid. He said that his was not a policy of appeasement. Rather he was proposing the "abandonment of the policy . . . of the use of the threat of military force and the determination of military might" for the establishment of U.S. domination.[46]

Critic Dwight Macdonald noted that the Truman Doctrine presented pacifists with an "impossible alternative." They would have to accept either Russian or American imperialism.[47] However, that is not the way they viewed it. The pacifists opposed both. The opposition of A. J. Muste was representative of religious-based pacifist groups. Muste spoke for the FOR before both the House and Senate committees and published a pamphlet titled "How to Stop Russia and Communism: The Crux of the Greek-Turkish Issue." Although unwilling to give in to Russian expansionism, he also rejected the use of military means to achieve that goal.

Muste noted that Greece and other war-torn areas urgently needed aid. Like other opponents, he opposed the bypassing of the UN and warned that the United States was embarking on a "radically new foreign policy, establishing a Monroe Doctrine for the entire earth." Muste felt that Truman was exaggerating the threat, and, in his Senate testimony, he mocked that threat, saying that the United States was "having a bad case of the jitters." Despite the fact that the United States had the largest overall military in the world, half the earth's wealth, and the Atlantic and Pacific were nearly U.S. lakes, "we stand before the world scared stiff."[48]

In his pamphlet, Muste elaborated on his beliefs about dealing with the threat of communism. He felt that Truman's aid proposals should be supported, but carried out under civilian auspices. Rejecting political or military action, he stated that the United States should refuse to adopt a policy of taking over Britain's imperialist commitments, and should reject proposals for unilateral political or military action, turning such problems over to the UN.[49]

The AFSC challenged the value of the military response of the Truman Doctrine, questioning the assumption that military force was the only language understood by the Russians. AFSC chairperson Henry J. Cadbury testified before the House Committee on Foreign Affairs on the request for assistance. He urged, as had many others, "scrupulous loyalty by our Government to the United Nations." Cadbury stated that the United States must find some other alternative, besides resistance or backing down, to deal with the communist threat. Such an alternative must, he said, be done piece by piece. He called for an isolationist policy, but not in the traditional sense. Cadbury told the committee: "Unlike the American tradition which is intervention for military purposes, and isolation in matters of public welfare the world over, I want to be an interventionist in public welfare and an isolationist when it comes to military intervention."[50]

The Quakers were also represented by the FCNL. Hitting on the major themes, Richard Wood of the FCNL stated that he favored relief, but not just for Greece and Turkey. Military aid, he told the Senate committee, was futile. Washington needed to get rid of the "naive" belief that it could deter other nations from policies that it disliked by the threat of force. The FCNL, according to its Executive Secretary E. Raymond Wilson, felt that the basic issue raised by the Truman Doctrine was whether the United States "should embark on a course of unilateral military aid to country after country *or* make an all-out effort to find some viable accommodation with the Soviet Union" and seek to achieve disarmament. Wilson argued that military aid could lead the country onto the path of military interventions and wars.[51]

The secular pacifist groups followed the same basic path as the religious groups in their critique of the Truman Doctrine. The NCPW, represented before the House committee by their head Frederick Libby, argued that the Truman Doctrine was "a declaration of war" against Russia. Libby favored an alternative that was neither "the Roosevelt policy of appeasement" nor "the Truman policy of aggressive belligerency." He proposed a policy of reconstruction separated from the anti-Russian slant of the Truman policy. Accepting Truman's statement that communism flourishes in misery and want, Libby favored a single-minded effort to relieve that distress. Later, Libby added to that argument, asserting that a futile challenge to Russia would bleed the United States white, and communism could not be defeated with threats of force. Finally, Libby also raised a point that was heard with more frequency as U.S. military programs began to evolve, and with the ongoing debate on UMT. He warned against the growing military influence in the United States. He wrote, "Not only does the Army want to indoctrinate our youth with the military point of view but it is grasping for control of our entire economy."[52]

Although he told the House committee that he was speaking as an individual, Frank Olmstead, the field director of the WRL, attacked the Truman Doctrine. He warned that the Truman policy, if it were to become a doctrine, would mean that the United States would use military power to keep communism from spreading. He said that Washington would have "to step in at all the weak points, and those weak points will be where the people are beginning to feel friendly toward Russia." That, Olmstead said, would mean that the United States would "have to ignore the will of the local people, imposing our will upon them by force of arms." That would be empire. Instead, he proposed a cooperative effort with the Soviets to end suffering and empires.[53]

The WILPF president, Mildred Scott Olmsted, wrote that American leaders were using the prestige and the power of the United States not to heal the terrible aftermath of two world wars but to deepen the divisions, to continue the destruction, and to fasten militarism on reluctant nations. The WILPF's Marshall told the house that there was no question that Greece needed technical and administrative advice, but the program as proposed appeared unrelated to the realities of the situation and needs in Greece. She stated that the disproportion between the amount that was set aside for military and for what was really needed, economic reconstruction, was startling.[54]

Because the Truman Doctrine implied an expanded U.S. role in the world, some groups objected that the U.S. role in Greece and Turkey was linked to and supportive of British imperialism. The *Christian Century*, in its March 26 editorial, stated that the "military minded statesmenship" did not see that by taking over Britain's imperial role, we would take on permanent liabilities, which had brought Britain's empire to ruin. The journal warned that the United States would take "an imperial position and hold it only at the cost of being feared and hated by the rest of the world." The concern that the rest of the world would come to hate the United States for its imperial role echoed elsewhere. The New York East Annual Conference of the Methodist Church condemned the Truman Doctrine because it would make the United States "hated by subject races everywhere for backing monarchy, reaction, and imperialism." This was even heard in the halls of Congress as Sen. Pepper argued the United States was stepping into British footprints in the imperial quicksands.[55]

Although historically African Americans have not played a major role in the foreign policy debates within the United States, with the advent of the Cold War, and what seemed like a growing support of the United States for imperial European powers, black Americans came to comment increasingly on U.S. policy. Opposition to racism and imperialism was strong enough in the African American community that the NAACP had to pay attention to it. Much of the black press opposed the Truman Doctrine. Black opposition centered on what they called the hypocrisy of calling for democracy abroad when it did not exist in the southern United States. Although the NAACP board of directors did not comment on the Truman Doctrine, Executive Director Walter White scorned the propping up of Great Britain and accused the United States of supporting a reactionary dictatorship.[56]

The pacifists and liberal internationalists were quite united in their view of the Truman Doctrine and aid to Greece and Turkey. They opposed the unilateralism of the policy, the military implication, the imperial implications, and the support it gave to a dictatorial regime. Many felt that instead the United States should undertake a massive assistance program, through the UN, to rebuild war-torn Europe. When the Truman administration proposed such a plan, divisions emerged within the ranks of the opposition.

THE EUROPEAN RECOVERY PROGRAM

The concern for the economic, and thus political, security of Western Europe led the Truman administration to develop the ERP. Working closely with the nations of Western Europe to coordinate economic needs, Washington funneled $13 billion in economic aid into that region. Administration officials believed that without such assistance the economies of Western Europe would have suffered "disastrous deterioration."[57] They believed that such a deterioration would lead Europeans down the road to totalitarianism because the communist parties would take advantage of economic chaos to seize power, or even, as in the case of Italy, to win elections. On May 8, 1947, Undersecretary of State Acheson delivered a speech in Cleveland, Mississippi, laying the groundwork for the program. He stated that the use of U.S. economic and financial resources would contribute to U.S. security by widening the economic margins upon which free institutions abroad were struggling to survive. Then in June, Marshall delivered his speech, inviting all European nations to join with the United States to rehabilitate their economies. The program assumed that a unified recovery program, supervised by Washington, would achieve economic recovery, secure political stability, weaken the political appeal of communist parties, and increase the well-being and security of the United States.[58]

Obviously, the purpose went far beyond the concept of humanitarianism, or even economic recovery. It was an attempt to assure political stability in Europe, especially Western Europe, which Washington believed essential for U.S. security and prosperity. Initially, Marshall and others urged Soviet and East European participation, but conditions for involvement were set that made it unlikely that the Russians or Eastern

Europeans would take part. Insisting on planning and exchanges of information, which would have subjected the Soviet economy to Western scrutiny, guaranteed that the Russians would reject the plan. Although the Russians attended the Paris meeting in June, it was all made easier after the Russians rejected participation and prevented the participation of Eastern European nations. Once the Russians were out of the way, the plan offered a convenient way to build popular support for the reconstruction of Western Europe and linked anticommunism to economic containment. The ERP was designed to protect the continent from the contagion of communism without a massive American rearmament.[59] Thus, the ERP became part of the containment program and contributed to further divisions in Europe.

The ERP also divided the liberal internationalists and pacifists at home over whether they would support the plan. Generally, the ERP had popular support. A Gallup Poll taken in July 1947 indicated that 57 percent of those who had heard of the Marshall Plan viewed it favorably, whereas only 18 percent viewed it unfavorably. Nearly a year later, in March 1948, 57 percent of those who had heard of it continued to view it favorably, and the opposition remained at 18 percent.[60]

On the political left, the ERP caused some division. The PCA at first gave it cautious support, but then, by the fall of 1947, after the Russian withdrawal from the program, they denounced the plan that they felt, along with the Truman Doctrine, was the cause for the dissolution of the wartime Soviet-American alliance. On the other hand, the ADA viewed it as an all important rallying point. For most liberals, the ERP was an affirmative departure from the Truman Doctrine and held out the promise of rebuilding Europe. The anticommunist left also responded enthusiastically to the plan.[61] Those who continued to favor a cooperative foreign policy with the Soviets, and pacifists who had long urged the United States to devote its resources to reconstruction of the war-torn nations, found themselves in a dilemma because of the political implications of the assistance program. Most religious organizations supported the program because of the ERP's emphasis on humanitarianism and reconstruction.[62]

LEFTIST, PACIFIST, AND LIBERAL SUPPORT FOR THE MARSHALL PLAN

Despite the fact that the ERP again avoided use of the UN, Clark M. Eichelberger, representing the AAUN, told the Senate Foreign Relations Committee he supported the program. He asserted that the success of the plan would mean stability for the nations of Europe and that the UN derives its strength from stable members. He expressed hope that the program would focus on economic needs and that military aspects could be held to a minimum, "with these nations finding their security through the larger union of the United Nations." However, he did regret that no effort was made to work out the program inside the UN and felt it important that the recovery program be connected to the UN wherever possible.[63]

Liberals in the ADA, already moving toward support for containment, overwhelmingly favored the Marshall Plan. David Lloyd, the ADA director of research and legislation, told the House Committee on Foreign Affairs that his organization viewed the plan as "the high point of our foreign policy since the war" and said that it was "essential to the maintenance of world peace." Lloyd said that the ADA believed that the United States faced a world crisis that needed immediate action, and without it, all plans for world prosperity and the UN itself would fail.[64] It was not surprising that the ADA would support the ERP. They had supported, though reluctantly, the Truman Doctrine. However, the support of other individuals and groups was more surprising.

Although he expressed either opposition to or serious reservations about most of the rest of the Truman foreign policy, James Warburg supported the Marshall Plan. He wrote Acheson in February 1948, "I agree with everything you say about the ERP." Nonetheless, he did disagree on the context in which the ERP could work. He told Acheson that it is not that the Russians are determined to prevent recovery but that they "are determined to prevent the success of *our* European recovery program." Warburg viewed the Marshall Plan as brilliantly conceived, and, after his opposition to the Truman Doctrine, he welcomed what he called a "return to reason." What he disliked was how it was sold to Congress "primarily as an instrument of power politics" to be used in the Cold War against Russia.[65]

Along with Warburg, another strong critic of the Truman Doctrine supported the ERP. Sen. Claude Pepper favored aid for European reconstruction. Though he advocated a UN program, he eventually voted for the March 1948 Marshall Plan bill. Pepper's vote for the ERP reflected a gradual shift on the part of the Florida senator toward support of the administration's foreign policy.[66] By April 1949, he had swung completely behind the Truman policy by voting for the North Atlantic Alliance, but perhaps not soon enough to save his Senate seat in the 1950 election.

With the ERP, the NAACP moved to support the Truman foreign policy. Walter White, the organization's secretary, called on Congress to vote the full sum requested by Truman and to extend it to Asia, Africa, and the Caribbean. White, however, used the opportunity to criticize European colonialism saying it "would be folly for the United States to help white Europe to rehabilitate that part of the world and permit it to continue to deny freedom and opportunity to colonial peoples."[67]

Norman Thomas strongly endorsed the ERP, telling the Senate committee that without U.S. assistance the chances that Western Europe would be "lost to Communist totalitarianism" were greatly increased. However, in his statement of support, he made a distinction between the Marshall Plan and the Truman Doctrine, saying that the ERP was not a mere extension of the Doctrine or subordinate to it. At the hearings, Thomas also took the opportunity to point out that too much money continued to be spent on armaments. He warned that "the plan and all our other hopes will be doomed unless . . . America will officially appeal to the nations for . . . the end of a frantic armament race." Thomas's PWWC noted in their newsletter of January 1948 that the defeat of the Marshall Plan would "gravely imperil democracy and peace in Western Europe."[68]

Among the leading pacifist supporters of the ERP was the WILPF. In various minutes, statements, resolutions, and public testimonies, the organization and its representatives spelled out their support in cautious terms. At the National Executive meeting in September 1947, the League noted that the policy committee did not want to support anti-Russian policies, but felt that aid must be given to Europe and that the Marshall Plan was the only available method of assistance. The WILPF supported the ERP generally, but wished it could be extended, facilitated through the UN, and not used for political purposes.[69] An October 1947 memorandum of the WILPF Policy Committee on the Marshall Plan stated, "Our policy should be . . . to get the Marshall Plan through Congress generally free of political and economic strings and as soon as possible." Within the organization, there was some concern about the ERP's political nature, and two WILPF branches went on record opposing the ERP on the grounds that it was aimed against the Soviets and would further divide the world. However, the National Board at their February 1948 meeting pointed out that, though it might have political strings that the League deplored, "there is no other alternative plan . . . [and] we must stand behind it."[70]

Katharine Lee Marshall, the legislative secretary of the WILPF, again represented the organization before both the House and Senate committees. She told the senate that the WILPF favored the inclusion of three points. First, there should be no conditions imposed that would restrain the political or economic development of other nations. Second, the plan should facilitate the use of appropriate UN organizations wherever possible. Third, the United States should repeat its invitation to all nations of Europe. Marshall told the house that "[l]ooking beyond the tensions of the moment, and remembering that the European recovery plan is designed to secure the peace, not to create an alliance for war, the United States should make it unmistakably clear that any European nation which should subsequently so choose is free to enter into the program."

She also took the opportunity to push beyond the ERP, calling on the United States to "accompany the inauguration of the Marshall Plan with a proposal that the nations of the world meet together to plan the abolition of all armaments." She noted that there was no point in rebuilding Europe if it was to turn into another battlefield.[71] Ironically, the Truman administration believed, too, that war threatened economic recovery, but argued that military security was essential to enable that recovery to succeed. That belief contributed to the Truman administration's decision to pursue a military alliance. It was also the fear that the ERP contributed to a division of Europe, was aimed against the Soviet Union, and would be used for military purposes that caused many others to oppose the plan.

THE OPPOSITION TO THE EUROPEAN RECOVERY PROGRAM

The best-known critic of the Marshall Plan was the former vice president, Henry Wallace. Throughout 1947, Wallace had been advocating a large-scale program of American aid for reconstruction, and so when Marshall presented his plan, Wallace received it favorably. However, by the end of 1947 Wallace had lost his enthusiasm, coming to feel that the economic objectives were being subordinated to military purposes. For many liberals, the plan was a constructive consequence of the valid criticism that Wallace had been leveling against the Truman administration. But for Wallace it had become a device of containment.[72]

Wallace explained his changed views in a March 1948 letter, writing that he was for "the spirit" of the original proposal, "administered through the United Nations with no political strings attached." However, he noted, he was against the ERP administered by the United States with political strings attached. Recognizing the desperate need for aid, he was willing to agree to a six-month stopgap measure, but if Congress would not then be willing to switch it to a UN basis, he would favor the termination of all aid after July 1, 1949.[73]

Wallace also explained his concern to the House Foreign Affairs Committee. The former vice president and commerce secretary told them that he reluctantly came to the conclusion that the ERP was the "wrong way" to help Europe. He said what Europe needed was a lend-lease program to fight hunger and chaos, but what they were getting was "a blueprint for war." Wallace felt that Marshall's June 1947 speech at Harvard seemed to "repudiate the Truman doctrine." To Wallace, the speech seemed to be a return to the principles of Roosevelt. But the State Department plan, he told the committee, completely abandoned these principles and "would foist a war economy" on the nation. Instead, he called for a proposal from the United States to the UN for the establishment of a UN fund for the reconstruction of war-devastated countries in Europe and Asia. Speaking in February 1948, Wallace stated that the ERP was a forerunner of a military alliance for Western Europe.[74]

Wallace's opposition to the ERP further alienated him from consensus liberals who supported the program. Most liberals were thrilled by the ERP and saw only minor flaws, including the bypassing of the UN. Further events in 1948 continued to drive a wedge between the Cold War liberals and Wallace. The communist takeover in Czechoslovakia was one of those events. At first, Wallace blamed it on the Truman Doctrine and the "get tough" policy. As his 1948 presidential campaign progressed, Wallace's lack of concern about communist backing for his Progressive Party candidacy also hurt him. Although Wallace was no communist and made clear his strong belief in what he called "progressive capitalism," he stated that he would utterly refuse to engage in Red-baiting and Russia-denunciation.[75]

Glen Taylor joined Wallace in his opposition of the ERP. Although Taylor admitted that Europe needed help to rebuild after the war, he believed that the UN should administer the relief rather than individual nations. The Idaho senator ridiculed the humanitarian arguments for the ERP, asserting that the real reason for the plan was economic self-interest. He presented it as a scheme to capture new markets for American products.[76]

Surprisingly, despite his advocacy of American assistance for war-devastated areas, A. J. Muste opposed the ERP. Although he felt that it held more promise than the Truman Doctrine for meeting human needs, he doubted that it was as great an act of generosity as the administration made it out to be. In a December 1947 letter, Muste listed the conditions under which he, as a pacifist, would accept the Marshall Plan. He felt it

should be for the purpose of promoting world recovery without discrimination as to race, creed or political belief; should not be used to build the military strength of any country or group of countries; [and] should not be directed economically or ideologically against the Soviet Union. . . . Furthermore, it should be accompanied . . . by a call for world wide disarmament.

Muste saw the ERP as a political act and was "all the things that it should not be" and was "in no sense a part of a campaign for world disarmament." Furthermore, the FOR leader compared it with the Munich agreement, saying that it was but a "breathing space" in preparation for war.[77]

Summing up most of the criticism about the ERP, James Reed, the secretary of the Foreign Service Division of the American Friends Committee on National Legislation, told the Senate Foreign Relations Committee that U.S. aid to Europe "should seek to unite Europe and not to split it into two parts permanently." In addition to the inclusion of efforts to reduce arms, Reed told the senators that the program "should be global" and "carried out in the closest possible cooperation with the United Nations."[78]

There was, however, one additional basis for opposition to the ERP. Although the NAACP supported the Marshall Plan, and began generally to support the administration's foreign policy, many African Americans were concerned about the effects of the ERP on the colonial world. Although the ERP could not be used explicitly for economic development or military counterinsurgency in the colonies, support for the European colonial powers did strengthen their hands in dealing with colonial rebellions. The ERP freed French, Dutch, and English "funds for the often bloody work of sustaining their empires." While publicly distancing themselves from counterrevolutionary actions in the colonies, U.S. officials privately acknowledged "that Marshall Plan aid was enabling the French to fight what became large-scale wars of 'pacification' in Indochina, Madagascar, and Algeria." ERP funds to the Dutch enabled that colonial power to fight in Indonesia. As a result of Truman's priority of the reconstruction of Western Europe and the containment of communism, the United States became the "guarantor of Europe's remaining colonies." Although opposed to colonialism, under heavy pressure the NAACP supported the Marshall Plan. Groups such as the CAA were weakened because of anticommunism and were under harassment from the Federal Bureau of Investigation.[79]

CONCLUSION

Despite the divisions that pacifists and liberal-internationalists had among themselves over the issue of the Marshall Plan, the basic ideas in opposition to the policy of containment that emerged full force during the debate over aid to Greece and Turkey remained part of the ideology of all the groups. Even those who supported the ERP often did so with reservations and expressed concern that this assistance not be used for political, military, or colonial purposes, and they expressed their concern about the survivability of the UN.

During 1947 and 1948, the main outlines of the containment policy emerged, and, despite the general support for it in congress and the public, criticism of the Truman foreign policy developed based on a set of convictions that continued to be articulated through the dangerous years of the Cold War. These ideas included support for a foreign policy that encouraged cooperation with the Soviet Union rather than confrontation, support for the UN as a means of maintaining the peace and bringing about world reconstruction, a belief that U.S. assistance should not be used for military or political purposes or in support of colonial or dictatorial regimes, and a belief in the necessity of some type of disarmament for peace to be maintained.

With the development of the NAT, most of the opposition groups and individuals had a target that briefly reunited them. They saw the treaty clearly as a military alliance and not economic assistance. To pacifists and liberal internationalists, it was a step toward provoking confrontation threatening the fragile peace and undermining the UN as a peacekeeping force.

NOTES

1. Richard M. Freeland, *The Truman Doctrine and the Origins of McCarthyism: Foreign Policy, Domestic Politics, and Internal Security* (New York: Alfred A. Knopf, 1972), 52–53; Robert A. Pollard, "Economic Security and the Origins of the Cold War: Bretton Woods, the Marshall Plan, and American Rearmament, 1944–50," *Diplomatic History* 9 (summer 1985): 280.

2. U.S. Department of State, *Bulletin*, March 23, 1947, 536.

3. Crabb, *Bipartisan Foreign Policy*, 58.

4. Morrell Heald and Lawrence Kaplan, *Culture and Diplomacy: The American Experience* (Westport, CT: Greenwood Press, 1977), 216, 221.

5. Gallup, *The Gallup Poll*, 1:639.

6. Crabb, *Bipartisan Foreign Policy*, 59; Heald and Kaplan, *Culture and Diplomacy*, 223; Paterson, *On Every Front*, 126–27.

7. Dunn to Marshall, June 17, 1947, Department of State, *Foreign Relations of the United States*, 1947, Vol. 3 (Washington, DC: Government Printing Office, 1972), 292–93.

8. Pollard, "Economic Security and the Origins of the Cold War," 280.

9. Vandenberg, ed., *The Private Papers of Senator Vandenberg*, 339; LaFeber, *The American Age*, 453.

10. Lawrence S. Wittner, *American Intervention in Greece 1943–1949* (New York: Columbia University Press, 1982), 80–81.

11. Acheson, March 20, 1947, U.S. Congress, House, *Assistance to Greece and Turkey: Hearings before the Committee on Foreign Affairs*, H.R. 2616, 80th Cong., 1st sess., 1947, 3–4. Hereafter referred to as *Greece and Turkey* (House).

12. Ibid., 31.

13. Ibid., 19; Acheson, U.S. Congress, Senate, *Assistance to Greece and Turkey: Hearings before the Committee on Foreign Relations*, S. 938, 80th Cong., 1st sess., 1947, 11. Hereafter referred to as *Greece and Turkey* (Senate).

14. Acheson, *Greece and Turkey* (Senate), 8–9, 47; Acheson, March 21, 1947, *Greece and Turkey* (House), 40.

15. Acheson, *Greece and Turkey* (Senate), 40.

16. Ibid., 39; Hamby, *Beyond the New Deal*, 176.

17. Acheson, *Greece and Turkey* (Senate), 43–44.

18. McAuliffe, *Crisis on the Left*, 23–25.

19. Ibid., 23, 32; Hamby, "Henry A. Wallace, the Liberals, and Soviet-American Relations," 163.

20. Barton J. Bernstein, "Walter Lippmann and the Early Cold War," in Pat-

erson, ed., *Cold War Critics*, 43, 48–49; Henry W. Berger, "Senator Robert A. Taft Dissents from Military Escalation," in Paterson, ed., *Cold War Critics*, 168, 194–95.

21. Fish, March 31, 1947, *Greece and Turkey* (House), 195, 202.

22. Anna Lord Strauss, April 8, 1947, *Greece and Turkey* (House), 273.

23. Clark Eichelberger, March 27, 1947, *Greece and Turkey* (Senate), 149–50; Robert D. Accinelli, "Pro-U.N. Internationalists and the Early Cold War: The American Association for the United Nations and U.S. Foreign Policy, 1947–52," *Diplomatic History* 9 (fall 1985): 394–95.

24. Walker, *Henry A. Wallace and American Foreign Policy*, 167–69, 173; Ronald Radosh and Leonard P. Liggio, "Henry A. Wallace and the Open Door," in Paterson, ed., *Cold War Critics*, 93–94.

25. Claude D. Pepper (with Hays Gorey), *Pepper: Eyewitness to a Century* (New York: Harcourt Brace Jovanovich, 1987), 153–54; Thomas G. Paterson, "The Dissent of Senator Claude Pepper," in Paterson, ed., *Cold War Critics*, 127.

26. Pepper, *Pepper*, 154–55.

27. Peterson, *Prophet without Honor*, 83–85.

28. Warburg, *The Long Road Home*, 245; David Farrer, *The Warburgs: The Story of a Family* (New York: Stein and Day, 1974), 156, 175.

29. Warburg, *The Long Road Home*, 236; Warburg to Acheson, May 9, 1947, Warburg Papers, Box 13, Acheson file, Kennedy Library.

30. Samuel Guy Inman, April 3, 1947, *Greece and Turkey* (House), 219, 224; Russell Smith, April 9, 1947, *Greece and Turkey* (House), 311; Mabel Vernon, April 9, 1947, *Greece and Turkey* (House), 317.

31. Popper, April 8, 1947, *Greece and Turkey* (House), 260–66. See also Popper, March 27, 1947, *Greece and Turkey* (Senate), 175.

32. Kingdom, March 31, 1947, *Greece and Turkey* (Senate), 183.

33. Schutzer, March 26, 1947, *Greece and Turkey* (Senate), 114, 113; Fleischman, March 26, 1947, *Greece and Turkey* (Senate) 116; Gausmann, April 8, 1947, *Greece and Turkey* (House), 276.

34. Joan Lee Byrniarski, "Against the Tide: Senate Opposition to the Internationalist Foreign Policy of Presidents Franklin D. Roosevelt and Harry S. Truman, 1943–1949" (Ph.D. diss., University of Maryland, 1972), 123, 161; Claude Pepper to the National Peace Conference, April 4, 1947, Papers of the National Peace Conference, DG 49, Box 12, Aid to Greece and Turkey, 1947, SCPC.

35. Lamont and Fairchild, April 9, 1947, *Greece and Turkey* (House), 298, 293; Melish, March 26, 1947, *Greece and Turkey* (Senate), 106.

36. Minutes of the Executive Committee of the PWWC, April 24, 1947, PWWC papers, DG-42, Reel 90.1, SCPC; Broads Mitchell, March 26, 1947, *Greece and Turkey* (Senate), 96–97.

37. Wallace, March 1947, *Congressional Record*, 80th Cong., 1st sess., Vol. 93, pt. 10, A1328–1329; Vol. 93, pt. 11, A1572; Wallace quoted in Walker, *Henry Wallace and American Foreign Policy*, 167–68.

38. Peterson, *Prophet without Honor*, 86–89; William C. Pratt, "Senator Glen H. Taylor: Questioning American Unilateralism," in Paterson, ed., *Cold War Critics*, 147.

39. Warburg to Acheson, May 9, 1947, Warburg Papers, Box 13, Acheson file, Kennedy Library.

40. Charles G. Bolte, *Greece and Turkey* (House), 334–35; March 26, 1947, *Greece and Turkey* (Senate), 95.

41. Alfred O. Hero Jr., *American Religious Groups View Foreign Policy* (Durham, NC: Duke University Press, 1973), 55.

42. Sikes, n.d., *Greece and Turkey* (House), 337; Cloward, March 31, 1947, *Greece and Turkey* (Senate), 198.

43. Marshall, April 8, 1947, *Greece and Turkey* (House), 283–84; Marshall, March 26, 1947, *Greece and Turkey* (Senate), 103–4.

44. "Resolutions Passed at Annual Meeting of WILPF," April 24–27, 1947, WILPF, Reel 130.94, SCPC.

45. *Christian Century*, March 26, 1947.

46. "Statement of Members of the New York East Annual Conference of the Methodist Church," n.d., *Greece and Turkey* (House), 331; Smith, April 3, 1947, *Greece and Turkey* (House), 232; Boss, March 31, 1947, *Greece and Turkey* (Senate), 204; Boss, April 8, 1947, *Greece and Turkey* (House), 266, 268, 270.

47. Quoted in Wittner, *Rebels against War*, 183.

48. Muste, n.d., *Greece and Turkey* (House), 327–28; Jo Ann Robinson, *Abraham Went Out: A Biography of A. J. Muste* (Philadelphia: Temple University Press, 1981), 138–39; Muste, March 26, 1947, *Greece and Turkey* (Senate), 98–99.

49. Muste, "How to Stop Russia and Communism: The Crux of the Greek-Turkish Issue," March 10, 1947, FOR, DG 13, A, 23, Releases 1946–47, SCPC.

50. Wittner, *Rebels against War*, 229; Cadbury, April 3, 1947, *Greece and Turkey* (House), 235, 238, 241–42.

51. Richard Wood, March 26, 1947, *Greece and Turkey* (Senate), 118; E. Raymond Wilson, *Uphill for Peace: Quaker Impact on Congress* (Richmond, IN: Friend's United Press, 1975), 246. Emphasis in original.

52. Libby, April 3, 1947, *Greece and Turkey* (House), 246–47; Libby to Rev. R. C. Menker, April 16, 1947, NCPW, DG 23, Reel 41.253, SCPC.

53. Olmstead, April 9, 1947, *Greece and Turkey* (House), 302–4.

54. Alonso, *Peace as a Women's Issue*, 171; Marshall, April 8, 1947, *Greece and Turkey* (House), 283–84.

55. Editorial, *Christian Century*, March 26, 1947; "Statement of Members of the NY East Annual Conference of the Methodist Church," n.d., *Greece and Turkey* (House), 331; Thomas Paterson, "The Dissent of Senator Claude Pepper," in Patterson, ed., *Cold War Critics*, 30–31.

56. Horne, *Black and Red*, 277, 281; Laville and Lucas, "The American Way," 580–81.

57. "Outline of a European Recovery Program," December 1947, Papers of Paul G. Hoffman, Box 23-ECA file, Outline of ERP, Truman Library, Independence, MO.

58. Harry Truman, *Memoirs*, vol. 2: *Years of Trial and Hope* (Garden City, NY: Doubleday and Co., 1955), 111–13, 119; U.S. Department of State, *Bulletin*, May 18, 1947, 994; Thomas Paterson, *Soviet-American Confrontation: Postwar Reconstruction and the Origins of the Cold War* (Baltimore, MD: Johns Hopkins University Press, 1973), 207.

59. Robert Dallek, "The Postwar World: Made in the USA," in Sanford J. Ungar, ed., *Estrangement: America and the World* (New York: Oxford University

Press, 1985), 45–46; Pollard, "Economic Security and the Origins of the Cold War," 280–81.

60. Gallup, *The Gallup Poll*, July 23, 1947, 1:661; March 3, 1948, 1:715.

61. McAuliffe, *Crisis on the Left*, 29–30; Hamby, *Beyond the New Deal*, 186, 193.

62. Wittner, *Rebels against War*, 183; Morton Gordon, "American Opposition to ERP and the North Atlantic Treaty: A Study of Anti-Administration Opinion" (Ph.D. diss., University of Chicago, 1953), 168.

63. Eichelberger, January 26, 1948, U.S. Congress, Senate, *European Recovery Program, Hearings before the Committee on Foreign Relations*, 80th Cong., 2nd sess., 3 parts, 1948, II:936–38. Hereafter referred to as *ERP Hearings*.

64. David D. Lloyd, February 4, 1948, U.S. Congress, House, Committee on Foreign Affairs, *United States Foreign Policy for a Post-War Recovery Program, Hearings*, 80th Cong., 2nd sess., 2 parts, 1948, II:992. Hereafter referred to as *Post-War Recovery Program*.

65. Warburg to Acheson, February 6, 1948, Box 13, Acheson file, Warburg Papers, Kennedy Library (emphasis in original); Warburg, *The Long Road Home*, 237; James P. Warburg, *Last Call for Common Sense* (New York: Harcourt, Brace and Co., 1949), 39.

66. Paterson, "The Dissent of Senator Claude Pepper," 131–32.

67. Walter White, January 27, 1948, *ERP Hearings*, II:952, 954.

68. Thomas, January 27, 1948, *ERP Hearings*, II:947, 951; PWWC News Bulletin, February 1948, PWWC, Reel 90.7, SCPC.

69. Minutes, National Executive Meeting, September 24, 1947, WILPF, Reel 130.13, SCPC.

70. "Statement of the Policy Committee on the Marshall Plan," October 24, 1947, WILPF, Reel 130.94, SCPC; Minutes, National Board of WILPF, February 13–15, 1948, WILPF, Reel 130.13, SCPC.

71. Katharine Lee Marshall, January 29, 1948, *ERP Hearings*, II:1103–4; February 12, 1948, *Post War Recovery Program*, 1191–92.

72. Radosh and Liggio, "Henry A. Wallace and the Open Door," 97–98; Hamby, *Beyond the New Deal*, 202–3.

73. Wallace to Anita McCormick Blaine, April 2, 1948, Wallace Papers, Reel 44.

74. Wallace, February 24, 1948, *Post-War Recovery Program*, 1581–83, 1594.

75. Alonzo L. Hamby, "Henry A. Wallace, the Liberals, and Soviet-American Relations," 165; Hamby, *Beyond the New Deal*, 230–31; Wallace to Blaine, April 24, 1948, Wallace Papers, Reel 44.

76. Peterson, *Prophet*, 91–92; William C. Pratt, "Senator Glen H. Taylor: Questioning American Unilateralism," in Paterson, ed., *Cold War Critics*, 156.

77. Robinson, *Abraham Went Out*, 139; Muste to E. Raymond Wilson, December 17, 1947, NCPW papers, Reel 41.254, SCPC.

78. James M. Reed, January 30, 1948, *ERP Hearings*, III:1144–45.

79. Thomas Borstelmann, *Apartheid's Reluctant Uncle: The United States and Southern Africa in the Early Cold War* (New York: Oxford University Press, 1993), 58–59, 67.

Future Secretary of State James F. Byrnes, President Harry Truman, and Commerce Secretary Henry Wallace wait in Washington for the train bearing the body of President Franklin Roosevelt from Warm Springs, GA, April 1945. (Courtesy of the Harry S. Truman Library, Office of War Information)

NAACP leaders W.E.B. Du Bois, Mary McLeod Bethune, and Walter White attending the 1945 founding meeting of the UN. (Courtesy of the National Park Service—Mary McLeod Bethune Council House NHS, Washington, DC)

Henry Wallace leaves the White House after discussing foreign policy differences with President Truman on September 18, 1946. (Courtesy of the University of Iowa Libraries)

President Truman signs and puts into effect the NAT, August 24, 1949. Looking on are representatives of NATO countries and Secretary of State Dean Acheson (third from the right). (National Park Service Photograph courtesy of the Harry S. Truman Library)

Key Marshall Plan figures: President Truman, Secretary of State George Marshall, European Cooperation Administration Head Paul Hoffman, and U.S. Special Representative to Europe W. Averell Harriman in the White House on November 29, 1948. (National Park Service Photograph courtesy of the Harry S. Truman Library)

FOR leader A. J. Muste. (Courtesy of the Papers of A. J. Muste, Swarthmore College Peace Collection)

WILPF leader Annalee Stewart. (Courtesy of the Records of the Women's International League for Peace and Freedom, Swarthmore College Peace Collection)

Sen. Claude Pepper (center) with Belgian Prime Minister Spaak and Belgian Ambassador, January 1950. (Courtesy of the Claude Pepper Library, Florida State University Libraries, Tallahassee, Florida)

Opponents beyond the water's edge: A. J. Muste, Norman Thomas, Eugene Dennis, W.E.B. Du Bois, and Roger N. Baldwin, May 27, 1956. (Courtesy of the Records of the Fellowship of Reconciliation, Swarthmore College Peace Collection)

4

OPPOSITION TO THE NORTH ATLANTIC TREATY

In April 1949, the United States institutionalized the containment policy by signing the NAT, which committed it to the defense of Western Europe. The NAT resulted from the deterioration of Soviet-American relations, which many critics of the Truman administration had feared. President Truman wrote that it was the threat of unpredictable Soviet moves that produced an atmosphere of fear and insecurity in Western Europe. Although the ERP was seen as a helpful measure, his administration believed that more had to be done to counteract the possibility that the Soviet Union would overrun Western Europe. If left unchecked, the administration felt that the entire economic recovery program would be paralyzed.[1] In addition to providing confidence for a successful recovery, as well as protection against a Soviet invasion of Western Europe, the NAT sought to counter internal communist subversion within Western Europe.[2]

The alliance emerged from a series of negotiations in 1948 and 1949. In March 1947, Britain and France had signed the Treaty of Dunkirk directed against a resurgent Germany. Then in March 1948, Britain and France joined with Belgium, the Netherlands, and Luxembourg in signing the Brussels Pact to defend Western Europe. The United States entered into alliance negotiations shortly after the signing of the Brussels Pact. During March and April 1948, the United States, Britain, and Canada held security talks in Washington. By their third meeting, the three agreed that the "objective is a security pact for the North Atlantic area."[3] The talks broadened into the Washington Exploratory Talks on Security by including all the Brussels powers. These negotiations, which eventually included Iceland, Italy, Norway, and Portugal, continued until April 1949 when the treaty was signed in Washington. In July, the Senate overwhelmingly ratified the pact by a vote of 82–13.

The strong support for containment, both in the Congress and the public as a whole, meant that there would be little opposition to the alliance of the United States with the nations of Western Europe. Nevertheless, isolationists, liberal internationalists, and pacifists continued their opposition to containment and opposed the ratification of the alliance. Lawrence Kaplan noted that historians have operated "on the assumption that the passage of the treaty was a foregone conclusion" because the Truman Doctrine had cleared the way. The overwhelming Senate vote seemed to indicate that. However, considering that the Truman Doctrine was a unilateral action along the lines of the Monroe Doctrine, the administration, according to Kaplan, expected to face significant opposition to treaty ratification. They expected opposition to come from three very different groups: the military establishment, which feared an overextension of U.S. military power; the traditional isolationists who would oppose an alliance with the Europeans; and what Kaplan called the advocates of a new international order.[4]

Although much has been written on the views of the military and the isolationists, very little scholarship has emerged on the third group. Here one finds the anti-imperialists, members of the Progressive Party and various noncommunist leftists, supporters of the UN, the antimilitarists, and the pacifists who were worried about a dangerous militarization of U.S. foreign policy. Generally, those who opposed the Truman Doctrine reemerged and reunited to criticize the NAT.

THE UNITED NATIONS AND THE NORTH ATLANTIC TREATY

Much of the debate over the NAT focused on its relationship to the UN or on the concern that this was another blow to the already weakened UN. Was the United States abandoning a universal security system for a traditional military alliance? The UN Charter is mentioned in several places in the NAT. In the Preamble, the parties "reaffirm their faith in the purposes and principles of the Charter of the United Nations." In article 1, the pact members pledge to attempt to settle international disputes by peaceful means "as set forth in the Charter of the United Nations." In article 5, the collective defense of the North Atlantic area is justified by noting that article 51 of the UN Charter gives nations the right of individual or collective self-defense.[5] The idea that the UN had failed and that the NAT was necessary to strengthen Western security was a common view held by the treaty's supporters. Secretary of State Dean Acheson, UN representative Warren Austin, Chair of the Senate Foreign Relations Committee Tom Connally, and leading administration officials defended the NAT, arguing that the UN was still important and that the pact did not bypass it.[6]

Scholars have disagreed over the UN–NAT relationship. Alan Henrikson argued that nothing in the treaty violated the UN Charter. He wrote that "[f]ar from intending to subvert the United Nations, substituting partisan collective defense for impartial collective security, the founders of NATO appear to have believed that they were doing what they could to strengthen the UN organization." He stated that the founders did not think of the NAT as a traditional alliance, instead viewing it as consistent with the original four-power cooperation that came out of World War II. NATO, Henrikson asserted, can be seen "as a kind of truncated three-power version of it." Nothing precluded Eastern European states from joining, except article 2 on "free institutions."[7] Since the end of the Cold War, NATO, in fact, has approved the expansion of membership to include some Eastern European nations, and perhaps ultimately it will include even Russia itself.

On the other hand, Roland Stromberg wrote that "by extracting" certain words from article 52 of the UN Charter, and ignoring others, "American officials erected a rationalization of the NATO alliance" that did "violence to the letter as well as the spirit of the original Charter." He noted the tremendous effort by the Truman administration to make it clear that the NAT was not an old-fashioned military alliance and that instead it was a kind of collective security, consistent with the UN Charter.[8]

Lawrence Kaplan wrote that the administration had to assure the nation that the policy of containment and the NAT fit into "the image of the world" that had replaced isolationism. This new image was one based on the collective security "implicit in the existence of the United Nations." He stated that the administration sought to avoid a direct conflict between a treaty of military alliance and a charter of collective security. "To accept one meant to deny the other." Kaplan noted that treaty supporters feared a revival of isolationism if they said that the UN had failed to keep the peace and "implied a need for the restoration of the old alliance system." Warren Austin was persuaded to say that the NAT would not weaken the UN but would in fact strengthen it. What they sought to do was to dress the treaty in language disarming both the old isolationists and the new UN supporters. However, as Kaplan noted, that effort failed.[9]

Most who felt that the pact was bypassing, or even contrary to the UN, opposed ratification of the treaty. E. Raymond Wilson and Barbara

Grant, writing for the FCNL, argued that the "treaty tends to over-shadow and circumvent the UN" in its procedures and expenditures. They noted that under article 5, the signatories became the judges in their own case, deciding on how to deal with the problem of aggression without any defined procedures or standards. Wilson and Grant wrote, "They are free to act without mediation, and become the judges of the adequacy of the United Nations Security Council actions." In its rela-tionship to the UN Security Council, they warned that the "size and importance of the nations signing this agreement cause it to overshadow the United Nations because it includes three of the five permanent mem-bers of the Security Council, all of the major colonial powers, and rep-resents more than 50 percent of the world's industrial capacity." They also challenged the validity of the use of article 52 of the UN Charter, which allowed for regional security arrangements, pointing out that ar-ticle 53 stated that no enforcement was to be implemented under regional agreements without Security Council authorization.[10]

During the debate over the ratification of the treaty, some administra-tion critics eventually agreed with pact supporters, hoping that some-thing more could evolve from the NAT and strengthen the UN. They did so despite their doubts. As Sen. Claude Pepper noted, when it be-came apparent that the UN was not yet able to keep the peace, the United States sought other alternatives. If the United States entered the pact, Pepper felt it "would find an acceleration in the peaceful progress being made in the present cold war." However, he did express hope that this was not "going to be the substitute for an effective United Nations."[11]

Most of the critics ignored the legalistic issue of a conflict between the UN Charter and the terms of the NAT. Instead, they focused on their conviction that the treaty weakened the UN. Seeing in the pact the final breakup of the World War II coalition that had been the basis of the UN, they made a final stand for renewal of peaceful cooperation with the Soviet Union.

PUBLIC OPINION, THE TRADITIONAL ISOLATIONISTS, AND THE VANDENBERG RESOLUTION

Despite the fact that the NAT would be a break with 150 years of traditional opposition to alliances with European nations, the American public overwhelmingly supported the pact. The Gallup Poll of February 25, 1949 indicated that strong support. When asked if the United States should join with Western European nations in agreeing to come to the defense of each other if attacked, 67 percent answered affirmatively, and only 16 percent opposed. Surveyed again on March 28, the numbers supporting an alliance jumped to 76 percent. When asked specifically, both on May 18 and July 8, if the Senate should ratify the NAT, 67 percent answered yes, and only 12 percent and 15 percent respectively, opposed ratification.[12]

Although the public either supported the alliance, or was sold on the necessity of it in conjunction with the UN, the old isolationists continued to oppose alliances. Although the old isolationists varied in motive for their opposition to the pact, most feared, as did the leftist critics, that the alliance would provoke rather than prevent war. Although the isolationist critics acknowledged the good faith of the NAT's proponents, they believed that supporters failed to perceive the treaty's provocative aspects.[13]

In addition to the provocative aspects of the treaty, the isolationist critique of the pact argued that it would lead to an overextension of U.S. resources, that it would cause the United States to seek world domination, and that it was unnecessary because Russia itself was overextended. They also raised the colonial issue, fearing that arms supplied to European allies would be used to suppress colonial peoples. Therefore, the NAT could seem an endorsement of colonialism. The isolationists also disliked the binding nature of the pact, fearful that congressional war powers would be circumvented. These critics felt that the treaty's sponsors were vague and evasive about the implication for those constitutional powers. The isolationists also wanted some congressional restraint to prevent executive military adventurism.[14]

Whereas Sen. Glen Taylor represented the most outspoken congressional critic from the left, the old isolationists were led by Sen. Robert Taft of Ohio. Taft focused his criticism on three elements. He felt that it obligated the United States to go to war if anyone attacked the other member nations, which would thus allow the president to take the nation into a war without the consent of Congress. He also felt that the pact would stimulate an arms race and indicated that he might have supported a treaty that had provided that there would be no obligation to offer arms to the European allies. Finally, he argued that the pact violated the UN Charter. Taft's criticism focused on the globalist interventionism of the Truman administration and in many ways reflected the position of the most severe left-wing critics.[15]

In the face of what the Truman administration feared would be strong opposition to the negotiation of an alliance with Western Europe, it worked with Sen. Vandenberg to pass a resolution placing the U.S. Senate on record as supporting such an alliance. The resolution, passed in June 1948, advocated the negotiation of regional and other collective arrangements for individual and collective self-defense in accordance with the UN Charter. Because Vandenberg was a Republican, it gave the movement toward an Atlantic alliance a bipartisan stamp of approval. The resolution passed with only four dissenting votes. Claude Pepper, supported by Taylor, led the opposition to the resolution. Pepper introduced an amendment to the resolution to strike out paragraphs that urged the development of regional and other collective security arrangements and U.S. association with them. What he left were statements urging Washington to achieve peace and security through the UN. Pepper felt that article 51 of the UN Charter did not envision a long, premeditated, formal regional military alliance. According to the Florida senator, article 51 limited the formation of regional pacts to spontaneous resistance to armed attack. Pepper, long an internationalist, did not want the United States to commit itself in advance to a blank check defense of Europe.[16] The Pepper amendment was defeated 6–61, and the Vandenberg resolution passed 64–4, with only Senators Pepper, Taylor, William Langer, and Arthur Watkins in opposition. The move toward an alliance had great strength and support in the Senate and the nation as a whole.

THE RELUCTANT SUPPORTERS

In the Senate, Vandenberg was one of the most outspoken supporters of the pact, and his resolution cleared its way. He called the NAT a fraternity of peace with "no obligation not already implicit in our signature to the United Nations Charter."[17] Although Vandenberg's support for the pact was expected, some opponents and mild supporters of containment decided to back the pact.

The AAUN opposed what it called old-fashioned military alliances in principle because they were inconsistent with collective security. The State Department did attempt to appease the pro-UN opinion by emphasizing the NAT's compatibility with the UN. Consequently, the AAUN did give the pact qualified support. However, the organization urged a congressional resolution calling for a UN-based multilateral treaty to supplement the NAT.[18] Stephen M. Schwebel, the chairperson of the Collegiate Council for the UN (the college affiliate of the AAUN), told the Senate Foreign Relations Committee that his organization believed "that the Atlantic Treaty will be a pillar of peace" if it is brought closer into harmony with the UN. Although the Council believed that the best hope for peace was to be found by the development of a universal collective security system through the UN, the NAT would reaffirm the crucial U.S. international role and bolster the defense of the peace-loving world.[19]

One of the surprising although reluctant supporters was Norman Thomas, whose own Socialist Party opposed the pact. It was his dislike of communism and support for democracy that led him to this point of view. Thomas, testifying in May 1949 before the Senate Foreign Relations Committee, stated that he favored ratification because to refuse it at this point "might be a tremendous jolt to governments and parties in Europe on which the hope of democracy depends." His testimony of support was also filled with much criticism of the alliance. Although he felt that the negotiation was motivated by a sincere desire for defense, he believed there were better ways to assure peace. Thomas feared that the NAT moved in the direction of a North Atlantic union which would "virtually junk the UN." He favored a world federation rather than a permanently divided Europe.[20]

Thomas had several reservations about the pact, or, as he put it, actions that should parallel it. First of all, he felt that the United States should make it absolutely plain that it would oppose the inclusion of Francisco Franco's Spain. Second, he felt that steps should be taken to make it clear "that the pact will not furnish moral or economic aid . . . to the wretched colonial wars . . . waged by the Netherlands and France." Third, he felt that the effect of the pact must be to reduce rather than increase arms expenditures. Fourth, the United States should appeal for an end to the arms race, if possible even before ratification. Although he recognized that the Soviet Union would not accept disarmament proposals, "an American appeal might be a beginning."[21] Despite the fact that many of his criticisms were those expressed by pact opponents, he supported the alliance.

The UWF also became reluctant supporters. The organization's vice president, Grenville Clark, in a draft statement on the NAT prepared in February, seemed to be moving away from support for such an alliance. He wrote that the UWF believed that the best hope for peace did not lie in more containment or alliances, but in new efforts to achieve a general East-West settlement, disarmament, and a revision of the UN Charter. Clark wrote that the UWF "cannot regard the proposed North Atlantic Alliance . . . as helpful to the causes of world order."[22]

Nonetheless, the UWF did endorse the pact. In a March 1949 memorandum to the executive committee of the UWF, Alexander Standish urged ratification as a temporary means of strengthening the United States. Seen as a temporary measure, the United States should then move toward strengthening the UN and making it a federal world government "of sufficient strength to assure permanent peace under world law."[23] The chairperson of the UWF Executive Committee, Cass Canfield, testified in support of the treaty before the Senate Foreign Relations Committee. He noted that "[a] difference exists between those who support the Atlantic treaty as a program to insure permanent peace and those supporting it as a temporary measure necessary for the defense of this country." Stating that he belonged to the latter group, Canfield urged the committee to make it clear that the pact "is an emergency measure" and combine it with efforts to amend the UN Charter so that the UN could be transformed into a limited world government.[24]

One of the most surprising of the reluctant supporters was Claude Pepper. Although he was the leading opponent of the Vandenberg resolution, the senator gradually shifted to support Truman's foreign policy. Shaken by the March 1948 coup in Czechoslovakia, he began to support the policy of containment, including the NAT, to stabilize the world to make it possible for the UN to work.[25] During the debates on the NAT, Pepper stated that the NAT was "a way of quieting things down, of giving these people the assurance they need, of taking a part of the military burden off them . . . it discourages aggression from any source outside their own individual territory, and pledges us to their territorial security." Still a supporter of the UN, Pepper argued that there was not time to alter the UN to accomplish that same purpose. However, he stated that he hoped "that this is not going to be the substitute for an effective United Nations."[26]

Despite the fact that Pepper, Thomas, the AAUN, and the UWF supported the pact, most of those opposed to containment continued in the opposition and spoke out against the NAT. Looking back at their arguments from the post–Cold War perspective, with NATO playing a peacekeeping role in the former Yugoslavia, it is obvious that some of the greatest concerns raised by the critics did not materialize. The pact did not lead to war. Many arguments raised in opposition to the pact had little long-term validity. However, as a general critique of the Truman foreign policy, there were some accurate points in the criticisms leveled at the NAT that encapsulated the opposition to the Truman foreign policy of containment.

To make sense of the wide-ranging criticism raised during the debate over treaty ratification, the most important points raised by the liberal internationalist and pacifist opposition can be arranged into five broad categories: (1) that the NAT weakened the UN and violated its charter; (2) that the NAT strengthened the dangerous military focus of the containment policy; (3) that with the NAT, arms sales to Europe would be emphasized over policies favoring economic recovery; (4) that the NAT strengthened the development of militarism and military decision making in U.S. society; and (5) that the NAT would lend support to European colonialism.

Although the isolationists discussed some of these issues, they also raised other issues, including the constitutional prerogatives of the Congress and the issue of entanglement. The internationalist opponents, however, did not fear entanglement. Speaking on the floor of the Senate, Glen Taylor noted that the press had referred to opponents of the pact as isolationists. He denounced isolationism and indicated his belief that "seeking to bypass, undermine, and destroy the United Nations is not internationalism" and that opposition to "alliances of a military nature" outside of the UN "which tend to weaken that organization certainly is not isolationism."[27] In fact, common to almost all of the left-liberal internationalist and pacifist groups was their desire to strengthen the UN through a greater U.S. commitment to that organization.

WEAKENING THE UNITED NATIONS

Although scholars and contemporary critics have discussed the legalistic issues of conflict between the UN Charter and the terms of the NAT, most critics emphasized their conviction that the treaty weakened the UN. Opponents from almost all perspectives viewed the pact as a threat to the potential new world order maintained by that international organization.

On the Senate floor, the most outspoken critic of the treaty from an internationalist perspective was Glen Taylor. Although his criticisms were wide-ranging, his most serious concerns related to the role of the UN. He believed that the United States should be making an all-out effort to build up the UN. He noted that he was elected to the Senate on his promise to the voters of Idaho that he would support an organization to maintain peace and "that organization was the United Nations." Taylor expressed determination "to oppose everything" that seemed "to have the effect of weakening the United Nations." The senator believed that the pact was going to weaken the UN and lead to an armaments race which could hasten a war instead of preventing one. He told his fellow senators that his "principal reason" for opposition to the NAT was that "[d]espite all the assurances to the contrary, I am still convinced that this pact ... [will] bypass, undermine, and weaken the United Nations."[28]

Outside of the Congress, the WILPF was one of the most outspoken supporters for the strengthening of the UN. In policy statements and in congressional testimony, the WILPF condemned the NAT as a threat to the UN. In an April 12, 1949 letter to the *New York Times*, sent two weeks after the text of the treaty was made public, the national board announced their opposition to the pact, saying that it would further divide and weaken the UN. Among a set of proposed policies to be presented to the WILPF's May 1949 annual meeting was an analysis of U.S. policy and the UN. The organization stated that loyalty to the UN demanded the acceptance of its decisions, which the United States has not done satisfactorily. The proposal noted that the ERP had bypassed the UN and that the pact "is a further blow to the health of the United Nations ... because it deepens the chasm between the West and the Soviet Union and involves a return to balance of power, instead of collective security." Although the League had supported world and regional cooperation, they felt that such cooperation should be in the form of economic and political cooperation, not military alliances. At the May meeting, the

League approved a resolution in opposition to the NAT. Their concerns included the potential of the NAT to replace the UN as well as to provide for arming certain nations in the UN against each other.[29]

Annalee Stewart, the president of the U.S. section of the WILPF, told the Senate Foreign Relations Committee that her organization believed that the inadequacy of the UN was due in part to the climate of fear and distrust in international affairs. Reflecting the official policy resolutions of the League, Steward stated that the task was to create a climate of cooperation among the member nations. Stewart argued that the pact was a blow to the health of the UN because it deepened the divisions between Washington and Moscow and was a return to old-style balance-of-power diplomacy. She noted that it was "never the real intent of the UN Charter to arm nations within the UN against each other."[30]

Charles F. Boss Jr., executive secretary of the Methodist Church's Commission on World Peace, told the Senate Foreign Relations Committee that his organization viewed the UN as "the keystone of our . . . national policy." Boss indicated that the Commission felt that the NAT weakened the UN because it was directed against a member nation. He stated that rather than opposing the pact at that point, the Commission was simply withholding its support. However, he noted later that if members had known that the pact was moving in the direction of rearmament, "they might have taken a position in opposition."[31]

In addition to Boss, the Methodists were represented before the committee by Mrs. Clifford Bender of the Women's Division of Christian Service of the Methodist Church. She told the senators that despite assurances, the NAT tended to overshadow and bypass the UN in its procedures, expenditures, and loyalty of member nations. Bender warned of the danger that the UN could splinter into armed camps and decline in prestige. When questioned on her position, Bender indicated that with modifications she would support adoption of the NAT but that without further adjustment she was opposed to ratification.[32]

Representing the Church of the Brethren Service Commission, A. Stauffer Curry said that his church looked "with great hopefulness upon the possibility of world brotherhood through the United Nations" and felt that the NAT would weaken that body. Instead, he called for an expansion of the UN role.[33]

One organization, the Committee for Peaceful Alternatives to the North Atlantic Pact, was founded specifically to oppose the treaty. Although it included communists, they did not dominate the organization, which continued to function after the ratification of the pact as the CPA. In their opposition to the pact, they cited the need for constructive alternatives, including greater support for the UN "whose primary business . . . is to settle differences among all nations and to maintain peace."[34]

The concerns expressed about the UN, though widespread, had little impact on the administration or Congress. Although high-level policy makers couched their arguments for regional security agreements within the confines of the UN Charter, Washington viewed the UN of little use in conducting a foreign policy aimed at the containment of the Soviet Union. NATO rather than the UN came to be the focus of U.S. diplomacy during the remainder of the Cold War.

MILITARY CONTAINMENT

Opposition to the military component of containment, represented by a military alliance, made up a second group of criticisms aimed at the Atlantic Pact. In the committee hearings and in other public statements in opposition to the treaty, critics charged that U.S. foreign policy was leading the nation in the wrong direction. It was leading in the direction of war.

The best-known critic of the NAT was Henry Wallace. In his testimony before the Senate committee, the former vice president argued that containment was not an American doctrine. First advocated by former British Prime Minister Winston Churchill in the struggle against Bolshevism, Wallace claimed that containment would end only in war. In a March letter, he wrote that the NAT was "another long step down the road to war." He felt that it would cause the militarization of the U.S. domestic economy and lead "to national insolvency, the surrender of our traditional freedoms, war, a possible military disaster, and certain sacrifice not only of life and treasure but of the very system of government which it is supposed to preserve." To Wallace, the NAT represented the failure of Truman's foreign policy, especially the Marshall Plan, which had aimed at "precluding the need for a military program in Europe."[35]

The strongest criticisms of military containment came from pacifist groups. The FOR issued a statement which emphasized its opposition to the spread of totalitarian communism, but noted that the United States had increasingly "come to depend upon military power" to accomplish that goal. The FOR argued that war had not ended totalitarianism or brought security, stating that America was "less secure than ever." In a May article in the organization's *Fellowship*, Alfred Hassler wrote that if the pact were ratified it "will be one of the more ominous indications of how completely this fear-ridden country has abandoned faith in itself and in every democratic value in favor of reliance on military power." FOR leader John Nevin Sayer, in a letter to Sen. Robert Wagner, noted that with the atomic bomb and biological weapons, the methods of warfare had undergone such a revolutionary change that "former strategies of defense which were based on preponderance of power in old fashioned military weapons" were "totally obsolete."[36]

The FOR was also among those groups testifying before the Senate committee. Dr. Phillips Elliot warned the committee that methods of military alliance and armament rivalries have been tried for centuries, and they "have led to disaster in the past." Elliot told the senators that the chief concern of the FOR was that the pact accepted the principle of a divided world, turning the nation away from the opportunity of great spiritual, not military, leadership.[37]

In his annual report to the NCPW, Frederick Libby also emphasized the danger of war. He wrote that the NCPW believed that the basic conflict with the Soviet Union was in the field of human welfare, not arms, and that "the arms race is the road to ruin and war." Libby told the Senate Foreign Relations Committee that the NAT was a "war pact" because it heightened the tension between the United States and Russia.[38]

Various Quaker organizations also were outspoken in their opposition to the alliance as a "war pact." Wilson and Grant argued that the entire program of a military alliance "misconceives the nature of the struggle with the Soviet Union, regarding it primarily as a military struggle rather than as an ideological one." An April 1949 statement by the Baltimore Yearly Meeting of Friends argued that military preparedness, rather than preventing war, was "actually conductive to it." They felt that the NAT would not end the Cold War but intensify it. The other peace churches agreed. Speaking for the Church of the Brethren, Curry expressed a fear that the NAT would be the means of stimulating aggression rather than deterring it. He noted that "the premise of the group I represent [is] that the threat of the use of force will only encourage aggression."[39]

The WRL was perhaps the most outspoken in the view that the pact was a preparation for war. In an April 1949 statement, the WRL denounced the NAT as an old-fashioned alliance. Such alliances were "usually a prelude to an impending international conflict." The WRL questioned the entire concept of deterrence, arguing that "aggressor governments do not suddenly become peaceable merely because menacing foreign opposition appears; on the contrary, its mere presence enables them to intensify the anxieties of their own peoples and strengthen their dictatorial systems." The WRL felt that the NAT accelerated the drift toward war and that those grim facts provided "sufficient reasons for opposing it." Edward C. M. Richards reiterated those points in his testimony before the Senate committee. He said that the pact, if ratified, would make for war.[40]

The theme that the NAT was a "war pact" was quite common among those who testified in opposition. The Rev. Dudley Burr, chairman of the People's Party of Connecticut, stated that the NAT would "bring war instead of peace because it is basically founded on a war philosophy." Richard Morford, the executive director of the National Council of American-Soviet Friendship and a Presbyterian clergyman, told the committee that he believed that "the implications of this pact and building up resistance for attack . . . will in effect be establishing a very tangible threat of war." The Rev. Lee Howe, president of the Northern Baptist Pacifist Fellowship, argued that such methods of containment would fail. He told the Senate committee, "We cannot stop communism or the spread of communistic ideas by a military alliance or the threat of the use of military power."[41]

Instead of support for a military alliance, those who felt that the NAT was leading toward military conflict with the Soviets argued that a greater effort should be made to resolve Soviet-American differences through negotiations. Additionally, they all echoed support for the UN and hoped instead that the United States would lend greater support to that international body.

ECONOMIC RECOVERY AND THE REARMAMENT OF WESTERN EUROPE

The third major theme of the critics of the NAT, and of particular concern to Congress, was the rearming of Western Europe under the pact's provisions. Article 3 of the NAT called upon members to give mutual assistance to alliance members. Most critics correctly believed that the United States would undertake the rearmament of Western Europe. The testimony before the Senate Foreign Relations Committee and the debates on the floor of the Senate brought out several points of opposition. Among the most cited was the belief that the rearmament of Europe was unnecessary and harmful. It was unnecessary because the Soviet Union was not a military threat to the West. It was harmful because it would threaten the economic recovery of Western Europe.

One of the most articulate and well-known critics of the NAT was James Warburg. In books, articles, congressional testimony, and memorandums, Warburg spoke out against the NAT. He was not, however, completely opposed to the treaty. In fact, he told Secretary Acheson that he favored the general idea of an Atlantic alliance "provided that our commitment would not tie the United States to any predetermined strategy of defense or theater of action in the event of war." He felt that he could support the alliance if it did not take "our eyes off the real danger—which is now not military but political."[42] However, he believed that the NAT as negotiated did just that. Not only did Warburg reject containment, he believed that the administration's position was filled with dangerous contradictions.

Warburg felt that the U.S. government was so obsessed with stopping Soviet expansion that it lost sight of the factors that made such expansion possible. The result was that the United States had allied itself "with the forces of reaction throughout the world instead of ally[ing] . . . with the forces of progress." He believed that the United States should throw its full military and economic weight behind the UN, with the end goal being world government. He told the Senate Foreign Relations Committee that he was an enthusiastic supporter of the Marshall Plan but "a persistent critic of the doctrine of physical containment." Warburg believed that expansion could best be halted as a by-product of a constructive American policy for peace.[43]

Prior to his congressional testimony, Warburg sent memos to congressmen and senators explaining his objections to the pact. In his memorandum of February 1, he cited five broad reasons for careful scrutinization of the pact. First, he noted that the geographic limits of the treaty implied that the United States would not protect nonsignatories, thus inviting aggression against them. Second, he argued that there was a congressional loophole because Congress preserved the right to declare war, which could create uncertainty and invite miscalculation by the Soviet Union. Third, he believed that the proposed rearmament would not provide Europe with an adequate defense unless West Germany were rearmed and U.S. troops were stationed in large numbers in Europe, which could both provoke a Soviet counterresponse. The final two reasons got to the heart of his criticisms. He wondered what the United States was combating. Warburg believed that the primary threat to Europe was not military but political, by which he meant communist subversion. Therefore, the best defense was a rapid rebuilding of the economic health of Western Europe. Warburg wrote, "To the extent that Western Europe turns from recovery to rearmament, its defenses against political penetration will be weakened." Finally, he warned against another Dunkirk. He felt that the treaty committed Washington to a strategy that would involve a reenactment of the British World War II retreat from the European continent. In summarizing his points, Warburg stated that the NAT, as an unsound and dangerous weapon to use in the Cold War, had led him to question the entire containment policy. He said it raised the question of whether the United States was "placing too little emphasis upon constructive efforts for peace and too much emphasis upon a purely negative policy of strategic containment." In a completely underlined passage, Warburg wondered if the United States had reached a point where the "cold war will cease to be a method of seeking a peace settlement and become, instead, merely the preparation for an atomic war tacitly assumed to be inevitable."[44] In a second memorandum, dated February 17, he argued that an adequate defense force in Western Europe would require a mobilization of manpower "sufficient to disrupt the present effort to achieve economic recovery."[45]

Warburg did recognize the danger of backing out of the pact at such a late date, but felt it should be made into a "useful form." He told Walter Lippmann that he favored a divorce of the pact from rearmament. In a February 26 memorandum sent to Secretary Acheson, Warburg indicated that he felt that the United States should "continue and reinforce our present efforts to secure Western Europe against *political* conquest by promoting economic recovery and political stability."[46]

In his testimony before the Senate committee, Warburg continued his emphasis on those themes, especially the need for a political rather than military security. He noted that the NAT represented a "negative approach" to peace, while programs such as the Marshall Plan were a "positive approach" because they attacked the causes of mass discontent. Sen. Tom Connally, the committee chair, asked Warburg if he favored giving military aid to Europe. In responding, Warburg elaborated on his position, stating that he believed it "extremely dangerous to divert them from recovery to rearmament." However, he would send the allies limited armed assistance for domestic use only to maintain stability, but "not to put them in a position to hold the Oder or the Elbe or the Rhine." He indicated that if the United States did intend to put them in a position to hold those locations, "then by all means let's do what it takes to hold those lines. We are not going to do that with the present plans." But again, he made it clear that he did not believe it possible to "create a force in Europe capable of holding the frontiers of western Europe against invasion without halting the entire recovery program." He noted that it was not clear to the American people or those in Europe what the "sum total" of the treaty and the arms program meant.[47]

Warburg was not the only critic of the rearmament of Western Europe through the alliance. On the Senate floor, Glen Taylor again led the opposition, pointing out that if the treaty were approved, "the arms will automatically follow ... [causing] greater and greater deficits ... by unlimited spending for an endless stream of armaments." He warned that the United States could not hope to arm the Europeans sufficiently to withstand the Russian Army. In this point, Taylor was joined by others, including the traditional isolationists. Sen. Kenneth Wherry of Nebraska noted that if the NAT were simply a statement like a "keep-off-the-grass policy," practically everyone could go along with it. However, if the treaty involved "an absolute commitment that we are to provide arms ... then the question before us is an entirely different one."[48] Yet most senators recognized and accepted the fact that the NAT would mean that more U.S. arms would be sent to Europe.

The religious and pacifist community also expressed their objections to military assistance. Mrs. Bender, of the Women's Division of Christian Service of the Methodist Church, noted that her organization opposed a policy committed to foreign military aid. It viewed such assistance as a hindrance to economic recovery by "diverting manpower, machines, and materials for defense purposes." Charles Boss, representing the Methodist Commission on World Peace, reaffirmed Methodist support for foreign aid to supply the basic necessities and full employment as the most effective bulwark against communism. He told the Senate committee, "We do not believe that primarily power prevents the spread of communism." Dr. Henry Cadbury, representing the FCNL and the chair of the AFSC, stated that the NAT "creates major competition in American foreign policy by setting up rearmament against recovery and makes our foreign policy increasingly subservient to military policy." Annalee Stewart of the WILPF stated her organization's belief that the NAT will interfere with the "constructive work of the European recovery program" by diverting the money and material needed for economic recovery to military purposes.[49]

The issue of military assistance was one that reunited many of the early critics of containment who had supported the ERP with other critics who had also opposed the Marshall Plan. Those who had supported ERP had done so because they viewed it as an effort aimed at humanitarian recovery. Now that U.S. assistance could be diverted into military programs potentially hurting recovery, they returned to the anticontainment fold and opposed the NAT.

MILITARISM AT HOME

Closely related to the points raised by the critics of rearmament and the containment policy were the concerns about the growth of militarism in the United States. The view that the United States had started down the road to militarism was based on the belief that the United States remained in the grip of wartime thinking because of the Cold War. With increasing military commitments and responsibilities, military influence in foreign policy also grew. Critics charged that this extension of military power threatened civilian supremacy and contributed to the ability of the military to sway public and congressional opinion.[50]

Fearful of a return to post–World War I isolationism, postwar liberals condoned what Arthur Ekirch called "the opposite extreme of a militant, interventionist nationalism, masquerading as idealistic internationalism." The result of the emerging conflict with the Soviet Union was "an unprecedented peacetime militarization of the American government and economy." Because of the Cold War, the American people were convinced of the necessity of military preparedness on virtually a wartime basis.[51]

Michael Sherry argues that American militarism emerged prior to World War II. He defined militarism as a "process by which war and national security became consuming anxieties and provided the memories, models, and metaphors that shaped broad areas of national life." Roosevelt, therefore, viewed the threat of Nazi Germany as rooted in lasting strategic and technical changes which stripped the United States of geographic isolation, making preparedness permanently essential.

Thus, the Soviet threat was not necessary to make the case for postwar preparedness. A threat preceded the Cold War, and Soviet postwar actions served only to confirm the necessity.[52] This militarism, then, came to influence not just policy, politics, and economics, but virtually all aspects of American culture and intellectual life.

Historically opposed to militarism, pacifist groups and churches were outspoken in their opposition to this postwar trend. In particular, they believed that the NAT strengthened the military influence on U.S. policy. Leaders of the WRL noted that they were "profoundly concerned that our Federal Republic has tended to make war its main business." They felt that preparation for war and later payment for its costs constituted the "leading items on the agenda of the national government." In his testimony before the Foreign Relations Committee, Edward Richards decried what the WRL viewed as "the progress of the militarization" of the United States and "the growth of the influence of military minded men" in determining U.S. foreign policy. Richards said that the NAT was "the crowning folly" of this militarization. The WILPF, in a resolution passed at their annual meeting in May 1949, cited four specific reasons for its opposition to the pact, including the extension of "military control over foreign policy."[53] In a 1948 policy statement, the WILPF expressed its concern about the military influence in American life, calling it "one of the most alarming trends in contemporary life." They believed that the appointment of military men to important government positions and the growth of military influence in other areas constituted "a threat of military domination." The WILPF felt this increased the danger of war and threatened democracy.[54]

Religious groups expressed similar reservations. The Church of the Brethren Service Commission issued a press release in March 1949 expressing alarm over several recent developments, including an increase in the control of public thought through military propaganda. Speaking for the Brethren Service Commission before the Foreign Relations Committee, A. Stauffer Curry presented several reasons for the church's opposition to the pact. Although he emphasized his belief that it would encourage aggression, Curry also expressed concern that the pact would intensify "the military domination of American life and thought."[55] The magazine *Christian Century*, which opposed the NAT, editorialized that the Atlantic Pact was "conceived by military minds," and "the sort of foreign policy whose wisdom seems self-evident to military minds." The editor's concern was that "it will hand over to the military services actual control" of U.S. foreign policy. Or, as James Finucane of the NCPW noted, "If we let the Army and the American Legion 'brass' impose their definition of 'preparedness' on the country, the American taxpayer would have to pay for 'fortifying the moon.' "[56]

Such arguments had virtually no impact in the Senate. Only Sen. Taylor expressed sympathy with this view. He told his colleagues in April 1949, "We are moving along toward militarism . . . and it is getting so it is almost a traitorous act to criticize any of the policies which are taking us down the road toward militarism."[57] Although other senators expressed some concern over the growth of executive power, there was no concern about the growth of what President Dwight Eisenhower would label the military-industrial complex, or what C. Wright Mills called the power elite. Only later in the Cold War did those worried about the development of militarism in the United States gain a significant audience.

SUPPORT FOR COLONIALISM

A final significant theme expressed by many in opposition to the NAT was a warning that the United States was becoming involved in support of European colonialism. Over the course of the Cold War, emerging nationalism in colonial nations caused a variety of problems for U.S. foreign policy, with Washington frequently supporting the colonial powers against indigenous demands for independence. Despite statements from treaty supporters, such as Sen. Connally, that the alliance had nothing to do with empire, historian Scott Bills has noted that the NAT contained clauses that "might pull the United States into colonial affairs." For example, in terms later popularized in the administration of President Ronald Reagan, State Department officials defended the Portuguese empire in Africa, calling it "authoritarian" rather than "totalitarian." The latter designation meant communist. The Portuguese control of the strategic Azores Islands led the United States to weigh more favorably the desires of the Portuguese government than demands by Africans for independence.[58]

Although the creation of the NAT did not mean that the United States formally agreed to defend colonial rule, the fact of alliance implied that colonies were viewed by Washington "as most important for how they could contribute to the stability of the Western European nations."[59] There was, in fact, one empire that was protected. Until Algerian independence in 1962, that part of the French empire was to be defended by NATO. The Algerian Department of France was included in article 6 of the NAT as a territory to be covered by the pact.[60]

There was always significant anticolonial sentiment in the United States, but it was often laced with economic self-interest. During World War II, American pronouncements encouraged colonial nationalists to believe they would receive support from the United States. However, American policy makers also believed that U.S. prosperity would depend on open access to foreign markets and raw materials. They also felt that complete independence was a radical idea, favoring instead a period of preparation before self-government was granted.[61]

Part of the difficulty faced by Washington was the fact that there were clashing views of the postwar world. For most American policy makers, tensions between the United States and the Soviet Union dominated their view of world affairs. However, for much of the rest of the world, especially the peoples of Asia, Africa, and the Middle East, the dominant international issue was colonialism and the control of their land and resources by Western Europeans. For these people, the Cold War and the communist threat were distractions from the historic opportunity provided by World War II for eliminating colonialism.[62]

Although there were divisions within the U.S. foreign policy bureaucracy between the Europeanists who argued the primacy of Europe and NATO and the Africanists who pushed for strong opposition to white control, even the Africanists argued their position from the Cold War perspective. They claimed that a continuation of white supremacy in Africa would drive the Africans to communism.[63] But with near unanimity, American policy makers believed that Soviet and communist expansion constituted a more significant threat to U.S. interests than did colonial tyranny. Outside the government, most critics were overwhelmed by anticommunist repression.[64]

Critics were concerned whether the pact, supported by American arms and men, would be used to protect access to raw materials in the colonies, suppress nationalist uprisings, and exploit cheap labor for the colonial powers. Farrell Dobbs, national chair of the Trotskyist Socialist Workers Party, criticized the NAT's inclusion of the Antonio Salazar government of Portugal and the potential for the inclusion of Francisco Franco's Spain. He also attacked the Dutch government for its suppression of Indonesian independence with the aid of U.S. dollars and arms, followed by its arrogant statement after the signing of the pact, that " 'Indonesia is outside the spirit of the pact.' "[65]

Anticolonial groups, including many African Americans who became more vocal in the postwar era, placed high priority on the colonial issue. Although some of their charges were invalid, they reflected the fact that the world was far more complex than Washington chose to view it. An example of criticism, which reflected an important though invalid concern, came in the statement by Dr. Joe Thomas, president of the United Congo Improvement Association, Inc., to the Senate Foreign Relations Committee. In explaining his opposition to the NAT, Thomas charged that because of the alliance with Belgium, the United States would be compelled "to go to war to defend Belgian slavery in the Belgian Congo." Also, the CAA's William A. Hunton indicated that he understood that revolts in Africa against the colonial powers could be interpreted by London and Washington "as a threat to Britain's territorial integrity and security, and all of the parties to the treaty would . . . be called upon to take joint action in crushing the revolt of these peoples by force of arms."[66]

Some criticisms relating to colonialism, however, were valid as well as significant. In her testimony before the Senate committee, Carolyn Hill Stewart questioned the peaceful intent of the colonial powers and worried that U.S. arms would be used against native insurgents. She wondered if the "entanglement and identification" that came with the treaty would force colonial peoples to turn to communism for support. Bishop William J. Walls of the African Methodist Episcopal Zion Church feared that the pact would indicate approval of the situation in the colonies, "bad as it is," and make it permanent. He feared that American arms and boys would be used to suppress "the democratic stirrings of peoples" seeking independence. Such a prospect, he said, "is not a pleasant one to Negro Americans." Aware that most of the colonial world was outside of the treaty's jurisdiction, the bishop warned, "The colonial powers which have signed the pact are notorious for their disregard for written commitments." Hunton also indicated a distrust for the European states, noting that they held hundreds of millions of peoples in subjugation. The NAT governments committed to live in peace, he noted, "are in fact today engaged in wars to maintain their domination over peoples of Burma, Malaya, Indonesia, Madagascar and Viet-Nam."[67]

Other critics of the treaty, while not emphasizing colonialism as the major reason for their opposition, did cite it as one of the problems they had with the pact. Methodist leader Charles Boss told the senators that there was no guarantee that U.S. arms would not be used to crush colonial peoples. At a special meeting in April 1949 on the NAT, the National Peace Conference discussed proposals to modify the pact "to make sure that it does not become a tool for . . . colonial domination abroad."[68]

The NAT, often given credit for contributing to peace and stability in Europe, ignored the brutal colonial policies of the European states. As Washington viewed the world through the lenses of Cold War anticommunism and its NAT allies, it sacrificed opportunities to encourage development in the emerging nations, often finding itself defending colonial or undemocratic regimes solely to prevent procommunist nationalists from gaining control. This deepened an American association with colonialism and contributed to U.S. involvement in the Vietnam War and other Third World conflicts.

CONCLUSION

With the Senate ratification of the NAT, the containment policy was in place in Europe. The NAT confirmed the defeat of the foreign policy ideals of the pacifists and the liberal internationalists. The explanations for the opposition of the various groups and individuals were ignored or, for that matter, never even heard by the Truman administration and Congress. The peace advocates had presented an alternative vision of the world in 1949. The Truman administration and Congress disregarded those ideals and ideas. By the time of the debate over the NAT, the two viewpoints were incompatible. Lawrence Kaplan has indicated that what was remarkable about the critics was not that they failed to exploit the vulnerabilities of the administration's positions, but that their constituencies were remarkably small, that "[t]hey lacked an audience."[69] The opposition to the NAT was given very little time to make its arguments before the Senate Committee on Foreign Relations. Libby even complained about the order of placement of groups opposed to the pact in the hearings. He wrote Sen. Connally, questioning the fairness to the NAT's opposition by listing Henry Wallace and Communist Party head Eugene Dennis first. Libby stated that by "giving primary position among opponents of the Pact to this reputed enemy of our form of government [Dennis], are you not by implication casting aspersions on the patriotism of the witness that will follow and by innuendo attempting to smear them as participants in a Communist Front against their will?"[70] With the exception of Wallace and Warburg, the senators paid very little attention to what the critics said about the pact. Nonetheless, the vision of the world they presented, even if it was unachievable in 1949, was a significant one and should not have been so completely ignored. Their emphasis on strengthening the economic foundation of the world, using negotiation in disagreements with the Soviets, developing the UN into an effective world organization, reducing armaments, preventing militarization of U.S. society, and recognizing the importance of the colonial world did contribute over time to reducing the tensions of the Cold War. However, in 1949, the Cold War consensus rejected those approaches. Unfortunately, they were then buried for several years by the events in Korea and a rising anticommunist hysteria at home.

NOTES

1. Truman, *Memoirs*, 2:263.

2. W. Averell Harriman, U.S. Congress, Senate, Committee on Foreign Relations, *North Atlantic Treaty, Hearings before the Committee on Foreign Relations*, 81st Cong., 1st sess., 1949, I: 190, 148. Hereafter referred to as *NAT* with the appropriate volume number.

3. Third Meeting of the U.S.–U.K.–Canada Security Talks, March 24, 1948, U.S. Department of State, *Foreign Relations of the United States*, 1948, Vol. III (Washington, DC: GPO, 1974), 66. Hereafter referred to as *FRUS*, followed by year and volume.

4. Lawrence S. Kaplan, "After Forty Years: Reflections on NATO as a Research Field," in Francis H. Heller and John R. Gillingham, ed., *NATO: The Founding of the Atlantic Alliance and the Integration of Europe* (New York: St. Martin's Press, Inc., 1992), 17–19.

5. The text of the NAT can be found in Kaplan, *NATO and the United States*, 219–21.

6. Thomas M. Campbell Jr., "NATO and the United Nations in American Foreign Policy: Building a Framework for Power," in Lawrence S. Kaplan and Robert W. Clawson, eds., *NATO after Thirty Years* (Wilmington, DE: Scholarly Resources, 1981), 133, 146–47.

7. Alan K. Henrikson, "The North Atlantic Alliance as a Form of World Order," in Alan Henrikson, ed., *Negotiating World Order: The Artisanship and Architecture of Global Diplomacy* (Wilmington, DE: Scholarly Resources, 1986), 114–18.

8. Roland N. Stromberg, *Collective Security and American Foreign Policy: From the League of Nations to NATO* (New York: Frederick A. Praeger, 1963), 193.

9. Lawrence S. Kaplan, *The United States and NATO: The Formative Years* (Lexington: University of Kentucky Press, 1984), 32, 40; Lawrence Kaplan, "Collective Security and the Case of NATO," 98; Lawrence Kaplan, "After Forty Years: Reflections on NATO as a Research Field," 20.

10. E. Raymond Wilson and Barbara S. Grant, "Some Questions and Comments about the North Atlantic Treaty and the Accompanying Rearmament Program," April 25, 1949, Friends Committee on National Legislation, DG 47, Series H, Box 20, North Atlantic Pact file, SCPC.

11. Claude Pepper, July 15, 1949, *Congressional Record*, 81st Cong., 1st sess., Vol. 95, pt. 7:9602–3.

12. George Gallup, *The Gallup Poll: Public Opinion 1935–1971*, Vol. II, 1949–71 (New York: Random House, 1972), 792, 800, 815, 829–30.

13. Ted Galen Carpenter, "The Dissenters: American Isolationists and Foreign Policy, 1945–1954" (Ph.D. diss., University of Texas at Austin, 1980), 239.

14. Ibid., 248, 241–42; Doenecke, *Not to the Swift*, 157–60.

15. Ronald Radosh, *Prophets on the Right: Profiles of Conservative Critics of American Globalism* (New York: Simon and Schuster, 1975), 168–70.

16. Bryniarski, "Against the Tide," 235–37.

17. Vandenberg, ed., *The Private Papers of Senator Vandenberg*, 497.

18. Accinelli, "Pro-U.N. Internationalists and the Early Cold War," 357.

19. Schwebel, May 10, 1949, *NAT* II: 657, 653.

20. Thomas, May 11, 1949, *NAT* II: 730–31.

21. Ibid., 731–33.

22. Grenville Clark, February 8, 1949, "Draft of Proposed Statement on NAT," Box 44, UWF, Warburg Papers.

23. Alexander Standish, "Memorandum to the Executive Committee of the United World Federalists," March 22, 1949, Box 44, UWF, Warburg Papers.

24. Cass Canfield, May 12, 1949, *NAT* III: 841–42.

25. Paterson, "The Dissent of Claude Pepper," 132–33.

26. Pepper, July 15, 1949, *Congressional Record*, 81st Cong., 1st sess., Vol. 95, pt. 7:9602–3.

27. Taylor, July 20, 1949, *Congressional Record*, 81st Cong., 1st sess., Vol. 95, pt. 7:9783.

28. Taylor, July 20, 1949, *Congressional Record*, 81st Cong., 1st sess., Vol. 95, pt. 7:9783, 9785, 9787; April 8, 1949, *Congressional Record*, 81st Cong., 1st sess., Vol. 95, pt. 3:4141.

29. Emily Greene Balch, Gertrude Bussey, and Annalee Stewart, letter to the *New York Times*, April 12, 1949, WILPF, Reel 130.25, SCPC; "Proposed Policies to Be Presented to the Annual Meeting, 1949," n.d., WILPF, Reel 130.13, SCPC; "Annual Meeting Resolutions," May 5–8, 1949, WILPF, Reel 130.13, SCPC.

30. Mrs. Alexander (Annalee) Stewart, May 13, 1949, *NAT* III: 429–31.

31. Boss, May 16, 1949, *NAT* III: 988, 990, 996–97.

32. Bender, May 16, 1949, *NAT* III: 1007, 1011–12.

33. Curry, May 12, 1949, *NAT* III: 836.

34. "Draft Letter to Senators for Endorsement by Individuals," June 24, 1949, CPA, CDG-A, SCPC.

35. Wallace, May 5, 1949, *NAT* II: 418, 431; Wallace to Herman Wright, March 24, 1949, Wallace Papers, Reel 45; Ronald Radosh and Leonard P. Liggio, "Henry A. Wallace and the Open Door," 104.

36. Executive Committee of the FOR, "The Atlantic Pact Is a Suicide Pact," March 1949, copy in possession of the author; Alfred Hassler, "The North Atlantic Security Alliance, Called a Force for Peace, Threatens Really to Be a Pact with Death," *Fellowship*, May 1949 in *NAT* III: 820; Sayer to Wagner, May 16, 1949, Sayer Papers, DG 117, Series E, Box 3, North Atlantic Pact file, SCPC.

37. Elliot, May 11, 1949, *NAT* II: 754–55.

38. F. J. Libby, "NCPW Annual Report," December 1949, NCPW Papers, Reel 41.17, SCPC; Libby, May 12, 1949, *NAT* III: 896.

39. Wilson and Grant, "Some Questions and Comments about the North Atlantic Treaty and the Accompanying Rearmament Program," April 25, 1949, Friends Committee on National Legislation, DG 47, Series H, Box 20, North Atlantic Pact file, SCPC; Baltimore Yearly Meeting of Friends, "Statement on the North Atlantic Pact," *NAT* II: 781; Curry, May 12, 1949, *NAT* III: 835.

40. WRL, "Statement on the North Atlantic Defense Pact by the War Resisters League," April 4, 1949, WRL, DG 46, Box 26, Atlantic Pact file, SCPC; Richards, May 17, 1949, *NAT* III: 1081.

41. Burr, May 10, 1949, *NAT* II: 708–9; Morford, May 11, 1949, *NAT* II: 805; Howe, May 16, 1949, *NAT* III: 1042.

42. Warburg, *The Long Road Home*, 256; Warburg, May 10, 1949, *NAT* II: 674.

43. Warburg, *The Last Call for Common Sense*, 33; Warburg, May 10, 1949, *NAT* II: 673.

44. Warburg, "Memorandum on the Proposed Atlantic Alliance," February 1, 1949, Warburg Papers, Box 50, memos to Congress, JFK Library (emphasis in original).

45. Warburg, *The Last Call for Common Sense*, 217.

46. Warburg to Lippmann, February 10, 1949, Lippmann file, Box 18, Warburg Papers, JFK Library; Warburg, "Proposal for Modification of Atlantic Security Pact," February 26, 1949, Acheson file, Box 13, Warburg Papers, JFK Library (emphasis in original).

47. James Warburg, May 10, 1949, *NAT* II: 672, 683–84, 691, 693.

48. Taylor, July 20, 1949, *Congressional Record*, 81st Cong., 1st sess., Vol. 95, pt.

7:9785; April 8, 1949, *Congressional Record*, 81st Cong., 1st sess., Vol. 95, pt. 3:4142; Wherry, July 20, 1949, *Congressional Record*, 81st Cong., 1st Sess., Vol. 95, pt. 7:9100.

49. Bender, May 16, 1949, *NAT* III: 1005–6; Boss, May 16, 1949, *NAT* II: 988, 998; Cadbury, May 11, 1949, *NAT* II: 762; Stewart, May 13, 1949, *NAT* III: 929–30.

50. Arthur A. Ekirch Jr., *The Civilian and the Military* (New York: Oxford University Press, 1956), 273–75; 277.

51. Arthur A. Ekirch Jr., *The Decline of American Liberalism* (New York: Atheneum, 1967), 319, 321–22.

52. Michael S. Sherry, *In the Shadow of War: The United States since the 1930s* (New Haven, CT: Yale University Press, 1995), xi, 32, 88.

53. George Hartmen (WRL) to senators, May 6, 1949, WRL, DG 46, Box 26, Atlantic Pact file, SCPC; Richards, May 17, 1949, *NAT* III: 1082–83; Annual Meeting Resolutions, May 5–8, 1949, WILPF, DG 43, Series A, Reel 130.13, SCPC.

54. WILPF, "Policies," 1948, WILPF, Reel 130.4, SCPC.

55. Press Release, Brethren Service Commission, March 25, 1949, Church of the Brethren, CDG-A, Brethren Service Commission file, SCPC; Curry, May 12, 1949, *NAT* III: 835–36.

56. "Shall the Generals Run Our Foreign Policy?" *Christian Century*, February 23, 1949; Finucane to Charles Nixdorff, July 19, 1949, NCPW, DG 23, Reel 41.255, SCPC.

57. Taylor, April 8, 1949, *Congressional Record*, 81st Cong., 1st sess., Vol. 95, pt. 3:4141.

58. Scott L. Bills, "The United States, NATO, and the Third World: Dominoes, Imbroglios, and Agonizing Appraisals," in Lawrence S. Kaplan et al., eds., *NATO after Forty Years* (Wilmington, DE: Scholarly Resources, 1990), 154; Scott L. Bills, "The United States, NATO and the Colonial World," in Lawrence S. Kaplan and Robert W. Clawson, eds., *NATO after Thirty Years* (Wilmington, DE: Scholarly Resources, 1981), 158; Noer, *Cold War and Black Liberation*, 6. Also see Borstelmann, *Apartheid's Reluctant Uncle*, 99–100.

59. Borstelmann, *Apartheid's Reluctant Uncle*, 114.

60. See the text of the NAT in Kaplan, *NATO and the United States*, 220.

61. Robert J. McMahon, *Colonialism and Cold War: The United States and the Struggle for Indonesian Independence, 1945–49* (Ithaca, NY: Cornell University Press, 1981), 44, 56–59, 60–61. On changing U.S. policies on colonialism, see William Roger Louis and Ronald Robinson, "The United States and the Liquidation of the British Empire in Tropical Africa, 1941–1951," in Prosser Gifford and William Roger Louis, eds., *The Transfer of Power in Africa: Decolonization 1940–1960* (New Haven, CT: Yale University Press, 1982), 44–46; Robert C. Good, "The United States and the Colonial Debate," in Arnold Wolfers, ed., *Alliance Policy in the Cold War* (Baltimore, MD: Johns Hopkins University Press, 1959), 222–33.

62. Borstelmann, *Apartheid's Reluctant Uncle*, 195.

63. Noer, *Cold War and Black Liberation*, 1–2.

64. Borstelmann, *Apartheid's Reluctant Uncle*, 202.

65. Wilson and Grant, "Some Questions and Comments about the North Atlantic Treaty and the Accompanying Rearmament Program," April 25, 1949,

Friends Committee on National Legislation, DG 47, Series H, Box 20, North Atlantic Pact file, SCPC; Dobbs, May 5, 1949, *NAT* II: 483.

66. Thomas, May 13, 1949, *NAT* III: 968; Hunton, May 13, 1949, *NAT* III: 965.

67. Stewart, May 16, 1945, *NAT* III: 1049–50; Walls, May 16, 1949, *NAT* III: 1024–25; Hunton, May 13, 1949, *NAT* III: 964.

68. Boss, May 16, 1949, *NAT* III: 990; Minutes of the National Peace Conference, April 4, 1949, WRL, DG 40, Series B, Box 12, National Peace Conference file, SCPC.

69. Kaplan, *The United States and NATO*, 46.

70. Libby to Connally, May 4, 1949, NCPW, DG 23, Box 430, North Atlantic Treaty file, SCPC. Because Dennis was under indictment for conspiracy to overthrow the government, he did not testify. See Joan Lee Bryniarski, "Against the Tide," 263–64.

5

MILITARY ASSISTANCE, THE KOREAN WAR, AND MCCARTHYISM

With the ratification of the NAT, the Truman administration moved to rearm its European allies. The Mutual Defense Assistance Program (MDAP) continued and accelerated the shift in emphasis from an economic to a military containment of the Soviet Union. Implemented at about the same time as the 1950 National Security Council document 68 (NSC-68) and the Korean War, the United States rearmed its NATO allies and began a massive buildup of its own military capabilities, both nuclear and conventional. The liberal internationalists and pacifists who had opposed a military approach to the challenges posed by the Soviet Union were able to mount only a weak protest to these foreign policies. The liberal internationalists themselves divided seriously over the role of the UN in Korea. Viewing it as a UN action, some former critics of containment supported the U.S. role in that war. In addition, many elements of the peace movement faced increased criticism from groups who felt that any disagreement with U.S. policy was communist inspired. The unjustifiable anticommunist assault weakened the credibility of much of the forces opposed to containment.

THE MUTUAL DEFENSE ASSISTANCE PROGRAM

Following from article 3 of the NAT, which called on signatories to provide for continuous self-help and mutual aid to enable the parties to resist aggression, the Truman administration launched the MDAP in 1949. Washington believed that economic assistance was not sufficient to defend the Western Europeans from aggressive Soviet designs. Secretary of State Dean Acheson argued that the Europeans needed a sense of security to accomplish economic recovery. Security for the European nations, according to Acheson, depended on their firm belief in their ability to defend themselves against armed aggression. He told the Senate Foreign Relations Committee and the Committee on Armed Services that the nations of Western Europe were virtually disarmed. Much of their resources had gone into economic recovery. Meanwhile, Acheson noted, the Soviets "continued to maintain the largest armed forces in the peacetime history of any country . . . and has used . . . its obvious military superiority to intimidate . . . smaller nations." This imbalance in forces "created a widespread sense of insecurity which has impaired the confidence in the future and has impeded the recovery effort."[1]

The MDAP concerned many Western Europeans and Americans. They worried about how the program would effect European economic recovery. As the program emerged from administration and congressional planning, it was clear that the rearmament of Western Europe was closely linked to the general postwar U.S. foreign policy. With the Soviet Union seen as the greatest threat to U.S. security, Washington feared the ability of the Soviets to conquer Western Europe, either militarily or through subversion. As part of containment, the ERP and NATO were aimed at lessening the internal and external communist threat in Europe. The MDAP became what Acheson called the third pillar in U.S. postwar foreign policy, aimed at containing and deterring the Soviet Union.[2]

Congress did not react quickly to the proposed MDAP. Lengthy hearings were held, the amount of the assistance was reduced, and requirements were tacked on. Opposition to the containment policy, however, was not one of the reasons for delay. The lack of enthusiasm in Congress had to do with an apparent shift in U.S. defense strategy that came with NATO and the MDAP. The rearmament program implied that NATO was based on a doctrine of large-scale land warfare in Europe, supported by U.S. strategic air power. To many in Congress, this seemed inconsistent with the strategic doctrine that underlay the low $15 billion defense budget.[3]

Although a plurality of Americans supported the MDAP, it was by a narrow margin. When asked by the Gallup Poll in September 1949 whether they supported the Truman administration's proposal to send war materials and money to countries who want to build up their military defenses against Russia, 46 percent approved, 40 percent disapproved, and 14 percent had no opinion.[4]

The overall reluctance to support the program was reflected by the length of time it took to get through Congress. Although it was introduced to Congress in July 1949, the MDAP was not approved until October, significantly two weeks after the administration announced that the Soviet Union had developed the atomic bomb.

THE OPPOSITION TO THE MUTUAL DEFENSE ASSISTANCE PROGRAM

Just as the MDAP can be linked closely with NATO and efforts of containment in Western Europe, the opposition to the MDAP came from the same groups who had opposed containment and the NAT. In fact, in some cases when testifying against the NAT, individuals had warned that the pact was linked with the rearmament of Europe. In that sense, one can view the critique of the MDAP as simply an extension of the opposition to the NAT.

Strongly linking the two, and expressing deep concern over the danger of wrecking economic recovery, James Warburg spoke out against rearmament programs during the Senate NAT hearings. When asked if he favored providing military assistance, Warburg stated that he felt it "extremely dangerous to divert them from recovery to rearmament" unless the military aid was primarily for the purpose of internal security. His concern was that it would take a massive amount of aid to put the Europeans in a position to hold the Oder, Elbe, or Rhine rivers, and the plans under development did not do that.[5]

Warburg explained his view concisely to Acheson in a January 1949 letter to the secretary of state. He wrote that rearmament would not provide an adequate defense unless it included either the remilitarization of West Germany or the stationing of large numbers of U.S. troops in Europe before any war started. He believed, then, that "the rearmament of Western Europe would not provide it with adequate defense against *military* aggression, [and] the rearmament program would seriously interfere with economic recovery and with our own effort to aid recovery."[6] In a memo to Senators Connally, McMahon, Pepper, and Vandenberg, Warburg noted another danger. He warned that to create a force in Western Europe "capable of holding off an invasion . . . involves creating a 'force in being' that is likewise capable of offensive action." Thus, the result could be that the United States would provoke the attack it was trying to prevent. He felt that Washington should not be committed in any way to a set strategy and should retain complete freedom of action in the conduct of a war against an aggressor.[7]

Warburg continued to emphasize this point, even after the onset of the Korean War. In a November letter to Acheson in which he indicated his support of the secretary's Asian policy, Warburg again stated that he did not believe that *"our undertaking to defend Western Europe against invasion in the event of war could be fulfilled."* He asserted that *"the only way to defend Western Europe against military aggression is to prevent that ag-*

gression from being undertaken." That could only be done through an alliance not committed to any preannounced strategy.[8]

Overall, Warburg saw U.S. policy as a negative policy of stopping
communism. He felt that the United States needed a positive purpose.
Two such positive purposes he advocated in a July 1950 University of
Chicago Round Table broadcast over NBC Radio. On the program, he
called for an end to the arms race and the initiation of a real war on
hunger and poverty. He stated that "unless we have disarmament, we
cannot have peace."[9]

Henry Wallace also publicly opposed the MDAP. In a July 1949 letter
to all the members of the Senate, Wallace expressed his concern that the
rearmament program would impose on the tottering Western European
economies "the enormous burden of additional arms which the Pact
[NAT] requires." He felt it wrong "to divert the energies and capital and
resources of these nations to further military preparedness when all resources are needed to prevent economic disaster."[10]

Wallace, officially representing the Progressive Party, testified before
the Senate Armed Services and Foreign Relations Committees in opposition to the rearmament program. He told the committees, in joint hearings, that he came because he believed "the security of the United States
and the world is threatened by the military assistance program." He felt
that shipping large quantities of arms to Europe would "undermine the
economy and military security of both the United States and Europe."
In his testimony, Wallace discussed some of the same concerns raised
during the NAT hearings by those opposed to the pact. In addition to
the economic issues, he also charged that the "entire foreign policy" was
not aimed at maintaining peace "but to prepare for war. It is not a defensive program, but an aggressive and provocative program." He stated
that Russia was different from Hitler's Germany and that there was no
indication that Russia wanted a war. The former vice president called
the current foreign policy "military insanity" and "economic suicide."
Repeating some of the themes expressed by Warburg, Wallace noted that
the administration took pride in preventing a Communist Party victory
in Italy in the 1948 elections by providing food and money. He wondered
whether arms would ensure that Italy will not be subverted and if arms
could alleviate the poverty and unemployment that could result in communist subversion. Finally, he also raised the colonial issue. He believed
that the arms program would bring to those areas the threat that their
aspirations for freedom would be repressed with arms supplied by the
United States.[11]

Speaking for the Young Progressives of America, Executive Director
Seymour Linfield brought up another theme of the opposition to the
NAT, arguing that the MDAP would mean a militarization of American
foreign policy. He feared it would "commit this country to chief reliance

on military force in its international relations and to mobilize armed strength as a means of diplomacy between nations."[12]

In addition to those well-known opponents of containment, pacifists and some church groups also spoke out against the MDAP. Frederick Libby of the NCPW believed the fight against the proposed program to rearm Europe began with the NAT and continued with the MDAP. The basis of his rejection of the program was that it assumed that peace could be based on the preponderance of military power.[13] In a June 1950 letter to the House Committee on Foreign Affairs, Libby stressed that communism was rooted in low standards of living and should thus be treated as a domestic problem. The militarization of nations, he argued, lowered living standards without increasing productivity.[14]

The Conference on Peaceful Alternatives to the Atlantic Pact, in an open letter to the Senate and House on the MDAP, argued that such a program would "lead to an armaments race which soon will take us into war." They felt it was "unthinkable that when the needs of the world are for economic survival, for food, clothing, shelter, that this money should be spent on arms."[15] Annalee Stewart of the WILPF told the Senate committees that the program was a detriment to peace. She stated that giving lip service to disarmament while leading an arms race was inconsistent and the only basic alternative to war was disarmament.[16]

Robert Yarnall of the AFSC testified that the program threatened to weaken the real safeguard against communism, which he called the general welfare. He also stated that a second reason for the AFSC opposition was that the MDAP sought to prevent war by the deterrent effect of the threat of force. He told the senators that the deterrent effect, "while generally less than is commonly assumed, is in the present case practically nonexistent." Preparation for war, he said, only increased its danger.[17] When testifying on the NAT, Bender of the Methodist Women's Division of Christian Service also expressed opposition to military assistance, noting several dangers. She said that military aid would hinder economic recovery, provoke fear, stimulate an arms race, and substantially increase the U.S. budget, threatening the domestic economy.[18]

A final group of opponents included a wide variety of leftist groups and spokespersons who reiterated many of the same themes. Among these was W.E.B. Du Bois, who submitted a written statement to the Senate committees for the CAA. He stated that the arming of Europe, at the expense of depressed classes in the United States, "is not so much to protect western Europe from the east as to enable it to put down colonial unrest among 250,000,000 colonial people and another half million of semicolonials."[19] Other opponents included representatives from the Peoples' Mandate Committee, the U.S. Committee for the Participation in the American Continental Congress for Peace, the National Economic Council, and the Communist Party.[20]

By the time that NATO and the MDAP were placed before the American public, the rearmament of Europe was not preventable by the minority who opposed it. The United States was firmly committed to the defense of Western Europe from potential Soviet aggression. For the Truman administration in 1949, that threat seemed to be growing. In that year, Mao Zedung and the communists had seized power in China, and the Soviet Union exploded an atomic device. The NSC began to reevaluate U.S. policy in terms of what the administration viewed as a greater threat. The result was NSC-68, which was initialed by Truman in April 1950. The document advocated a new and different containment strategy than that developed by George Kennan in 1946–47. Where Kennan's strategy had focused on economic instruments of containment, the policy that came from NSC-68 emphasized a military containment.[21]

NSC-68 accepted the viewpoint that the Soviets sought world domination and were seeking to create overwhelming military force. Comparing the Soviet and Western Bloc economies, the NSC warned that the Soviets had created a war economy while the West was attempting to raise standards of living. This meant that the readiness of the West to support a war was declining relative to that of the Russians. In discussing an American response, the NSC considered four possible courses of action, three of which were forcefully rejected. They rejected a continuation of current policies, a policy of isolation, and a preemptive war. The fourth possibility, "[a] more rapid build-up of political, economic, and military strength in the free world than is now contemplated," was chosen. To accomplish this, the NSC recommended eleven actions, including a huge increase in U.S. military expenditures and a substantial increase in the military assistance programs.[22]

Although not all administration officials accepted the conclusions of the document, by 1950 most U.S. policy makers accepted the view that the Soviet Union was a revolutionary state bent on world conquest. With this viewpoint, the United States set out to develop "a posture of defense sufficient to enable the US to deter a direct Soviet attack."[23] Despite the turn toward a more militarized foreign policy and greater expenditures on weapons, disarmament advocates continued their efforts to turn American policy, and indeed the world, around.

CONTINUED DISARMAMENT EFFORTS

In the late 1940s and early 1950s, as proponents of peace saw their postwar hopes shattered by the Cold War and what they viewed as a dangerous militarization of American foreign policy, ideas on disarmament and the fear of the growth of militarism kept groups and individuals active in an attempt to bring changes to American policy. Political defeats, the Korean War, and the Red Scare shrank the ranks of the noncommunist peace movement, limiting it to a diminishing number of pacifist groups.

The WILPF continued its efforts to encourage disarmament. Having watched with concern "the extension of militarism and rearmament throughout the world," the WILPF called for world disarmament and reconstruction. The international WILPF proposed breaking the deadlock in the UN on disarmament by recommending that all nations agree to stop simultaneously and at once the production of atomic bombs. This was to be enforced through inspections under the UN, in possession of a police force capable of arresting individual violators.[24]

In December 1949, the NCPW issued its "Program for Peace—1950." The NCPW stated that true national security required understanding, justice, goodwill, and cooperation on the part of all peoples. Security, the statement read, "cannot be achieved by national or international armed force." In regard to U.S. foreign policy, the NCPW stated that the United States "must neither appease nor threaten the Soviet Union. War itself, more than the Soviet Union, is today our most dangerous foe." In addition, they called for cooperation in a program of universal disarmament, a program of economic outreach, and a policy toward the UN that was more constructive and aimed at peaceful cooperation.[25]

The peace churches continued to state their concerns about the growth of militarism. The Brethren Service Commission of the Church of the Brethren expressed alarm over increased control of U.S. foreign policy by the army and the navy through the NSC, the increased control of the public through military propaganda, and the increased control over America's scientists through military domination of university research projects. The Mennonites, at a 1950 conference on nonresistance, stated that they could not compromise with war: "In case of renewed compulsion by the state in any form of conscription of service or labor, money or goods, including industrial plants, we must find ways to serve our countries and the needs of men elsewhere."[26]

The PWWC, though not pacifist and not opposed to all elements of the Truman containment policy, continued to push for disarmament and new programs against hunger and poverty.[27] Although they had given support to much of the containment policy, the UWF also continued efforts to strengthen the UN to achieve disarmament. Alan Cranston, the UWF president, wrote that the purposes of the organization were to seek peace through disarmament, enforced by a strengthened UN.[28] Despite the ratification of the NAT, the Committee for Peaceful Alternatives (CPA) continued its efforts to change U.S. policy. The CPA based itself on three principles: There can be no victor in an atomic war; peaceful coexistence of nations with different social and economic systems is possible and imperative; and no difference between nations can be so great that mutual annihilation is the only answer. In addition to various other proposals in 1951, including calling for an end to the Korean War, the CPA advocated a mutual reduction of weapons through a general disarmament under the UN.[29]

Through the final years of the Truman administration, these groups, and others, held several conferences in an effort to find solutions to the dangerous deadlock in the Cold War and the rapid increase in the arms race. From September 28 through 30, 1949, the Consultative Peace Council brought peace movement activists together in Pendle Hill, Pennsylvania, to explore the possibilities of launching a disarmament campaign. Much of the discussion centered on the U.S.–Soviet conflict and the growing militarization of U.S. policy. John Swomley noted that in the United States the idea that air power is peace power had become a creed that the average citizen was caught up in through parades, air shows, newsreels, and various other items promoting national strength. Others noted that the atmosphere of distrust, which they felt started with the Greek-Turkish aid program, had to be eliminated.

The conference divided over the type of disarmament to advocate. One participant challenged the whole concept of treaties and political disarmament agreements, stating that if disarmament had to wait until security was guaranteed, "we probably won't get it." He wondered if military men would ever go along with disarmament and if instead they should be circumvented or ignored and go instead to the people advocating unilateral disarmament. Another disagreed, "believing that talk of unilateral disarmament is futile." Other participants favored various different tactics, including a people's conference to work out a treaty and develop a formula for universal disarmament supported by an international organization to solve economic and political problems. This latter proposal would begin with the United States unilaterally taking some steps in the direction of divesting itself of certain types of weapons.

John Swomley attempted to reconcile the differences between universal and unilateral disarmament advocates. He noted that since the organizations represented were part of an international movement, they could ask members in other countries to oppose their own nation's militarism, to work for disarmament and to call upon their fellow countrymen to work for it, and to work for universal action in the UN. To Swomley, the campaign "must necessarily . . . be for universal disarmament." The conference agreed, recommending that the objective was a reduction of arms and ultimately universal and total disarmament.[30]

A second conference was held by religious leaders from May 8 through 11, 1950, in Detroit. This conference, organized by pacifists, sought to form a Church Peace Mission to promote a dialogue between pacifists and nonpacifists. The FOR wanted to provide an occasion for a united Protestant approach to the question of war, calling on the church to take a clearer position against war.[31] When they gathered in May 1950, there

were four hundred delegates and an additional four hundred participants.

The conference adopted several statements. One was the "Theological
Roots of Christian Pacifism," which stated that pacifism was a phase of
total Christian life. The statement noted that the Gospel required them
to relate love to every aspect of life and that they "can not reconcile
violence, and especially war, with the practice of love." Therefore, they
stated that "we must refuse voluntary participation in war."[32]

A second statement dealt with the social and political implications of
their religious beliefs. It called upon Christian churches to move out in
an act of faith by which they no longer supported war or its preparation
as an instrument of national policy, declaring that "the moral leadership
of the United States should be directed persistently toward enlarging
confidence, faith, and goodwill within the United Nations." It also called
for the total disarmament of national military establishments, which
would require "international inspection and controls, and the enforcement of law upon individuals by international civilian police." The participants asserted that the UN should move toward becoming a world
government.

The statement was strongly anticontainment. In looking at Soviet-
American relations, it stated that the conference felt "the present United
States policy of 'containment' of Soviet expansion with its predominant
reliance upon military might is failing, and is contrary to Christian principles." The statement argued that the result of the policy is a solidifi-
cation of the support of the Russian people for their government, a
tightening of the "iron curtain," and a stimulation of the atomic arms
race. Instead, the conferees proposed a policy of active goodwill aimed
at removing restrictive and retaliatory measures that caused fear and
suspicion.[33]

A third conference in 1950 was held in Chicago May 29–30 and was
sponsored by the CPA. The CPA was an organization that worked with
parties of the political left. Because of those leftist leanings, Muste expressed some concern about the organization and its executive secretary,
Willard Uphaus. The FOR leader wrote that Uphaus was "a swell guy
personally" and he had no reason to think that Uphaus was a communist, but he was aware that Uphaus would work with Communist Party
people and in Muste's opinion, "has no judgment whatever when it
comes to that." Muste was also concerned about the participation of the
Progressive Party in the CPA. He noted that the party continued to advocate that a genuine peace party had to be built on the basis of inclusion
of communists, as well as others. Muste did not deny the party the right
to build such an organization, but feared that opposition to it would
contribute to growing anti-Russian hysteria. However, he was convinced
that part of the strength of the pacifist movement "derives from the fact

that it has never engaged in organizational collaboration with totalitarians of any kind."[34]

The conference began on May 29 at the St. James Methodist Church in Chicago with about seven hundred in attendance representing thirty-one states. Despite Muste's concern, about half of those in attendance represented church groups, and another quarter were from the Progressive Party, some of whom were also members of the Communist Party.[35]

Kermit Eby of the University of Chicago gave the keynote speech. He called for a determination of the peoples of the world to compel their governments to seek peaceful alternatives to war, and because the United States had greater freedom than the Soviet Union, it was the greater responsibility of Americans to put pressure on their government. In implementing this "will to peace," the United States, Eby stated, must not withdraw from the world, returning to isolationism. Implementation did not mean reliance on "utopian" solutions like world government. Instead, he said, "I believe that peace is the continuing by-product of the decisions painstakingly made from day-to-day in the political arenas of our respective governments." He believed that a free and open discussion of foreign policy ideas was necessary. Pointing out an increasing problem for critics of foreign policy, Eby stated that "At this moment, the citizen finds himself upon the horns of a dilemma. He is either for the 'cold war,' and hence a good patriotic American, or he is against it, and hence a Communist, fellow-traveler, or God knows what kind of a demon."[36]

Although discussions at the conference revealed no clear viewpoint, there was a general opposition to the course of the Cold War. However, their opposition was for a variety of reasons. Throughout the conference, participants emphasized that they were not seeking to establish another peace organization, though a decision was made to continue the CPA with a board of officers. They also agreed that no communist should be appointed to that continuing board. Although there was opposition to cooperation with the communists, the conference was definitely a united front effort and intended to remain that way. All efforts to include a plank in their documents that favored democracy and rejected totalitarianism were defeated. The leaders of the conference attempted to keep the platform broad and inclusive. Nonetheless, a committee of pacifists did get approval of a statement that noted that as Americans they had a special responsibility to change U.S. government policies that continued the Cold War, but also asserted "that the Russian people have the same responsibility in regard to their own government." They also included the following statement: "We are . . . united in devotion to democratic principles and methods."[37]

The conference adopted documents which reflected the desires of this diverse group of Cold War critics. First, they emphasized the importance of local peace groups. In their "Appeal to the American People for Peaceful Alternatives to the Cold War," they stated that the objective was "the formation and full participation of local groups so that a veritable network of such independent groups shall arise throughout the nation." Specifically, they proposed thirteen ways to push for alternatives, including efforts at organizing locally, lobbying congress, working in the UN, supporting peaceful uses of atomic energy, using economic resources for peace, protesting violations of civil rights, combating "warmindedness," and circulating the speeches and documents from the conference.[38]

The CPA conference demonstrated the growing issue faced by the peace movement—its association with the communists, real or perceived, in the context of the growing Red Scare. The CPA conference was able to deal with it and still conduct their business, but as the years progressed, and with the onset of the Korean War, it became more difficult. Nonetheless, they battled on, and, in addition to the Korean War, they continued to challenge the growing military involvement of the United States in Europe.

THE GREAT DEBATE: GROUND TROOPS TO EUROPE

When the NAT was approved by the Senate, the administration presented an argument to Congress and the American people that it was a mutual assistance pact designed to deter or repulse a Russian attack on Western Europe. The administration never suggested that it intended to station large numbers of U.S. troops in Western Europe, or that a U.S. officer would command a NATO defense force. In fact, the idea of deploying U.S. troops to Europe under article 3 had been ruled out by Secretary Acheson in 1949. However, on September 9, 1950, President Truman announced that U.S. troops would be sent to Europe, changing the nature of the American role from that of occupation forces designed to contain Germany to combat forces to contain the Soviet Union. The United States would now directly participate in the maintenance of the balance of power in Europe.[39]

The so-called "Great Debate" resulted from this Truman decision. The debate contained various elements, including the struggle between the two political parties in the Senate, the struggle for control of foreign policy between the legislative and executive branches of the government, and the issue of whether the troops should be sent. One scholar has argued that the debate cannot be simplified into one between isolationism and internationalism. Instead, it was a debate over the future direction of U.S. policy. Was containment to be continued? How was it to be done?[40] Ultimately, Truman was forced to compromise with Congress and only four divisions were sent. The Senate Foreign Relations and

Armed Services Committees held joint hearings in February 1951 on the Wherry Resolution. Named after Sen. Kenneth Wherry of Nebraska, the resolution stated that no ground forces should be assigned to NATO duty in Europe pending formation of a policy by Congress.[41]

The opposition to the commitment of the extra troops to Europe consisted of three categories. There were the old line isolationists, the advocates of U.S. air power, and what one scholar called the "feeble remnants" of one-worlders, who argued it would further divide the world.[42] Most dissenters in the Senate did not question the central assumptions of the administration that the Soviets were dangerous and should not be permitted to expand. They also believed that the United States should contribute to stopping Soviet expansionism. Most of the critics were fiscal conservatives who were distrustful of the presidency. The debate of 1951 centered on the congressional desire to protect that institution from an unbridled executive.[43]

Although the peace movement had indeed been enfeebled, some leftist internationalists and pacifists did speak out in opposition to the commitment of the ground troops. They, too, expressed concern about the growth of presidential power. Referring to Truman's entrance into the Korean War without congressional authority and deciding to send ground troops to Europe without consultation with Congress, C. B. Baldwin, the secretary of the Progressive Party, told the Senate Foreign Relations and Armed Services Committees that there was a grave danger that there may be a further abdication of the power of Congress to the president. He stated that there had been no genuine debate on foreign policy because the American people had been offered no real alternative. Arguing that containment was a failure, Baldwin called for a policy based on coexistence with the Soviet Union.[44]

A new organization, formed after the start of the Korean War, American Women for Peace (AWP), also spoke out against the troop deployment. AWP emerged from the Congress of American Women (CAW), which was formed in February 1946 by U.S. representatives to the first World Congress of Women held in Paris in November 1945. The World Congress attracted representatives from forty-one different nations, including the Soviet Union, and founded the Women's International Democratic Federation. The Federation had a strong feminist platform and "embraced the overall concept of world peace and universal disarmament" as an ultimate goal of the organization. The CAW was the U.S. branch of the federation and included professionals, labor leaders, African American women, and the chair of the Women's Commission of the Communist Party. By 1949, the CAW had over two hundred and fifty thousand members, but then it felt the fury of the Red Scare. It was placed on the U.S. attorney general's list of subversive organizations, and rather than register as "foreign agents" with the Department of Justice, the CAW disbanded in January 1950. Several of the leaders of the CAW went on to participate in the AWP which was founded in August 1950.[45]

The acting chair of AWP, Clementina J. Paolone, testified before Congress against sending troops to Europe, telling the committees that sending troops to Europe was "both terrifying and dangerous to the health and welfare of this country." Repeating a familiar theme of the postwar peace movement, Paolone stated that efforts should be made to improve the standard of living all over the world through the UN. That, she said, was "better than to send bullets."[46]

Frederick Libby of the NCPW expressed concerns about the military's control of policy. He told the committees that it was time Congress resume control of foreign policy in cooperation with the president and "relegate the Pentagon to its true position, which is not that of policymaking, but the subordinate position of implementing the policy on which the President and Congress have agreed."[47]

Robert Havighurst, the chair of the executive board of the National CPA, submitted a statement to the committees. He stated that the CPA believed that the proposal to garrison Europe would not prevent war or help European morale. An improvement of morale, Havighurst stated, "cannot be accomplished while the resources of the world are being depleted by armaments race and East-West tension is being increased through actions such as the proposal to send additional American troops to Europe." The New York division of the CPA also submitted a statement expressing concern that U.S. foreign policy was leading the nation step-by-step into a "major catastrophe."[48]

Although the Senate mustered more votes against sending troops to Europe than any containment policy since aid to Greece and Turkey, the majority supported the consensus policy established by the Truman administration.[49] The peace movement was at a near standstill, and liberal internationalists had lost their battle for a more cooperative policy toward the Russians. These weaknesses were made clear with the minimal opposition to the war in Korea. That war, fought under UN authority, further divided the internationalists because some critics, including Henry Wallace, viewing the role of the UN in the war as the significant factor, abandoned opposition to the Truman policies and supported the war.

THE KOREAN WAR

On June 24, 1950, North Korean troops attacked across the thirty-eighth parallel that had separated communist North Korea from the U.S.–backed South Korea. On June 25, President Truman committed the United States to stopping that invasion and the nation to a war that was to last three years and take the lives of thirty-three thousand Americans and much larger numbers of South and North Koreans and Chinese. The Cold War had become hot. The history of the events leading up to the war, and of the war itself, is filled with continuing historical controversy.[50] However, from the administration's point of view this was a Soviet-initiated war which challenged the policy of containment and could have significant implications for a divided Europe.

Rather than asking for a congressional declaration of war, Truman took the issue to the UN. On June 25, the UN Security Council, with the Soviets boycotting the meetings in protest of the exclusion of the People's Republic of China from the UN, condemned the North Korean invasion and called for a cease fire and withdrawal of North Korea's armies to the thirty-eighth parallel. Two days later, the UN Security Council called on UN members to help South Korea. Truman appointed as commander of U.S. forces Gen. Douglas MacArthur, who then took control of the UN effort. U.S. troops were ordered into combat on June 30.[51]

Despite the growing importance of military programs, such as the MDAP, to the containment policy, the Korean invasion caused U.S. policy makers to complete the shift away from economic means to military means of containment.[52] One might think that this would have caused the peace movement to rally against the war and military containment. Instead, the war, in which the UN played an important role, weakened those forces and caused most liberals to rally behind Truman's policies.[53] Lawrence Wittner argues that the war "dealt the final hammerblow to the fragile postwar peace movement." The only ones left to oppose Korea were the pacifists, communists, and the die-hard isolationists. Robert Kleidman also viewed the war as a "devastating blow to a weakened peace movement, widening its internal divisions and escalating the repression of dissenters." He wrote that for the next few years the peace movement was reduced "to a small core of activists, outside the mainstream of politics and culture." Nonetheless, this group of pacifists and left-leaning internationalists continued to propose alternatives to the military policies of the Cold War and the buildup of nuclear weapons.[54] From this group, in the later 1950s, emerged a larger antinuclear movement and eventually a movement to oppose American actions in Vietnam. But with Korea, and with the concurrent Red Scare, the peace movement did reach its lowest postwar point.

KOREA AS A TURNING POINT FOR SOME OPPONENTS

For many peace activists, the war in Korea was a decisive turning point. In the United States, there was very little opposition to the war, and some of the best-known critics of the containment policy broke with their former associates and supported the UN actions. Some did so because they viewed the war in Korea as a UN police action.[55]

One of the biggest surprises was the change in the viewpoint of Henry Wallace. On July 15, 1950, Wallace issued a statement supporting the Truman policy in Korea, and on August 8, he resigned from the Progressive Party. At a July 6 executive committee meeting of the Progressive Party, Wallace indicated that he would not countenance criticism of the United States when it was at war. He blamed the Soviets for the start of the war and indicated his support for the UN and the United States. This, he said, was not a renunciation of his previous point of view, but reflected his support for the UN, whose sanction he felt was necessary.[56]

Wallace received a lot of criticism for his decision to support the war. In a series of letters, Muste wrote Wallace about the apparent switch. In August, Muste questioned the soundness of his course, saying that "now that the United States is involved in war you support it and the United Nations." Muste noted that if previous actions "taken by the Truman administration were without justification and did not deserve support," it seemed "that the actions which grow out of them are also unjustified and undeserving of support." In November, Muste expressed admiration for Wallace's courage in switching positions, but "as a pacifist, I regret that you should now find yourself . . . supporting the administration in the war in Korea." In December, Muste explained his pacifism to Wallace. He stated that "the force that is employed in modern war is itself so indiscriminate, destructive, and demonic, that it seems to me impossible any longer to suppose that it even serves to restrain evil and violence. It seems to me rather to enlarge them."[57]

Wallace received much criticism from within the Progressive Party. One party member from Los Angles, Raymond Cox, wrote Wallace, criticizing the former party presidential candidate for aligning himself with "militarists and reactionaries." Cox questioned Wallace's belief that it was his duty to support the war, right or wrong, writing that "it is your patriotic duty to immediately come to the aid of your country by speaking out for peace." Carl vonder Lanchen, a Progressive Party National Committee member from Oklahoma, questioned Wallace, writing that "Now you are either saying the American people ought to support any war its governmental administration gets into or, perforce, our government is always right."[58]

Wallace actively defended himself. Although he continued to state that he believed that he knew of no party members who were communists, they nonetheless were following a course that would wreck the party. He wrote, "Those on the left in the US see American strong arm methods increasing in action but I can assure you that such actions are as nothing when compared with what has been going on in Czechoslovakia in recent months." Nonetheless, party members continued to view his action as strengthening the "forces of reaction."[59]

Wallace had favored cordial relations with the new People's Republic of China and urged that they be seated in the UN. He wrote Mao Zedong in September 1950 that he consider fundamentals of a peaceful understanding with the United States as a preliminary to settling the Korean and Formosa problems. He felt that the Korean War would delay admittance and that their eventual participation in the war meant that they had come to be loyal to Moscow.[60]

In 1951 and 1952, Wallace continued to attempt to clarify his positions. He stated that his critics were mistaken in believing that he supported Truman's policy. He wrote to Harry Weinberg that since September 10, 1946, his foreign policy "has been quite different from Truman's." Although he still supported the UN in Korea, that did not mean he backed all its policies. He continued to propose a complete settlement between the United States and the Soviet Union to disarm step-by-step. In a May 1951 letter, Wallace told Susanne LaFollette that late in 1949 he became convinced that the Soviets "definitely wanted the cold war to continue" and did not want to live in a state of nonaggressive peace with the West. However, he wrote former Roosevelt aide Rex Tugwell that "we are combatting communism in the wrong war. The methods we are using are quite likely to result either in making communism stronger or in replacing communism with . . . anarchy." One other individual who supported Wallace and also switched his position was Glen Taylor. Taylor supported the attempt to halt the North Korean attack because it was a UN action.[61]

Another Wallace supporter was Norman Thomas. Thomas wrote Wallace that he believed that he "showed a rather rare type of courage." For Thomas, the North Korean attack on the South left no alternative but to support armed intervention. He feared that any other course would convince the Russians that the West would yield indefinitely to communist aggression. The Socialist Party leader felt that pacifism in 1950 would result in surrender to totalitarianism. According to his biographer, the war in Korea even convinced Thomas that disarmament was impossible for the time being. The war also temporarily ended Thomas's opposition to conscription. In 1951, he testified before the Senate Armed Services Committee supporting the retention of the draft. During the war, Thomas sounded like an individual who had accepted the consensus foreign policy of the Truman administration. However, after the Korean War he returned to an antimilitarist program.[62]

Thomas, along with intellectuals and activists such as Sidney Hook, Reinhold Neibuhr, and A. Philip Randolph, signed a declaration aimed at socialists around the world. They clarified the position of democratic socialists that the intervention in Korea was "in support of the UN" and the "beginning of world law against military aggression" and was not a drive toward imperialist profit or power. The declaration stated that

American capitalism did not lead to imperialism. American democracy "is today grimly resolved to protect peace by military strength."[63]

Another Truman critic who supported UN efforts in Korea was James Warburg, who proposed policies that he believed would lead to a settlement with the Chinese. His proposals called for a withdrawal of all foreign powers from Korea combined with a cessation of hostilities. If the Chinese did not agree, then the United States would have to declare war. However, like Wallace, Warburg sought a broader settlement with the People's Republic. He hoped that once hostilities ended "the United States would hope to see a renewal of the traditional friendship which has existed between the peoples of China and the United States." What that would mean would be that the United States would no longer recognize the legitimacy of the former Nationalist Government of China. However, in 1951 when the administration announced that it would never recognize the communist regime, it seemed to Warburg that "our declared objective becomes the overthrow of that regime," which he found unacceptable.[64]

Between the defeat of Wallace in 1948 and the Korean War, many liberal internationalists and leftists moved toward support of the consensus containment policy. Barton Bernstein has noted that many surrendered to the Cold War consensus and a safer political position. As they fell into line "[o]nly slowly were they allowed to forget their political 'errors' and to cast off the label of 'pariah' they had worn."[65] Pacifist David Dellinger had a different view of those changes. He wrote that pacifists themselves had naively "failed to anticipate the extent to which the leaders of the established antiwar organizations would be seduced by the support of the U.N. for a 'police action.' " According to Dellinger, the fact that the war was fought under the UN flag created a confusion in liberal circles and made pacifist leaders such as Muste hesitant about getting too far out in front in opposition to the war.[66]

THE OPPOSITION TO THE KOREAN WAR

Opponents of the Korean War can be divided into several different categories, each opposing the war for different reasons. One scholar divided them into three groups: moralists/pacifists, ideologues/leftists, and pragmatists. The first category included groups like the FOR and WRL, the second included the Communist and Socialist Parties, and the third included groups and individuals who initially supported the war, but came to feel that its liabilities outweighed the assets in pursuit of a military victory.[67]

Although the focus of this work has been on the first two groups, it is important to note the reasons for the pragmatic opposition. These critics, many of them in Congress, gave opposition to the war a legitimacy. Congressional opposition came from three sources: the belief that the executive decision to enter the war was a usurpation of congressional power; the belief that a limited war would not achieve the desired ends; and conviction that it was politically opportune to disavow the war. Although many in Congress came to hold those views, the only one who opposed the war from the beginning was the leftist congressman Vito Marcantonio from New York.[68]

Aside from Marcantonio, the first critics of the war were pacifists and leftists. They hoped that they could create a mass movement that could force the United States out of the war. However, their efforts were hampered by a number of factors. There was no effective leadership or program or organization. There was ideological division among the groups that prevented mutual cooperation. There were also external factors, such as harassment by local, state, and federal officials. Nonetheless, the efforts did serve notice to the nation that there was an opposition to the Korean War.[69]

The most outspoken pacifist critic of the war was A. J. Muste. He wrote numerous articles and delivered a multitude of speeches in opposition to the war. In July 1950, just after the war's beginning, Muste issued a general statement of policy titled "Pacifists and the Korean Crisis." In this work, he indicated that the program for this generation is no more war, and the program for the Korean crisis was stop the war. Noting that the U.S. intervention in Korea had resulted from the Truman Doctrine of containment, which he argued aimed at establishing an American empire, he wrote, "It represents the policy of white or western aggression in the Orient." Muste stated that pacifists opposed Russian military measures "as unequivocally as we condemn American military measures." He indicated his opposition to communism was not "by means such as war which actually promotes its growth."[70]

Muste also wrote "Korea: Spark to Set a World Afire?" In this essay, he argued that if the American people have accepted the Korean extension of the Truman Doctrine, then they have committed themselves to World War III. Although he was not sure it would be soon, the situation was "ominous." Muste attacked what had become a consensus liberal position in the Cold War. He said the problem, from the liberal point of view, was that if the West failed to resist, then communism overruns the earth. If the West continues to resist via warfare, then the result will be world war, chaos, and the triumph of totalitarianism. The liberal solution then was that the United States would keep up its military security and not let the Russians get away with any aggression. While doing that, liberals favored stopping support for undemocratic regimes in Asia, and supported racial equality at home. Muste wrote, "Riding these two horses going in opposite directions does not work . . . nations always put their money and moral steam first into H-bombs, and never have enough of either left to do anything adequate about economic rehabilitation and social change. Moreover, military 'necessity' leads to alliances with the very elements that oppose all idealistic or progressive measures." In this essay, Muste took on the issue of the UN, and the fact that many justified the war because of the UN and the concept of a "police action." He rejected the entire concept of Korea being a police action, pointing out that it was a war, fought by soldiers on both sides.[71]

With the dismissal of Gen. Douglas MacArthur as the commander of U.S. forces in the Far East in 1951, Muste saw at least a ray of hope. He wrote that it "demonstrates that military control over American foreign policy is not yet complete and cannot yet be open and avowed." However, he warned that this was not to be seen as a reversal or slackening in the trend toward increasing military control. The FOR leader noted that MacArthur "had the support of important elements in Congress and of powerful interests, as well as millions of individuals, in the country; and that the effect is in no sense that MacArthur is considered disgraced."[72]

In addition to Muste, other pacifists spoke out against the war. Muste's own FOR issued a statement that rejected the concept of "police action," calling it a war, which also placed it in the context of a dangerous expansion of the Truman Doctrine.[73] In July 1950, the executive committee of the WRL called for an immediate mediation of the war, possibly by India under the leadership of Prime Minister Jawaharlal Nehru.[74]

The WILPF also opposed the war, despite their support for the UN. In 1948, the WILPF had been granted a consultative status as a nongovernmental organization to the Economic and Social Council of the UN. In this role, they had recommended that the UN institute an agency for child welfare, which became the United Nations International Children's Emergency Fund in 1950.

The WILPF had a problem with the way the United States was using the UN during the Korean crisis. They issued a statement that the decision of June 27, 1950, to use military force before adequate discussion of the June 25 Security Council resolution was premature and determined by U.S. pressure. With the cease-fire order only sent 48 hours before, they believed "that not enough time had been given to put into operation other methods short of force provided for in Article 33." The organization noted that whatever the intention of the UN in approving military action of the United States in Korea, "it falls short of dealing with the basic problem which is not limited to the regional difficulty but includes the broader problem of the two world power struggle." Therefore, the WILPF recommended the seating of the People's Republic of China in the UN and a meeting of the Security Council with the Soviets and Chinese communists present, where North Korea and South

Korea would present their arguments. They concluded their statement, reaffirming their traditional position opposing the use of military force and stating their regret that "military intervention of outside forces has turned the United Nations into an instrument of war rather than of peace." They believed it "disastrous that military action was taken before every effort had been made to solve the problem by mediation."[75]

The WILPF continued throughout the war to encourage U.S. leaders to end the war peacefully. The firing of MacArthur led the WILPF to state that the action had created a favorable climate for negotiations, and had prevented a World War III. The president of the U.S. Section, Elsie Picon, wrote Secretary Acheson in 1951 that the UN had accomplished its mission of expelling the aggressors from South Korea, and, therefore, it was time for negotiations. To break the stalemate of the negotiations once they had been started, the WILPF encouraged the establishment of an immediate cease-fire, and then, because the UN was responsible for the entrance of UN forces into the conflict, let all other issues of the armistice be left to the UN Security Council.[76]

The NCPW also opposed the Korean intervention. In a "Statement on the Korean Crisis" of July 1950, the NCPW noted that the actions in Korea were based on the Truman Doctrine, which called for containment of Russia and communism by force. The statement indicated that at this point, all over the world, Russia and the United States are "locked in a conflict of power, in countering military might with military might." It argued that the fact that Washington's actions in Korea received UN approval did not alter that basic conflict. The UN action of calling upon members to give military assistance meant that the UN itself had been drawn into the battle. Having been told repeatedly that containment, that is, meeting force with force, would lead to peace, the NCPW noted that it had not proved to be so. Their statement continued, "We cannot now approve, support, or condone that policy as it plainly leads to a further intensification of the armaments race, and extension of military lines around the entire world, and the threat that an incident on this far-flung battle line may over night plunge the world into an atomic war."[77]

In the July 1950 NCPW publication *Peace Action*, Frederick Libby wrote that there were several considerations about the Korean crisis. He noted that the United States was saved from killing the UN because of the Russian boycott and that the United States could not rely on such good fortune again. He also noted, perhaps with greater future implications, that, at the time, it was only Americans shooting Koreans. "If this is to be repeated in other parts of the world—perhaps, Iran, or French Indo-China . . . it will be hard for us to escape being 'stuck' with the charge of 'Imperialism.' " In addition to calling for UN initiated truce negotiations, he suggested several measures to strengthen the UN, including universal membership, negotiations through the UN with Russia for disarmament, and transferring to the UN the American "self-assumed but illegal policing of the world."[78]

In addition to the pacifists, there were remnants of the progressive left who continued to oppose containment and, particularly, the Korean War. One of the most outspoken critics of the war was the independent journalist I. F. Stone. To Stone, who published his own newsletter, the war had to be ended, but so did the Cold War. He called for a complete rejection of the containment policy.[79]

One new group emerged to oppose the Korean War. In response to the outbreak of the war, the AWP was formed in New York City in August 1950 as a service center for all women's peace committees. At a meeting in October 1950, the AWP issued a declaration of principles. With an emphasis on gender, the group noted that because the privilege of giving birth belongs uniquely to women, it is the responsibility of all women to preserve life, and "especially to protect it from the dangers of useless and criminal warfare." They called for a strengthening of the UN as an instrument of peace and the banning of all instruments designed for mass destruction.[80]

Throughout the war, the AWP continued its criticism of U.S. policy. In a press release of October 4, 1950, AWP leader Dr. Clementina Paolone stated alarm at the decision to cross the thirty-eighth parallel. Paolone warned that a bitter and prolonged war would result and called for the immediate cessation of hostilities. In April 1951, the group led a protest at the UN calling for an end to the war in Korea. In May 1951, Paolone wrote to Truman to express approval of the firing of Gen. MacArthur, hoping that it was a first step "in the reversal of a disastrous foreign policy" and again calling for a cessation of hostilities in Korea.[81]

The CPA also spoke out against the U.S. Korean policy. In a "Statement of Policy," the committee indicated that they were not in complete agreement on the use of military intervention by the UN in Korea, though they were united on the principle that peace could be won and maintained through "persistent work with peaceful alternatives." In the future, where aggression occurs, the CPA urged that the UN first explore peaceful means and negotiation before invoking military sanctions. In a specific statement on Korea, the committee proposed that Prime Minister Nehru use his good offices to arbitrate the conflict and that the UN appoint a commission to seek a peaceful solution to the war, including a cease-fire. They called on the U.S. government to "reaffirm our traditional respect for the independence and autonomy of other nations," and, in indicating their support for "collective action and collective decisions," called on the United States to support UN efforts to end the war.[82]

Although Henry Wallace split with the Progressive Party over the Korean issue, the party continued its opposition to the war. The party condemned American intervention in Korea under the UN mantle and the use by the Truman administration of the crisis in Korea to increase war preparations and further anticommunist hysteria. Corliss Lamont, the party's treasurer, took the official line one step further by also deploring the resort to violence and military aggression on the part of the North Koreans, though the party statement of July 15, 1950 did not include such a condemnation. The party continued its antiwar stance through the entire war, and their 1952 presidential candidate, Vincent Hallinan, called for an acceptance of a cease-fire at the demarcation line and turning over the problem of exchange of war prisoners to nonmilitary representatives for negotiation.[83]

The American Peace Crusade (APC), led by Willard Uphaus, was also active in the antiwar efforts. The organization, which developed from the Second World Peace Congress in Sheffield, England, in November 1950, held its first meeting in July 1951 in Chicago. The goal of the APC was to be a center of information and action on peace and to work closely with other movements. According to Uphaus, the APC was not arguing the right or wrong of U.S. military involvement in Korea. He wrote in his biography, "Our crusade was to end the fighting. It seemed to me in the face of the tragedy in Korea, a tragedy that might spread and engulf the world, we were striving for something universal in humanity." The organization had the support of some prominent individuals, including W.E.B. Du Bois, writer Howard Fast, and scientist Linus Pauling. They sponsored several demonstrations against the war and wrote Secretary of Defense George Marshall calling for an end to the war.[84]

Despite the general acceptance of the Cold War policies by the leading civil rights organizations such as the NAACP, there were a number of African Americans who objected to U.S. actions in Korea. Ten days after the war started, Paul Robeson called for a "hands-off Korea" policy at a rally in Harlem to criticize military involvement in Asia. One of the few black newspapers to oppose the war was the *California Eagle*, which opposed sending the troops because it would not bring peace to Korea. One of the paper's writers, Raphael Konigsberg, suggested that the South Korean government of Syngman Rhee may have provoked the North's attack to bring American entry into the conflict.[85]

In addition to working with the APC, Du Bois continued writing for the CAA. In a July 1950 statement, he called for an end to foreign intervention in what he called a civil war and said that the UN had acted in undue haste. Incorporating elements of race, capitalism, and military intervention, the Du Bois statement argued that apartheid in South Africa was more of a threat to peace than were the hostilities in Korea.[86]

African American women emerged as leading dissenters against the policy in Korea. Many members of black women's clubs became radicalized by the prospect that fighting in Korea could lead to all-out nuclear war. Others were persistent critics of the Truman administration's foreign policies. Civil rights advocate Mary Church Terrell, who was also a member of the WILPF, opposed the war "partly because she feared that a male relative might be drafted and partly because she feared a nuclear war." Charlotta Bass, an editor of the *California Eagle*, repeatedly condemned U.S. involvement in the war.[87]

Despite the efforts of small groups of devoted activists, the Truman administration, and then the administration of President Dwight D. Eisenhower, could ignore protests. Although the American people became frustrated with the war, and many wanted to find an end as quickly as possible, it was not because of the efforts of the peace movement. By 1950, and certainly through the Korean War years, the peace movement of left-liberal internationalists and pacifists became an insignificant force in American politics and policy making. The Cold War consensus had few challengers in position of influence. Defeat after defeat had weakened the strength of the opponents of containment, and the Korean War and use of the UN had severely divided the critics of military containment. Not insignificantly, the emergence of hysterical anticommunism, which linked any opposition with communism, contributed to the weakening of the movement.

ANTICOMMUNISM

As historian Charles DeBenedetti wrote, politics in Cold War America "veered into a fogbank of rightist repression." By the early 1950s, only very few doubted the need for a powerful security state and the need to be vigilant against external and internal subversion. The peace movement "tumbled to the lowest point of its twentieth century influence."[88]

With the emergence of Loyalty Boards, the discovery of atomic spies, the accusations against and the trials of Alger Hiss and the Rosenbergs, and the charges of Sen. Joseph McCarthy, the United States entered into a new period of repression. As the fear of communism spread, it became apparent that the peace movement would be one of its victims. Senators Taylor and Pepper became its political victims, both losing their Senate seats. Taylor warned about the dangers of repression in 1949. He stated, "We are moving along toward militarism in this country and it is getting so it is almost a traitorous act to criticize any of the policies which are taking us down the road toward militarism. . . . It seems to me that in our great anxiety to fight communism we are succumbing to totalitarian practices in our own country." Henry Wallace expressed the same idea in 1948 when he wrote, "I am more worried about appeasing native born fascists than I am about appeasing Russia. Those who call me an appeaser today are the same breed of people as those who initiated the Anti-Comintern in the later thirties."[89] Nonetheless, though suspect themselves, many peace activists threw themselves into a defense of civil liberties.[90]

One of the most serious problems faced by the movement in the context of what came to be known as McCarthyism was getting their point of view across to the public because of the association of the movement with communism. As the FOR put it, "Peace itself has to a great extent become a 'bad word' in this country, and the open discussion of alternatives to the government's policy in Korea a difficult matter."[91]

The various peace organizations devoted much of their time distinguishing themselves from the communists and defending the political rights of communists. The WILPF was determined, despite similarities in tactics with the communists, to remain clearly in the hands of the genuine pacifists. Its members fell under suspicion for their antiwar activities. They felt the strong arm of McCarthyism from the national office down to their local branches. Membership did not grow, it was at times difficult to find meeting places, and members became suspicious of each other. The organization was ripping apart from within.[92]

Often for the noncommunist left-liberals and pacifists, it was a matter of how to react to the communists who frequently called for the same policies. Should activists cooperate in a united front, or should they exclude communists from their ranks? This issue, until the emergence of the New Left in the early 1960s, divided the American left.[93] The FOR executive committee, in the midst of the Korean War and the Red Scare, explained their policy. Based on their religious pacifist position in opposition to totalitarianism of all kinds, including communist totalitarianism, they stated, "[I]t has never been and is not now the policy of FOR to support or collaborate with the Communist movement or Communist Parties."[94]

However, that did not mean they would not have contact with communists, including such prominent ones as Du Bois. The FOR noted that it was its policy to exclude no one from human fellowship and that they would strive to win communists and others to the way of nonviolence and reconciliation. It was also the policy of the FOR "to defend the civil rights and liberties of all individuals and groups, and this applies specifically to Communists." The purpose of the statement was defensive as the FOR not only felt it was necessary to disassociate themselves from communists, they were careful throughout to make sure they would not appear even as sympathizers. They stated that they did not imply any "whitewashing of the war ('defensive') policy of the Russian government or advocate 'appeasement.' " The FOR restated its position that they did not believe that such evil could be overcome by violence.[95]

Although not opposed to cooperation with nonpacifist individuals and groups, the FOR felt it wise to refrain from organizational collaboration in activities with the Communist Party or other communist organizations in the form of united fronts. Such organizations, the FOR argued, are seen by the communists as a means to build their party and advance the aims of the communist movement and Russian foreign policy. Indeed, as Lawrence Wittner has argued, the main aim of the Soviet antinuclear movement was to stigmatize nuclear weapons, thereby undermining the U.S. military advantage. In addition, they hoped to project the image of the Soviet Union as a peace-loving nation to attract new party recruits.[96]

The FOR and other peace groups therefore faced dilemmas when confronted with what were called Soviet Peace Offensives. The most significant effort of these "offensives" was the circulation of the Stockholm Petition. As the Soviets launched a peace offensive, and with the United States already in the grip of the Cold War consensus, this offensive was viewed with great suspicion. Those who came to be associated with the offensive were viewed as either communists or dupes, and it contributed to the belief, which lasted throughout the Cold War years, that peace activists were communists.[97]

This offensive started at the August 1948 World Congress of Intellectuals for Peace held in Poland. The idea of the conference was that intellectuals could lead the opposition to the rearmament of Germany and the formation of NATO. The Polish conference set up a series of meetings. One of the most important was the Waldorf Conference held in New York in March 1949. The Waldorf Conference placed blame on the United States for threats of war. This position reflected the Communist Party line, but was also held by many noncommunists. Although the conference basically held to the communist line, it also attracted noncommunists who were opposed to the growing militarism of U.S. foreign policy and the increasingly repressive atmosphere in the United States. A second conference was held in April in Paris. At this meeting, a Permanent World Peace Committee was established. At the committee's third meeting in Stockholm in March 1950, it "proclaimed a new campaign for signatures on a petition to ban the atomic bomb"—the Stockholm Petition. Secretary of State Acheson called the petition Soviet propaganda and made it clear that the United States would not refrain from using atomic weapons just because it would be labeled as a war criminal if it used them.[98]

The FOR and NCPW both rejected the Stockholm Petition. Libby wrote, "We ought to be glad that Russia is circulating a peace petition." But, he noted, "there is no question that the prohibition of atom bombs would be greatly to Russia's advantage . . . since this is the only weapon we have with which to balance with all Russia's incomparable manpower equipped with 'conventional weapons.' " He reasserted his belief that universal disarmament, "down to rifles," was the only policy that made sense.[99]

The FOR, which also rejected the Stockholm Petition, noted that an indication of how that peace movement was used for totalitarian means could be found in the fact that the peace organizations promoted by the Communist Party ruled out antitotalitarian declarations that would criticize Soviet foreign policy.[100] In particular, the FOR was highly critical of the Mid-Century Conference for Peace held in Chicago in May 1950. One historian has argued that the FOR's efforts to draw lines between its peace efforts and those that had the support of communists may have contributed to a weakening of the peace movement. The organization's attempts to warn people away from the Chicago conference even created a rift within the FOR. The FOR, after the conference, noted that though it passed a declaration that it was united in devotion to democratic methods, it refused to pass a statement in opposition to totalitarianism.[101]

Although not all pacifists shared the views expressed by Muste and the FOR, all U.S. pacifist groups, including the WRL and FOR, adopted policies of nonparticipation in communist-organized peace activities. The FOR and Muste continued to call for American-Soviet negotiations while refusing to cooperate with Communist Party members. The FOR noted that the best way to test a project was to demand the inclusion of a statement in opposition to war preparations in both the United States and Soviet Union, and to oppose totalitarianism.[102]

Despite the refusal to participate in united front organizations, the pacifist organizations did speak out forcefully for civil liberties for communists. In November 1949, the FOR issued a statement of concern over the trial and conviction of eleven national leaders of the Communist Party under the 1940 Smith Act, which outlawed conspiracy to advocate the overthrow of the U.S. government. They noted, "It is our earnest hope that the Supreme Court will eventually declare this law unconstitutional; and failing this, that congress will repeal it." The FOR noted that recent history demonstrated that unpopular or unorthodox ideas may be threatened with proscription. Such action would contribute to the totalitarianism that they sought to defend the United States against. The FOR stated its belief that "[l]imiting freedom of expression and yielding to hysteria are not effective ways to combat Communism." Instead, communism and other forms of dictatorship could be prevented by "removing the conditions of poverty, insecurity, discrimination and repression that breed social unrest."[103]

The WILPF also spoke out against the growing repression in the nation. Annalee Stewart told the House Un-American Activities Committee that the League, which viewed the guarantee of freedom of speech as necessary to a democracy, was concerned about the "growing tendency to interfere with freedom of opinion by the use of loyalty tests." She noted the danger that "[a]ny organization, whether permanent or temporary, which is working for social or economic change could . . . be considered subversive." She told the committee that "The best *defense* of freedom is the *practice* of freedom."[104]

Even the Catholic Worker Movement, which aside from conscription took few stands on the issues of the Cold War because the group preferred to be "announcers" not "denouncers," took a stand in opposition to the McCarran Internal Security Act of 1950, which, among a number of items, made it illegal to do anything that could contribute to the establishment of a totalitarian dictatorship and required communist organizations to register with the attorney general. They felt that it represented a movement away from freedom toward totalitarianism, and although they differed with the Communist Party over the issue of means to achieve social justice and the concept of atheism, they respected the party's freedom as a minority group in the United States.[105]

CONCLUSION

By 1950, with several failures to derail the Truman containment policy and with the growing association of peace and leftist groups with communism, the peace movement had little effect in the early 1950s on U.S. policy, or at least far less than they had had just a few years before. The arms race and the rearming of Europe went ahead full speed, disarmament looked like a distant dream, and a war raged in Korea. The movement, in addition to attacks from the outside caused by a growing anticommunist hysteria, faced division within over how to deal with American communists and Soviet-backed peace initiatives. By 1953, it appeared that the movement was over and that it had little affect on American life. However, the ideas stayed alive, and it had a greater impact than was evident at the time. In the process of criticizing the various Truman containment initiatives, the opponents had developed a coherent, though perhaps not always practical, alternative to containment.

NOTES

1. U.S. Congress, Senate, Committee on Foreign Relations and Committee on Armed Services, *Military Assistance Program: Joint Hearings before the Committee on Foreign Relations and the Committee on Armed Services*, 81st. Cong., 1st sess., 1949, 6–7. Hereafter referred to as *Military Assistance Program*.

2. Acheson, *Military Assistance Program*, 6. For the development of the MDAP, see Lawrence S. Kaplan, *A Community of Interests: NATO and the Military Assistance Program 1948–1951* (Washington, DC: Historical Office, Office of the Secretary of Defense, 1980); E. Timothy Smith, *The United States, Italy and NATO, 1947–52* (New York: St. Martin's Press, 1991), chapter 6.

3. See James Nathan and James Oliver, *The United States Foreign Policy and World Order* (Boston: Little, Brown and Co., 1976–81), 98–99.

4. September 7, 1949, Gallup, *The Gallup Poll*, II:845.

5. Warburg, May 10, 1949, *NAT* II: 683.

6. "Proposal to Acheson from Warburg," January 27, 1949, Warburg Papers, Box 13, Acheson file, JFK Library. Emphasis in original.

7. Memo, Warburg to Senators Connally, McMahon, Pepper, and Vandenberg, n.d. (but most likely after May 10, 1949), Warburg Papers, Box 50, Memos to Congress, JFK Library.

8. Warburg to Acheson, November 21, 1950, Warburg Papers, Box 13, Acheson file, JFK Library. Emphasis in original.

9. *University of Chicago Round Table*, "Turning World Resources to World Welfare," Number 643, July 23, 1950, AFSC, DG 2, II, Box 6, Literature 1950, SCPC.

10. Wallace to each member of the Senate, July 5, 1949, Wallace Papers, Reel 46, University of Iowa.

11. Wallace, August 19, 1949, *Military Assistance Program*, 185–90.

12. Seymour Linfield, August 18, 1949, *Military Assistance Program*, 179.

13. Libby to Rothburn Willard, August 22, 1949, NCPW, DG 23, Reel 41.287, SCPC; Libby, August 19, 1949, *Military Assistance Program*, 249.

14. Libby, "Case Against the M.A.P. as of June 26, 1950," NCPW, DG 23, Box 430, SCPC.

15. CPA, "Open Letter," August 22, 1949, *Military Assistance Program*, 250.

16. Stewart, August 22, 1949, *Military Assistance Program*, 251.

17. D. Robert Yarnall, August 19, 1949, *Military Assistance Program*, 199, 201.

18. Mrs. Clifford Bender, May 16, 1949, *NAT* III: 1005–6.

19. Du Bois, *Military Assistance Program*, 229.

20. Ibid., 180, 236, 238, 244, 255.

21. John Lewis Gaddis, *Strategies of Containment: A Critical Appraisal of Postwar National Security Policy* (New York: Oxford University Press, 1982), 82–83.

22. NSC-68, *Foreign Relations of the United States*, 1950 (Washington, DC: GPO, 1977), I: 237–85.

23. Daniel Yergin, *Shattered Peace: The Origins of the Cold War and the National Security State* (Boston: Houghton Mifflin Co., Sentry edition, 1977), 235; Memo of the Ad Hoc Committee on NSC-68, *FRUS*, 1950, I: 302. For examples of opposition in the administration, see Smith, *The United States, Italy and NATO*, 121–22.

24. *Four Lights* (WILPF newsletter), July 1951, WILPF, Reel 130.4, SCPC; Elizabeth Haswell to Branch leaders, August 16, 1949, WILPF, Reel 130.25, SCPC.

25. NCPW, "NCPW Program for Peace—1950," December 21, 1949, NCPW, DG 23, Box 487, Releases 1950, SCPC.

26. Brethren Service Commission Press Release, March 25, 1949, CDG-A, Church of the Brethren, Brethren Service Commission file, SCPC; "Declaration of Christian Faith and Commitment," November 9–12, 1950, IX-7-2 Peace Section, Peace Conferences and Study Papers, 1950 Winona Lake Materials, Mennonite Archives, Goshen, IN.

27. Madeleine Trimmer (administrative secretary of PWWC) to Joseph Brower, May 26, 1950, PWWC, Reel 90.2, SCPC.

28. Cranston to Warburg, October 19, 1950, Warburg Papers, Box 44, UWF file, JFK Library.

29. Committee for Peaceful Alternatives, "What It Is, What It Does," July 1951, CDG-A, CPA, SCPC.

30. Conference on Disarmament, Minutes, September 28–30, 1949, WRL papers, RG 40, Series B, Box 12, Miscellaneous literature, SCPC.

31. Boyer, *By the Bomb's Early Light*, 347–48; Report to the Mennonite Central Committee Peace Section Executive Committee, June 6, 1949, IX-7-8 MCC Peace Section, Minutes and Reports, 1948–50, Mennonite Archives.

32. "Theological Roots of Christian Pacifism," May 8–11, 1950, I-3-5.11, Peace Problem Commission, GFH file, Data #62, Detroit Conference 1950 file, Mennonite Archives.

33. "Some Social and Political Implications of Our Faith," May 8–11, 1950, I-3-5.11, Peace Problem Committee, GFH File, Data #62, Detroit Conference 1950 file, Mennonite Archives.

34. Muste memo on the Mid-Century Conference for Peace, May 1, 1950, CPA, CDG-A, SCPC.

35. Willard Uphaus, *Commitment* (New York: McGraw-Hill Book Co., Inc., 1963), 80; Herman Will Jr., "Report on Mid-Century Conference for Peace," June 5, 1950, CPA, CDG-A, SCPC.

36. Eby, "Requirements for Peace," May 29, 1950, CPA, CDG-A, SCPC.

37. "Report on Mid-Century Conference for Peace," CPA, CDG-A, SCPC.

38. "Appeal to the American People for Peaceful Alternatives to the Cold War," CPA, CDG-A, SCPC.

39. Ted Galen Carpenter, "United States NATO Policy at the Crossroads: The 'Great Debate' of 1950–1951," *International History Review* 8 (August 1986): 414–15; Phil Williams, *The Senate and U.S. Troops in Europe* (New York: St. Martin's Press, 1985), 36–39.

40. Williams, *The Senate and U.S. Troops in Europe*, 50–51.

41. David R. Kepley, "The Senate and the Great Debate of 1951," *Prologue* 14 (winter 1982): 219.

42. Carpenter, "The Dissenters," 298.

43. Kepley, "The Senate and the Great Debate of 1951," 213.

44. Baldwin, February 20, 1951, U.S. Congress, Senate, *Assignment of Ground Forces of the United States to Duty in the European Area, Hearings before the Committee on Foreign Relations and Committee on Armed Services*, 82nd Cong., 1st sess., 1951, 238–40. Hereafter referred to as *Assignment of Ground Forces*.

45. Alonso, *Peace as a Women's Issue*, 185–90. Also see Harriet Hyman Alonso, "Mayhem and Moderation: Women Peace Activists during the McCarthy Era," in Joanne Meyerowitz, ed., *Not June Cleaver: Women and Gender in Postwar America, 1945–1960* (Philadelphia: Temple University Press, 1994).

46. Paolone, February 20, 1951, *Assignment of Ground Forces*, 260, 262–63.

47. Libby, February 20, 1951, *Assignment of Ground Forces*, 266–67.

48. Statement by Havighurst, February 26, 1951; New York CPA, n.d., *Assignment of Ground Forces*, 790, 805.

49. There were 23 votes against aid to Greece and Turkey, 17 against the ERP, 13 against the NAT, and 21 against the deployment of troops. See Goldman, "The Conservative Critique of Containment," 262.

50. For the history of the Korean War, see, among many others, Bruce Cumings, *The Origins of the Korean War* (Princeton, NJ: Princeton University Press, 1981); Callum MacDonald, *Korea: The War before Vietnam* (New York: Free Press, 1987); Rosemary Foot, *The Wrong War* (Ithaca, NY: Cornell University Press, 1985).

51. LaFeber, *The American Age*, 490–91.

52. Pollard, "Economic Security and the Origins of the Cold War," 287.

53. McAuliffe, *Crisis on the Left*, 76.

54. Wittner, *Rebels against War*, 201–2; Kleidman, *Organizing for Peace*, 25–26.

55. Wittner, *One World or None*, 316.

56. Yarnell, *Democrats and Progressives*, 112; Walker, *Henry A. Wallace and American Foreign Policy*, 208–9.

57. Muste to Wallace, August 8, 1950; Muste to Wallace, November 13, 1950; Muste to Wallace, December 27, 1950, Wallace Papers, Reel 47, University of Iowa.

58. Raymond Cox to Wallace, August 1, 1950; Carl vonder Lanchen to Wallace, August 1, 1950, Wallace Papers, Reel 47, University of Iowa.

59. Wallace to Curtis MacDougal, August 15, 1950; MacDougal to Wallace August 19, 1950, Wallace Papers, Reel 47, University of Iowa.

60. Walker, *Henry A. Wallace and American Foreign Policy*, 210; Wallace to Mao Zedong, September 30, 1950, Wallace Papers, Reel 47, University of Iowa.

61. Wallace to Harry Weinberg, February 20, 1951; Wallace to Susanne LaFollette, May 17, 1951; Wallace to Tugwell, January 20, 1952, Wallace Papers, Reel 48, University of Iowa; Peterson, *Prophet without Honor*, 164.

62. Thomas to Wallace, September 8, 1952, Wallace Papers, Reel 49, University of Iowa; Bernard K. Johnpoll, *Pacifist's Progress: Norman Thomas and the Decline of American Socialism* (Chicago: Quadrangle Books, 1970), 265, 272.

63. "To Our Friends in Europe and Asia," January 17, 1951, PWWC, DG-62, Reel 90.4, SCPC.

64. "A Maximum American Proposal for Settlement with China," December 1950; Warburg to Acheson, May 21, 1951, Warburg Papers, Acheson file, Box 13, JFK Library.

65. Barton J. Bernstein, "Review Essay: 'Henry A. Wallace and the Agony of American Liberalism: A Political Pariah in the Cold War.'" *Peace and Change* 2 (fall 1974): 66.

66. David Dellinger, *From Yale to Jail: The Life Story of a Moral Dissenter* (New York: Pantheon Books, 1993), 153.

67. Matthew Edwin Mantell, "Opposition to the Korean War: A Study in American Dissent" (Ph.D. diss., New York University, 1973), 2–3.

68. Ibid., 5–6, 20.

69. Ibid., 31.

70. A. J. Muste, "Pacifists and Korean Crisis," July 21–25, 1950, FOR papers, DG 13, A, 24, Releases January–July 1950, SCPC.

71. A. J. Muste, "Korea: Spark to Set a World Afire?" 1950 (?), FOR copy in possession of the author. Also published in Nat Hentoff, ed., *The Essays of A. J. Muste*, 331–54.

72. A. J. Muste, "The MacArthur Case," April 1951, DG 13, A, 24, Releases 1951, SCPC.

73. FOR, "The Meaning of Korea," 1950, personal copy.

74. Minutes of the Executive Committee, WRL, July 10, 1950, DG 40, A, Box 2, SCPC.

75. Catherine Foster, *Women for All Seasons: The Story of the Women's International League for Peace and Freedom* (Athens: University of Georgia Press, 1989), 25–26; National Policy Committee of the WILPF, "Statement of the Korean Crisis," 1950, WILPF, Reel 130.37, SCPC.

76. Picon to Acheson, May 5, 1951, WILPF, Reel 130.37, SCPC; WILPF, "The Recall of MacArthur," May 16, 1951, DG 47, Series L, Box 15, Korean War file 3, SCPC; WILPF National Board Resolutions, October 12–14, 1951, WILPF, Reel 130.82, SCPC. See also Picon to Truman, October 23, 1950, WILPF, Reel 130.97, Washington Newsletter no. 13, SCPC.

77. "Statement on the Korea Crisis," July 1950, NCPW, Reel 41.254, SCPC.

78. Libby, "We Get Bogged Down in Korea," in *Peace Action*, July 1950, NCPW, DG 23, Box 438, U.S. foreign policy Korea file, SCPC.

79. For Stone's critique, see Norman Kaner, "I. F. Stone and the Korean War," in Paterson, ed., *Cold War Critics*, 261.

80. "The Peacemaker," Vol. 2, no. 4 (May 1951); "Declaration of Principles," in "The Peacemaker," Vol. 1, no. 2 (November 1950), AWP, CDG-A, SCPC.

81. Press Release, October 4, 1950, AWP, CDG-A, SCPC; "The Peacemaker," Vol. 2, no. 4 (May 1951), AWP, CDG-A, SCPC.

82. CPA, "Statement of Policy," December 1950, CPA, CDG-A, SCPC; CPA, "Statement on Korea," July 27, 1950, CPA, CDG-A, SCPC.

83. Corliss Lamont, "Statement on Korea," July 30, 1950, Wallace Papers, Reel 47, University of Iowa; Speech by Vincent Hallinan, September 6, 1952, PWWC papers, Reel 90.5, SCPC.

84. Willard Uphaus, *Commitment*, 83, 107, 109; Gerald Robert Gill, "Afro-American Opposition to the United States' Wars of the Twentieth Century: Dissent, Discontent and Disinterest" (Ph.D. diss., Howard University, 1985), 466; APC, "Statement of the Delegation of the American Peace Crusade," March 15, 1951, APC, CDG-A, SCPC.

85. Gill, "Afro-American Opposition to the United States' Wars of the Twentieth Century," 72–73.

86. Ibid., 74–75.

87. Ibid., 78–79.

88. DeBenedetti, *Peace Reform in American History*, 156–57.

89. Taylor, April 8, 1949, *Congressional Record*, 80th Cong., 2nd sess., Vol. 93, no. 3, 4141; Wallace to Don Murphy, January 13, 1948, Wallace Papers, Reel 44, University of Iowa.

90. Wittner, *Rebels against War*, 215.

91. "Preamble to Report on Civil Liberties," adopted by the National Council of the FOR, December 1950, NCPW, Reel 41.254, SCPC.

92. Report of Mildred Scott Olmsted, administrative secretary WILPF, January 29–31, 1953, WILPF, Reel 130.4, SCPC; Alonso, *Peace as a Women's Issue*, 159.

93. For a discussion of the divisions in the early New Left, see James Miller, *"Democracy Is in the Streets": From Port Huron to the Siege of Chicago* (New York: Touchstone, 1987).

94. FOR, "The Peace Movement and United Fronts," July 1950, FOR, DG 13, A, 24, Releases, January–July 1950, SCPC.

95. Ibid.

96. Wittner, *One World or None*, 171.

97. Robbie Lieberman, " 'Does That Make Peace a Bad Word?' American Responses to the Communist Peace Offensive, 1949–1950," *Peace and Change* 17 (April 1992): 199.

98. Ibid., 199–200, 210–12.

99. Libby to William Orton, July 25, 1950, NCPW, Reel 41.225, SCPC.

100. FOR, "The Peace Movement and United Fronts."

101. Lieberman, " 'Does That Make Peace a Bad Word?' " 218; FOR, "The Peace Movement and United Fronts."

102. Wittner, *One World or None*, 206–7. An example of the WRL's view can be found in the minutes of the executive committee in which they felt that they needed to let the American people know that the Communist Party use of the word "peace" was "not peace at all." See WRL, Minutes of the Executive Committee, July 10, 1950, DG 40, A, Box 2, SCPC.

103. FOR, "Statement by the Executive Committee of FOR on the Trial of Communist Party Leaders," November 19, 1949, FOR, DG 13, 3, Minutes 1942–49, SCPC.

104. Stewart, "Testimony against the Nixon Bill," May 3, 1950, in Washington Newsletter, no. 11, WILPF, Reel 130.97, SCPC. Emphasis in original.

105. William D. Miller, *A Harsh and Dreadful Love: Dorothy Day and the Catholic Worker Movement* (New York: Liveright, 1973), 228–29.

6

THE ALTERNATIVES

For when a people is divided within itself about the conduct of its foreign relations, it is unable to agree on the determination of its true interest. It is unable to prepare adequately for war or to safeguard successfully its peace.[1]

We are deeply convinced that ... alternatives do exist and that the people of this land still have the power to choose them. Our people can still refuse to let the fateful choice be made for them by those who promise peace and yet steadily prepare for war.[2]

After World War II, with the onset of the Cold War, Truman administration officials, along with congressional leaders, attempted to end divisions and create a foreign policy of consensus. At least until divisions emerged over Vietnam, the postwar foreign policy of the United States included what Richard Melanson called the three elements of consensus. There was policy consensus that included public and elite agreement on strategy and tactics of foreign policy. There was a cultural consensus that included broad agreement on appropriate sets of private and public values. Finally, there was procedural consensus, which refers to a presidential-congressional understanding about which branch performs which tasks.[3]

The consensus foreign policy of the Cold War years centered on the active containment of the Soviet Union. Viewing the Soviets as the primary threat to U.S. interests in the world, the Truman administration rallied both the Congress and the public behind an activist foreign policy that committed the United States to the defense of Europe and other far-flung areas of the world. After having convinced many reluctant congressmen to support the policy, the administration announced containment to the world with the Truman Doctrine of 1947. Nonetheless, many critics remained. However, the election of 1948 solidified the bipartisan consensus and discredited the liberal critique of the Cold War.[4] In that election, Truman and the Democratic consensus internationalists portrayed Henry Wallace as a communist dupe, driving one of the key leaders opposed to containment from public life. After that, the consensus internationalists ended meaningful debate of U.S. foreign policy for nearly two decades.[5]

Although the consensus weakened with the emergence of antinuclear activists in the mid and late 1950s, it did not completely collapse until the nation itself was torn apart by the escalation of the Vietnam War. Meanwhile, the policy gained popular support. It was supported by the media and the large pool of talent that came to be called the foreign policy establishment. They supported a commitment to the assertion of American global power. Any questioning of that globalism, or as it was called, internationalism, risked exposure as a communist or a reactionary isolationist.[6] That was what drove Wallace, Warburg, and others from the scene, and resulted in the marginalization of peace activists for over a decade.

This containment policy also had a domestic cultural impact, what historian Elaine Tyler May called domestic containment.[7] The challenge of communism became a basis for the creation of an American identity that included family and religion. The United States was a nation called to global responsibility and was seeking a common identity, a moral legitimacy, a civic duty and an ideological purpose.[8] This, too, came under challenge during the 1960s.

The procedural consensus, that is, the relationship between the Congress and the president, involved an acceptance of the role of presidential leadership in the realm of foreign affairs. The Congress gave the president wide latitude in dealing with the Soviet Union and emerging crises, such as the Korean War, throughout the 1950s and well into the 1960s. Again, it was Vietnam, and the Watergate scandal, that led to significant challenges of presidential authority. However, more than the other two, this element of consensus has remained intact as Presidents Ronald Reagan, George Bush, and Bill Clinton have sent U.S. troops into several nations with only minimal congressional consultation.

Despite the Cold War consensus and their growing marginalization, groups and individuals stood up in opposition to what they viewed as a dangerous foreign policy leading the United States into a potentially atomic war. It has been repeatedly argued here that these individuals and groups had little, if any, impact on the decision making of the Truman administration in the early Cold War years. Lawrence Kaplan has indicated that what was remarkable about the critics was not that they failed to exploit the vulnerabilities of the administration's positions, but that their constituencies were remarkably small, that "[t]hey lacked an audience."[9] Nonetheless, their ideas promoting world reconstruction, democracy, human rights, and the elimination of poverty and colonialism did set high standards for the United States and the world to follow. However, what is more significant is the long-term impact that these individuals had on the later peace movement and on scholars who have looked at the Cold War from a historic perspective. Furthermore, the opposition brought new groups to the scene, including women's peace groups and African American organizations, which spoke out against the direction of U.S. policy.

Most historians would agree that the deepening Cold War, Truman's continuation of atomic testing, the decision to pursue the hydrogen bomb, and the outbreak of the Korean War ended the peace movement by 1950. This led some groups, like the Catholic Worker Movement, to return to their roots by concerning themselves with issues of social justice.[10] Other organizations, such as the WILPF and the FOR, suffered membership declines. Groups such as the CPA were viewed as communist sympathizers and therefore had no impact on policy making. Eventually, Wallace and Warburg found themselves aligning with the administration on the issue of the Korean War. The critics dwindled, reaching a state of near inactivity, but the opposition continued to keep its flames alive. It is out of these embers that a new antinuclear and antiwar movement emerged in the later 1950s and grew rapidly with the deepening U.S. involvement in Vietnam. The groups that emerged later raised the same criticisms that had been presented and ignored in the late 1940s.

ALTERNATIVE PROPOSALS

Despite their differences, the pacifists, liberal internationalists, and other peace activists of the late 1940s and early 1950s challenged consensus policies and the emerging national security state with powerful analyses and attacks upon the policy justifications and institutions that were organized in the postwar world. They proposed different ways of interpreting and realizing security in a fragile world filled with nationalism and scientific-industrial interdependence.[11]

The critical opposition presented an alternative view of the world that was not isolationist. They supported an activist American world role, and it was this view that led to their opposition to containment. As James Warburg noted in a March 10, 1949 speech on Atlantic defense, "In ordinary circumstances, I do not think it is incumbent upon one who criticizes a proposal to offer a substitute. If you see a man about to walk off a precipice, it is enough to shout a warning." However, in this case, he noted, "these are not ordinary circumstances."[12]

Their criticisms and proposals centered on four main issues. First and foremost was their support for the UN and its potential use to bring about some type of disarmament. Although most originally saw it as a weak institution, it was all there was, and they felt that the United States should do all it could to support the UN. As the U.S. policy veered away from the UN with the assistance to Greece and Turkey, critics coalesced around the belief that the United States was undercutting the UN with a unilateral program that could lead to confrontations with fellow UN member, the Soviet Union. Instead, they felt that Washington should deal with the conflict in Greece through the UN. Each successive program, especially the ERP and NATO, seemed to do more damage to the UN.

Sen. Glen Taylor held that an all-out effort had to be made to build up the UN and reach agreements on disarmament. He remarked that the Truman administration should "quit this business of even entertaining the thought that we should not negotiate with the Russians." If all possible measures were taken and failed, then he said that the United States "should look to ourselves for our own defense."[13] Others also supported serious negotiations to end the Cold War. The CPA proposed more support for the UN, "whose primary business it is to settle differences among all nations and to maintain peace." The Committee, in advocating peaceful negotiations, asserted that "[d]ifferent political and economic systems can exist together in peace."[14]

The problem with this critique of U.S. foreign policy in the early years of the Cold War is that the UN was not functioning as its founders had hoped. The emerging Cold War saw confrontations between Washington and Moscow in the UN. Lack of cooperation between the powers contributed to the U.S. decision to act on its own in Greece and later with the ERP and NATO. By 1949, however, it appeared unlikely that the UN was capable of defusing Soviet-American tensions. Nonetheless, pacifist and peace movement critics continued to pursue these other alternatives.

When the United States did decide to use the UN, the Russians were boycotting the Security Council and the result was a war in Korea fought under the UN flag. This caused divisions among the peace activists. Although the pacifists and liberal internationalists may have been a bit advanced of their time in placing hopes in the UN, perhaps if some of their other suggestions had been supported, the UN might have been made into an effective force. In fact, Muste noted that though many felt

that the use of military force by the UN in Korea had "made" that organization an effective power, quite the opposite was true. He felt that,
after the war, the UN was no longer the center of attention and the
"important discussions no longer even take place in the United
Nations."[15] With the Cold War deepening, the Russians and Americans
carried their conflict into the international organization, which then became an arena for attacking each other. That is not to say that the UN
was totally ineffective, but it was only effective when the powers could
agree. The critics had hoped that the two governments could find more
grounds for agreement through greater cooperation in that organization.

The second criticism/proposal coming from the peace forces was a
warning that U.S. policy, with its growing hostility toward the Soviets,
would lead to war and create a militarized America and a dangerously
armed world. The fear of war was legitimate despite the fact that, in
retrospect, the United States and the Soviet Union never fought a war
against each other. Both the United States and the Soviet Union engaged
in an arms race that lasted as long as the Cold War, and in some ways
continues to the present. The development of larger and more effective
nuclear weapons made war increasingly dangerous and threatening to
human existence if they were ever used. The threat of war and its escalation into nuclear conflict haunted the critics of containment in the
postwar years and became one of the key issues that rejuvenated the
peace movement in the 1950s.

In both nations, the influence of the military in policy making was
strengthened. In the case of the United States, the Joint Chiefs of Staff
was formalized as part of a larger national security structure that included the new Department of Defense. The creation of the NSC to ad-
vise the president on matters of economic, foreign, and military policy
increased the military's influence in the White House. For the first time
in its history, the United States maintained a large standing army in
peacetime. That standing army remained deployed in Europe, Asia,
Latin America, and, indeed, around the world. This military was,
through most of the Cold War period, conscripted and thus increasing
the role of the military in the everyday lives of Americans. Although it
never fought the Soviet Union, that military soon found itself in a war
in Korea, and not long after that, in Vietnam. In addition, there were
many smaller engagements that U.S. forces participated in during the
Cold War.

In their critique of the NAT for the FCNL, Wilson and Grant called
for persistent attempts to end the Cold War through negotiations, extension of genuine third-party judgment of the UN, reduction of armaments,
and extension of resources for recovery instead of the threat and use of
force. Wilson clarified what was meant by negotiation in a letter to Sen.
Frank Graham. He noted that he was not talking about "surrender or

appeasement," nor "the abandonment of fundamental principles of liberty and freedom." As an example, he noted that though the Baruch proposal for international control of atomic energy was generous, the United States had not made a proposal for general disarmament. Wilson wrote that World War I unleashed communism in Russia, and World War II had vastly spread its grip. The idea that it could be contained by military force had to be replaced by an emphasis on investment in the health and well-being of countries "in the process of making up their minds between democracy and communism."[16]

In a memorandum on Russian-American relations for the AFSC, Robert Frase concluded that a Western European Alliance rearmed and guaranteed by the United States presented "a very confused picture." In general, he stated, it seemed to be leading in the direction of a continually growing level of armaments, a stagnation or decline in living standards, and an indefinite continuation of tensions and the danger of war. In the memo, Frase lists and discusses the various alternatives, including nonaggression pacts, Atlantic Federation concepts, world government, and preventive war. Among the alternatives that had some positive results was economic aid, which "can be regarded as a means not only of maintaining non-communist governments . . . but of helping to provide a practical demonstration that the long-term economic, social, and political goals of the Communist doctrine itself can be achieved without the use of means which endanger those goals." Supportive also of disarmament initiatives, Frase concluded that such efforts only seemed feasible "as an integral part of a much broader attempt at international equilibrium." What he supported was a broad negotiated general settlement on geographic, military, economic, ideological, and UN-related issues.[17]

Cadbury of the FCNL summed up the Quaker point of view. He told the Senate Foreign Relations Committee that they still believed that among nations, as between individuals, there is "a language beside force that is understood, and an ultimate capacity for response to straightforward, patient, tolerant attempts at mutual understanding."[18] NCPW head Frederick Libby discussed some specific alternatives similar to those proposed by the other critics. He suggested two alternative lines of policy. One was to halt the arms race, stabilizing war expenditures at their current figures. A second alternative was to accept a Soviet proposal to work out a plan for a worldwide reduction of arms. Either of these two, according to Libby, could lead to a Big Four conference to settle the biggest differences.[19]

The critics may have been wrong about actions such as the aid to Greece or the creation of NATO bringing the world closer to war, but they were not wrong about the increased influence of the military in both American government and culture.

The third proposal or criticism of the consensus policy centered on economic issues. Most of the critics felt that since the United States was the world's richest nation, it had an obligation to help the poorer nations of the world. Pacifists such as Muste and liberal internationalists such as Warburg felt that the best way to deal with communism was not through an arms buildup or military alliances but through economic assistance to those in need, both in war-torn Europe and in what became known as the Third World. Muste continually pointed out that communism had spread by the conditions of war. He believed that a world with greater economic equality would reject communism.

Warburg, although viewing economic assistance as a means of containment in Western Europe, firmly believed that U.S. economic assistance could prevent the spread of communism, whereas military programs might weaken the economies of Europe. To Warburg, economic recovery was essential. He felt that creating an adequate defense establishment would require a mobilization of manpower and resources sufficient to disrupt recovery and economic self-support for Western Europe. Warburg believed that to whatever extent recovery was impeded, Western European defense against political penetration would be weakened. However, he was convinced that because the principal opponents of the NAT would be isolationists and communist sympathizers, instead of opposition, or even a lukewarm attitude toward the pact, he ultimately favored ratification while pushing modifications. These modifications included limiting the geographic scope of the pact; abandoning the attempt to force, promote, or assist rearmament of the continental powers; the liquidation of colonial wars; and the coordination of American, British, and Canadian forces, so that maximum power could be brought to bear instantly on any potential aggressor. He also called for a tripartite treaty between the United States, Britain, and the Soviet Union to guarantee the demilitarization of Germany, the control of the Ruhr for all, and to provide for the withdrawal of the three nations' troops from Germany.[20]

Henry Wallace also spoke out in favor of cooperative alternatives to containment. Instead of military alliances, he favored the conclusion of a different type of treaty, one that would establish a unified and democratic Germany stripped of its war potential. He wanted both blocs to agree to refrain from interference in the internal affairs of other nations; to give up military bases in other UN nations and to halt arms exports; to resume unrestricted trade and allow the free movement of citizens and ideas; to reduce arms; and to establish a World Reconstruction and Development Agency within the UN to rebuild Europe and to assist developing nations.[21]

Supporting the ideas of negotiation, disarmament, and economic recovery, the WILPF defined reconstruction to mean building democracy through adequate housing, education, health efforts, and the protection of civil rights and liberties. Stauffer Curry emphasized the religious motivations for Church of the Brethren efforts to provide relief in war-torn areas, including an effort to provide heifers-for-relief. The Heifer Project, initiated by Dan West, was an effort to provide relief to the hungry.[22]

Programs such as the Marshall Plan did get the support of some pacifists and liberal internationalists, but programs of military assistance, such as the aid to Greece and Turkey, the NAT, and the MDAP were strongly criticized. For one thing, such programs were attacked because they were viewed as diversions away from needed economic development programs. First heard in the case of the aid to Greece and Turkey, then in the NATO hearings, and ultimately in discussions about U.S. military aid programs around the world, the critics believed that much of the military assistance was being used to prop up dictatorial and colonial regimes. Indeed, throughout the Cold War era, much U.S. assistance was given to support nondemocratic regimes around the world because they opposed communism. Often these regimes committed brutal human rights abuses.

Finally, the critics believed that U.S. support of Europe, especially with the development of the NATO and the MDAP, placed the United States on the side of colonialist powers. Although, as pointed out above, NATO itself was not directed toward the preservation of European colonial empires, the programs that followed, such as the MDAP and the Mutual Security Administration (which combined military and economic assistance to Western Europe), indirectly had that effect. By assisting the Western Europeans with military equipment to defend their territories from a potential Soviet attack, the United States enabled them to send weapons to maintain their colonial empires. The most obvious cases are that of the French in Indochina, the Dutch in Indonesia, and the Portuguese in Angola and Mozambique. Although these were not significant issues to the general public, and even Indochina became important only when the United States became involved in efforts to maintain an independent South Vietnam, they were discussed by the anticolonial critics of the Truman administration in the late 1940s and early 1950s. In 1948, the PWWC noted, concerning Vietnam, that "[d]ecent Americans are happy to aid France to recovery but do not want to give direct or indirect aid to French imperialism." They also charged that the "State Department . . . has aided Dutch imperialism by military equipment, loans to Holland and apparently by pressure in the UN."[23] Muste noted that the result of the war in Korea was an intensification of the battle in Indochina. Again, warning that one of the consequences of war was the spread of communism (and using terminology associated with the domino theory), Muste stated that "the fall of Indochina might well start a chain reaction that would spread to other nearby countries, areas remarkably rich in strategic supplies that we need and want to keep out of Russian hands." He felt that Indochina could have repercussions in other colonial territories, including North Africa. He saw the dangers of war then leading to a potential loss of France because of the strong Communist Party in that nation.[24] But always to Muste it was war itself that led to the spread of communism.

These anticolonial critics felt that programs such as Point Four, proposed by President Truman in 1949 to provide scientific and technical assistance to underdeveloped areas, should receive more funding. However, that did not occur because Congress was reluctant to spend money and the costs of the Korean War were too great.[25]

Although the critics may have been wrong about the dangers of war with the Soviet Union, it was the policy of containment and their willingness to support noncommunist regimes in the Third World that led the United States into wars in the Cold War era. The United States placed the colonial world into the bipolar struggles of the Cold War. Revolutionary change, peaceful or violent, anywhere in the Third World could represent gains for the Soviet Union and losses for the United States. Washington placed these issues into the context of the Cold War. However, critics such as Muste had noted that these changes had little to do with communism and in some ways had been unleashed by U.S. actions. There was little the United States could do to hold back the tide of anticolonialism. Viewing the whole world through the lens of the Cold War, the United States found itself deeply entangled in the Third World.

DEALING WITH AN "EVIL EMPIRE"

It is impossible to determine without a time machine whether the ideas of the pacifist and internationalist critics could have avoided the forty-five years of Cold War, or if they could have made the Cold War less severe. Certainly some of their ideas were feasible, especially those programs aimed at economic development. Would a greater emphasis on economic, instead of military, assistance have made the world more peaceful? That is impossible to answer. Certainly some conflicts would have been avoided. Would a less military-oriented foreign policy have brought the two rival powers together earlier? Could it have prevented the massive nuclear arms race of weapons that most agree were unusable because of their excessive destructive capacity? Certainly the ideas presented by critics of atomic weapons should have been given more consideration.

At the end of the World War II, the Truman administration quickly came to believe that it was impossible to get along with Stalinist Russia. Many historians, such as John Lewis Gaddis, argue that, though there were differences between Adolf Hitler's Germany and Stalin's Russia, it is quite difficult "to see how there could have been any long-term basis for coexistence" with either.[26]

One of the problems that faced the advocates of a peaceful approach to the Russians was the question of how to deal with Joseph Stalin's brutal dictatorship. How does one trust what was later called "an evil empire"?[27] In an attempt to answer that question, James Finucane of the NCPW noted that even if one accepted the argument that Russians were the devil incarnate, peace advocates such as himself still believed that "there is something of the divine spark in even the worst of humans." He noted that tradition had the devil as a fallen angel with many of the insights and graces of the heavenly variety. He also reminded his readers of the American legend of Daniel Webster and the devil, when Satan was argued out of the soul of a good New Hampshire farmer. All this was to point out that the devil cannot be shot or destroyed with an atomic bomb; instead, mankind had to learn to solve problems without resorting to war.[28]

Although Finucane's ideas were hypothetical and perhaps unrealistic, the most radical and far-reaching alternative proposal came from the pacifist A. J. Muste, who claimed to have a program that would stop communism without war. To begin with, he favored a domestic program that would create a democratic society which would fill others with a desire to be like the United States. Second, he advocated a foreign policy aimed at supporting "democratic tendencies and forces everywhere." Third, Muste called for a foreign policy that was imaginative and friendly, built on a cooperative economic program aimed at raising living standards and stabilizing economic life. To accomplish that, the FOR leader argued that the United States "would have to be willing to put [in] something like the money, effort and brains" it has put into war. Fourth, he indicated that such a program must include the readiness to join in universal disarmament and world government, and even setting an example by unilateral disarmament. Such a program would be aimed at the status quo, which was upheld by the United States. Muste wrote that the world was undergoing a revolution—economic, technological, social, political, and spiritual. This revolution was not launched by the communists. In fact, he noted the United States, with its technology and its gospel of human freedom and equality, "had a good deal to do with putting ideas into the heads of Asiatics and Africans." This was a revolution that neither the United States nor the Soviets could stop.[29]

Muste's answer to war was a spiritual one. He believed that if the American people had the courage and faith to launch the "true human revolution" by placing themselves in the service of mankind and practicing nonviolent resistance to aggression, the price would be high, but it would be an "utterly different historical deed than that of a nation which joined other nations in atomic suicide." In 1950, after the beginning of the Korean War, Muste issued a new series of proposals aimed at accomplishing his goals. First, the United States should support efforts to bring about a cessation of hostilities in Korea. Second, he urged that the UN cease to be a war agency because participation on one side in the war between great powers can only destroy the body. Third, he called on the United States to abandon its war method and replace it with a nonviolent program, "including racial equality at home and abroad, and a concentrated effort at raising the standard of living of the masses." Fourth, he believed that there should be a strenuous effort to spread pacifism. Fifth, he stated that individuals and groups who reject war should go patiently about "weaving strands of human fellowship."[30]

The FOR summed up much of the concern of the opposition and its hope for a different future. The group addressed the belief of most consensus supporters that Russian peace proposals were not genuine, pointing out that to ignore them was to turn one's back on peace and accept war as inevitable. Instead, such peace offensives should be confronted; if in fact they were phony, the only way to counter them was "with a genuine and all-out peace offensive." When the United States stopped spending all its money and labor on instruments of war, "we shall be forced to build a society of equals" that could give adequate help to lift the weight of poverty and ignorance "from the children of all peoples." Then the "[v]ast multitudes of . . . colored peoples of the earth will be our friends. . . . The multitudes of earth's needy will no longer be moved to envy or hostility against us or constitute an easy prey for totalitarian Communism."[31]

Henry Wallace noted the obvious in his testimony against the MDAP: the United States must live in the same world with the Soviet Union. He argued that there was not a single point on the globe where American interests conflicted with the Russians that could not be resolved "without long-range bombers and propaganda hand-outs." Summing up the points of the critics, he advocated working within the UN framework to meet the needs of the world for economic rehabilitation, and the demands of the colonial peoples for freedom and a rising standard of living. He felt that, as the strongest nation in the world, the United States should take a lead in such a program.[32] Those ideas certainly would have set an example for the world to follow.

THE IMPACT OF THE CRITICS

The critics of containment faced a difficult task. Their plans could have no impact without a wide audience, and the Truman administration was unwilling to listen. That became clear with the firing of Henry Wallace in 1946. Convinced by the administration of the dire threat of Soviet expansionism, Congress also was unwilling to give serious consideration to the critics. Those who were sympathetic were labeled isolationist or communist dupes and often lost elections, as in the case of Claude Pepper. The public was convinced of the Soviet threat and not only supported containment of the Soviet Union, but also became immersed in a culture that encouraged a domestic containment, and took on a variety of forms, including McCarthyism. This made it impossible for the critics to find supporters anywhere, and thus, they became marginal figures for over a decade.

Nonetheless, many of these same groups and individuals had a significant impact beyond the late 1940s and early 1950s. Critics of containment included African Americans and women who spoke out against these programs. They emerged as important postwar groups in foreign policy public opinion. African American critics, who focused on the issue of colonialism and connected it to domestic issues such as segregation, made a major contribution to the peace movement. Although their role remained small, black opposition to containment could not be completely overlooked at a time when the United States was trying to uphold its democratic image in the world. Although women had been active in the peace movement and in various social causes since the early 1800s, they played an increasingly prominent role in the 1930s and 1940s. The WILPF survived the years of marginalization to remain a significant activist force in the Vietnam War era.

Another impact of the opposition came with its influence on the revival of the peace movement in the mid 1950s. Charles DeBenedetti argues that the later peace movement emerged from these liberal internationalists and radical pacifist organizations, including the FOR and WRL.[33] Although their activism was limited in the early 1950s, the postwar critics of containment had formulated a coherent critique. Much of this was echoed by the later noncommunist left.[34] The support for the UN; opposition to the arms race, war, and militarization; assistance for economic development; and anticolonialism can be found in much of the New Left opposition to American society.

One of the leading documents of the New Left, the 1962 Port Huron Statement of Students for a Democratic Society (SDS), reflects many of the same concerns. In that founding document, the SDS decried the development of the military-industrial complex and the "general militarization of American society." The statement argued that "[w]ar can no longer be considered as an effective instrument of foreign policy" and that "the American military response has been more effective in deterring the growth of democracy than communism." The SDS called for a reconsideration of the "increasingly outmoded . . . North Atlantic Treaty Organization." In the colonial world, the SDS charged that the United States had sided with the old colonialists and that "[i]mmediate social and economic development is needed." Foreign aid, they stated, "should be given through international agencies, primarily the United Nations," and that would "enhance the importance of the United Nations itself."[35] Many similar examples can be found in the SDS statement. What is clear is that the ideas that were rejected in the late 1940s were finding new life in the early 1960s and came to have a significant impact in American society. The second time around these ideas contributed to a breakdown of the postwar consensus and the renewal of a foreign policy debate.

The Cold War intellectual and historical revisionists who emerged in the 1960s and were critical of the containment policy also reflected the ideas of the immediate postwar critics. Justus Doenecke noted that the arguments used by historians against aid to Greece and Turkey "strongly resembled the attacks made upon the Truman Doctrine" by the Cold War critics of the time. He noted that it was not surprising that these revisionists pointed to the Greek and Turkish examples as evidence that Washington had been involved in counterinsurgency since the beginning of the Cold War.[36] Doenecke also discussed the emergence in the 1960s of a group of writers, including Sen. William Fulbright and author Ronald Steel, whom he called "neoisolationists," and who called for the curtailment of U.S. overseas commitments. Like the old isolationists, they emphasized domestic priorities, opposed unrestricted presidential power, favored curbing military spending, and denied that the Soviets sought military conquest. He placed these in a category separate from the political New Left, noting that the New Left, rather than seeking U.S. isolation, sought the world's isolation from the United States.[37]

Professional historians also drew from the previous critics to argue that the United States could have done more to prevent the Cold War, but because Washington was interested in expansion itself and in building up U.S. power, no serious negotiations were ever attempted. Of particular importance was William A. Williams, who argued in *The Tragedy of American Diplomacy* (1959) that it was time to stop blaming the Soviet Union and other communist nations for all the evil in the world and for the United States to come to grips with its own internal dilemmas. However, Williams might be viewed as a bridge between the earlier and later critics. As early as 1952, in a critique of containment, Williams argued that freedom was not nurtured by states preparing for war. Instead, he wrote, it would find more opportunity to flower "in the atmosphere of mutual accommodation achieved and maintained through negotiated settlements."[38] Whether neoisolationist or not, certainly both the writers and the political New Left used arguments that had long simmered among the critics of containment.

CONCLUSION

With the emergence of a new generation of critics coming from the pacifist movement, the historical or intellectual professions, and the political left, consensus foreign policy came under renewed attack in the

1960s. The catalyst and the focus of this attack came to be the U.S. in-volvement in South Vietnam. This criticism did not just focus on the single issue of Vietnam, but came to question the value of a consensus foreign policy. With critics emerging prior to the escalation of U.S. in-volvement in Vietnam, it was not just the issue of the war that led to the collapse of consensus. Other factors included a growing vulnerability to Soviet nuclear missiles, the unacceptable costs of policing the world, de-colonization, and a growing economic competition with Europe and Ja-pan.[39]

Since the collapse of consensus, foreign policy decisions have faced greater public debate. In 1976, Secretary of State Henry Kissinger said that " 'the principal danger we face is our own domestic divisions.' "[40] Politicians and diplomats have struggled to develop a consensus policy. As Richard Falk has noted, however, bipartisanship as such was not the problem. The United States, instead of following a "conflict-oriented and expansionist" bipartisan policy, could have dedicated itself to the avoid-ance of a Cold War or to disentangling responses to Third World na-tionalism from the dynamics of East-West rivalries.[41] With the end of the Cold War, the way is open for the ideas that were buried by the early Cold War and that reemerged in the 1960s. Disarmament, a strong UN, and world economic development are just as relevant today as the world attempts to construct a post–Cold War order.

NOTES

1. Walter Lippmann, *US Foreign Policy: Shield of the Republic* (New York: Pocket Books, 1943), 1.

2. Committee for Peaceful Alternatives, "Statement of Policy," December 1950, CDG-A CPA, SCPC.

3. Richard Melanson, *Reconstructing Consensus: American Foreign Policy since the Vietnam War* (New York: St. Martin's Press, 1991), 3.

4. Barnet, *The Rockets' Red Glare*, 281.

5. Divine and Herman, "Internationalism as a Current in the Peace Move-ment: A Symposium," 180–81.

6. Godfrey Hodgson, "Disorder within, Disorder without," in Sanford J. Un-gar, ed., *Estrangement: America and the World* (New York: Oxford University Press, 1985), 140–41.

7. See Elaine Tyler May, *Homeward Bound: American Families in the Cold War Era* (New York: Basic Books, 1988).

8. Allan C. Carlson, "Foreign Policy, 'the American Way,' and the Passing of the Post-War Consensus," *This World* (spring/summer 1983): 19, 25. On the do-mestic impact of containment see also Alan Nadel, *Containment Culture: American Narratives, Postmodernism and the Atomic Age* (Durham, NC: Duke University Press, 1995).

9. Kaplan, *The United States and NATO*, 46.

10. McNeal, *Harder than War*, 73.

11. DeBenedetti, "The American Peace Movement and the National Security State, 1941–1971," 125.

12. Warburg, "The Atlantic Defense Pact and the Proposal to Rearm Western Europe," 10–11; James Warburg, CDG-A, SCPC.

13. Taylor, July 20, 1949, *Congressional Record*, 81st Cong., 1st sess., Vol. 95, pt. 7:9785.

14. "Draft Letter to Senators for Endorsement by Individuals," June 24, 1949, CPA, CDG-A, SCPC.

15. Muste Lecture #2, Pendle Hill Lectures, April 7, 1954, Muste papers, DG 50, Reel 89.3, SCPC.

16. Wilson and Grant, "Some Questions and Comments about the North Atlantic Treaty and the Accompanying Rearmament Program," April 25, 1949, FCNL, DG 47, Series H, Box 20, North Atlantic Pact file, SCPC; Wilson to Graham, July 7, 1949, FCNL, DG 47, Series H, Box 20, North Atlantic Pact file, SCPC. See also Wilson, *Uphill for Peace*, 248–49.

17. Robert W. Frase, "Memorandum on Russian-American Relations," February 2, 1949, AFSC, DG 2, Series II, Box 5, Literature: US–Russia 1949 file, SCPC.

18. Cadbury, May 11, 1949, *NAT* II: 760.

19. Libby, May 12, 1949, *NAT* III: 906.

20. Warburg, "The Atlantic Defense Pact and the Proposal to Rearm Western Europe," 8–9; Warburg, "Memorandum," March 22, 1949, Warburg Papers, Kennedy Library; Warburg, "Proposal for Modification," February 26, 1949, Warburg Papers, Box 13, Acheson file, Kennedy Library.

21. Wallace, May 5, 1949, *NAT* II: 432.

22. Stewart, May 13, 1949, *NAT* III: 937; Curry, May 12, 1949, *NAT* III: 835. On the Heifer Project, see Glee Yoder, *Passing on the Gift: The Story of Dan West* (Elgin, IL: Brethren Press, 1978), 100–124.

23. PWWC News Bulletin, February 1948, DG 62, PWWC, Reel 90.7, SCPC.

24. Muste, April 7, 1954, Pendle Hill Lectures.

25. LaFeber, *The American Age*, 519.

26. John Lewis Gaddis, "The Tragedy of Cold War History," *Diplomatic History* 17 (winter 1993): 10–11.

27. For a discussion of the concept of the evil empire, see ibid., 1–16.

28. James Finucane, "How to Deal with the Devil," *Peace Action*, April 1950, NCPW, DG 23, Box 487, Releases 1950 file, SCPC.

29. A. J. Muste, *A Pacifist Program—1949* (New York: Fellowship Publications, 1949).

30. A. J. Muste, "Korea: Spark to Set a World Afire?" 1950[?], FOR, copy in possession of the author. Also published in Nat Hentoff, ed., *The Essays of A. J. Muste*, 331–54.

31. "The Atlantic Pact Is a Suicide Pact," statement by the executive committee of the FOR, March 1949. A copy is in the possession of the author.

32. Wallace, August 19, 1949, *Military Assistance Program*, 191–92.

33. Charles DeBenedetti and Charles Chatfield, *An American Ordeal: The Antiwar Movement of the Vietnam Era* (Syracuse, NY: Syracuse University Press, 1990), 13, 21. For more on the impact of radical pacifists, see James Tracy, *Direct Action:*

Radical Pacifism from the Union Eight to the Chicago Seven (Chicago: University of Chicago Press, 1996).

34. Kleidman, *Organizing for Peace*, 26.

35. "The Port Huron Statement," in Miller, *"Democracy Is in the Streets,"* 340, 346, 348, 358, 360–61.

36. Doenecke, *Not to the Swift*, 78.

37. Ibid., 244–45.

38. Paul M. Buhle and Edward Rice-Maximin, *William Appleman Williams: The Tragedy of Empire* (New York: Routledge, 1995), 111; William A. Williams, *American Russian Relations 1781–1947* (New York: Rinehart and Co., 1952), 283. Also see William A. Williams, *The Tragedy of American Diplomacy* (New York: Delta Books, 1959).

39. Barnet, *Rockets' Red Glare*, 351; Falk, "Lifting the Curse of Bipartisanship," 129–30.

40. Kissinger quoted in McCormick, *America's Half-Century*, 181.

41. Falk, "Lifting the Curse of Bipartisanship," 129.

BIBLIOGRAPHY

ARCHIVAL SOURCES

Archives of the Mennonite Church, Goshen, IN

Mennonite Central Committee Peace Section

John F. Kennedy Library, Boston, MA

James Warburg Papers

Swarthmore College Peace Collection, Swarthmore College, Swarthmore, PA

American Friends Service Committee
American Women for Peace
Church of the Brethren
Committee for Peaceful Alternatives
Fellowship of Reconciliation
Friends Committee on National Legislation
Mennonite Central Committee
Methodist Commission on World Peace
A. J. Muste Papers
National Council for the Prevention of War

National Peace Conference
National Service Board for Religious Objectors
Post War World Council
John Nevin Sayer Papers
Norman Thomas Papers
War Resisters League
James Warburg Papers
Women's International League of Peace and Freedom, U.S. Section

Harry S. Truman Library, Independence, MO
Papers of Paul G. Hoffman

University of Iowa, Iowa City, IA
Papers of Henry A. Wallace

PUBLISHED DOCUMENTS

Congressional Record. 1945–1950. Washington, DC.
Gallup, George H. *The Gallup Poll: Public Opinion 1935–1971*, 2 vols. New York: Random House, 1972.
O'Sullivan, John, and Alan Mechler, eds. *The Draft and Its Enemies: A Documentary History.* Urbana: University of Illinois Press, 1974.
Public Papers of the Presidents of the United States: Harry S. Truman, 1948. Washington: GPO, 1964.
U.S. Congress. House. *Assistance to Greece and Turkey: Hearings before the Committee on Foreign Affairs.* 80th Cong., 1st sess., 1947. H.R. 2616.
———. *United States Foreign Policy for a Post-War Recovery Program, Hearings before the Committee on Foreign Affairs.* 80th Cong., 2nd sess., 1948.
U.S. Congress. Senate. *Assignment of Ground Forces of the United States to Duty in the European Area, Hearings before the Committee on Foreign Relations and Committee on Armed Services.* 82nd Cong., 1st sess., 1951.
———. *Assistance to Greece and Turkey: Hearings before the Committee on Foreign Relations.* 80th Cong., 1st sess., 1947. S. 938.
———. *The Charter of the United Nations, Hearings before the Committee on Foreign Relations.* 79th Cong., 1st sess., 1945.
———. *European Recovery Program, Hearings before the Committee on Foreign Relations.* 80th Cong., 2nd sess., 3 parts, 1948.
———. *Military Assistance Program: Joint Hearings before the Committee on Foreign Relations and the Committee on Armed Services.* 81st Cong., 1st sess., 1949.
———. *North Atlantic Treaty, Hearings before the Committee on Foreign Relations.* 81st Cong., 1st sess., 1949, 3 vols.
———. *Universal Military Training, Hearings before the Committee on Armed Services.* 80th Cong., 2nd sess., 1948.
U.S. Department of State. *Bulletin.* 1947.

———. *Foreign Relations of the United States*, 1947, Vol. III. Washington, DC: GPO, 1972.

———. *Foreign Relations of the United States*, 1948, Vol. III. Washington, DC: GPO, 1974.

———. *Foreign Relations of the United States*, 1950, Vol. I. Washington, DC: GPO, 1977.

MEMOIRS AND COLLECTED ESSAYS

Dellinger, David. *From Yale to Jail: The Life Story of a Moral Dissenter*. New York: Pantheon Books, 1993.

Hentoff, Nat, ed. *The Essays of A. J. Muste*. New York: Bobbs-Merrill Co., Inc., 1967.

Kennan, George F. *Memoirs, 1925–1950*. Boston: Little, Brown and Co., 1967.

Muste, A. J. *A Pacifist's Program—1949*. New York: Fellowship Publications, 1949.

Pepper, Claude D. (with Hays Gorey). *Pepper: Eyewitness to a Century*. New York: Harcourt Brace Jovanovich, 1987.

Truman, Harry S. *Memoirs*, vol. 2: *Years of Trial and Hope*. Garden City, NY: Doubleday and Co., 1955.

Uphaus, Willard. *Commitment*. New York: McGraw-Hill, 1963.

Vandenberg, Arthur H., Jr., ed. *The Private Papers of Senator Vandenberg*. Boston: Houghton Mifflin, Co., 1953.

Warburg, James P. *The Last Call for Common Sense*. New York: Harcourt, Brace and Co., 1949.

———. *The Long Road Home: The Autobiography of a Maverick*. New York: Doubleday and Co., 1964.

Wilson, E. Raymond. *Uphill for Peace: Quaker Impact on Congress*. Richmond, IN: Friend's United Press, 1975.

BOOKS

Adler, Selig. *The Isolationist Impulse: Its Twentieth-Century Reaction*. New York: Abelard-Schuman, 1957.

Alonso, Harriet Hyman. *Peace as a Women's Issue: A History of the U.S. Movement for World Peace and Women's Rights*. Syracuse, NY: Syracuse University Press, 1993.

Bacon, Margaret Hope. *One Woman's Passion for Peace and Freedom: The Life of Mildred Scott Olmsted*. Syracuse, NY: Syracuse University Press, 1993.

Barnet, Richard J. *The Rockets' Red Glare: When America Goes to War, the Presidents and the People*. New York: Simon and Schuster, 1990.

Borstelmann, Thomas. *Aparteid's Reluctant Uncle: The United States and Southern Africa in the Early Cold War*. New York: Oxford University Press, 1993.

Bowman, Rufus D. *The Church of the Brethren and War, 1708–1941*. Elgin, IL: Brethren Publishing House, 1944.

Boyer, Paul. *By the Bomb's Early Light: American Thought and Culture at the Dawn of the Atomic Age*. New York: Pantheon Books, 1985.

Buhle, Paul M. and Edward Rice-Maximin. *William Appleman Williams: The Tragedy of Empire*. New York: Routledge, 1995.

Chatfield, Charles. *The American Peace Movement: Ideals and Activism*. New York: Twayne Publishers, 1992.

———. *For Peace and Justice: Pacifism in America 1914–1941*. Boston: Beacon Press, 1971.

Chernow, Ron. *The Warburgs; The Twentieth-Century Odyssey of a Remarkable Jewish Family*. New York: Random House, 1993.

Crabb, Carl Van Meter, Jr. *Bipartisan Foreign Policy, Myth or Reality?* White Plains, NY: Row, Peterson and Co., 1957.

Cumings, Bruce. *The Origins of the Korean War*. Princeton, NJ: Princeton University Press, 1981.

DeBenedetti, Charles. *Peace Reform in American History*. Bloomington: Indiana University Press, 1980.

DeBenedetti, Charles and Charles Chatfield. *An American Ordeal: The Antiwar Movement in the Vietnam Era*. Syracuse, NY: Syracuse University Press, 1990.

Divine, Robert A. *Second Chance: The Triumph of Internationalism in America during World War II*. New York: Atheneum, 1967.

Doenecke, Justus D. *Not to the Swift: The Old Isolationists in the Cold War Era*. Lewisburg, PA: Bucknell University Press, 1979.

Ehrman, John. *The Rise of Neoconservatism: Intellectuals and Foreign Affairs 1945–1994*. New Haven, CT: Yale University Press, 1995.

Ekirch, Arthur A., Jr. *The Civilian and the Military*. New York: Oxford University Press, 1956.

———. *The Decline of American Liberalism*. New York: Atheneum, 1967.

Farrer, David. *The Warburgs: The Story of a Family*. New York: Stein and Day, 1974.

Flynn, George Q. *The Draft, 1940–1973*. Lawrence: University Press of Kansas, 1993.

Foot, Rosemary. *The Wrong War: American Policy and the Dimensions of the Korean Conflict*. Ithaca, NY: Cornell University Press, 1985.

Foster, Catherine. *Women for All Seasons: The Story of the Women's International League for Peace and Freedom*. Athens: University of Georgia Press, 1989.

Freeland, Richard M. *The Truman Doctrine and the Origins of McCarthyism: Foreign Policy, Domestic Politics, and Internal Security*. New York: Alfred A. Knopf, 1972.

Fried, Richard M. *Nightmare in Red: The McCarthy Era in Perspective*. New York: Oxford University Press, 1990.

Gaddis, John Lewis. *Strategies of Containment: A Critical Appraisal of Postwar National Security Policy*. New York: Oxford University Press, 1982.

Graebner, Norman. *The New Isolationism: A Study in Politics and Foreign Policy since 1950*. New York: Ronald Press, 1956.

Hamby, Alonzo L. *Beyond the New Deal: Harry S. Truman and American Liberalism*. New York: Columbia University Press, 1973.

Heald, Morrell and Lawrence Kaplan. *Culture and Diplomacy: The American Experience*. Westport, CT: Greenwood Press, 1977.

Heale, M. J. *American Anticommunism: Combating the Enemy Within, 1830–1970*. Baltimore, MD: Johns Hopkins University Press, 1990.

Hero, Alfred O., Jr. *American Religious Groups View Foreign Policy*. Durham, NC: Duke University Press, 1973.

Hershberger, Guy Franklin. *War, Peace, and Nonresistence*. Scottdale, PA: Herald Press, 1944.

Holsti, Ole R. and James N. Rosenau. *American Leadership in World Affairs: Vietnam and the Breakdown of Consensus*. Boston: Allen and Unwin, 1984.

Horne, Gerald. *Black and Red: W.E.B. Du Bois and the Afro-American Response to the Cold War, 1944–1963*. Albany: State University of New York Press, 1986.

Johnpoll, Bernard K. *Pacifist's Progress: Norman Thomas and the Decline of American Socialism*. Chicago: Quadrangle Books, 1970.

Jonas, Manfred. *Isolation in America 1935–1941*. Chicago: Imprint Publications, 1990.

Kaplan, Lawrence S. *A Community of Interests: NATO and the Military Assistance Program, 1948–1951*. Washington, DC: Historical Office, Office of the Secretary of Defense, 1980.

———. *NATO and the United States: The Enduring Alliance*. Boston: Twayne Publishers, 1988.

———. *The United States and NATO: The Formative Years*. Lexington: University of Kentucky Press, 1984.

Kleidman, Robert. *Organizing for Peace: Neutrality, the Test Ban, and the Freeze*. Syracuse, NY: Syracuse University Press, 1993.

Kuehl, Warren F. and Lynne K. Dunn. *Keeping the Covenant: American Internationalists and the League of Nations, 1920–1939*. Kent, OH: Kent State University Press, 1997.

LaFeber, Walter. *The American Age: United States Foreign Policy at Home and Abroad since 1750*. New York: W. W. Norton, 1989.

Levering, Ralph B. *The Public and American Foreign Policy, 1918–1978*. New York: William Morrow and Co., 1978.

Lifton, Robert Jay and Greg Mitchell. *Hiroshima in America: Fifty Years of Denial*. New York: G. P. Putnam, 1995.

Lippmann, Walter. *US Foreign Policy: Shield of the Republic*. New York: Pocket Books, 1943.

Lynch, Hollis R. *Black American Radicals and the Liberation of Africa: The Council on African Affairs, 1937–1955*. Ithaca, NY: Cornell University African Studies and Research Center, 1978.

MacDonald, Callum. *Korea: The War before Vietnam*. New York: Free Press, 1987.

Marabell, George Peter. *Frederick Libby and the American Peace Movement, 1921–1941*. New York: Arno Press, 1982.

May, Elaine Tyler. *Homeward Bound: American Families in the Cold War Era*. New York: Basic Books, 1988.

McAuliffe, Mary Sperling. *Crisis on the Left: Cold War Politics and American Liberals 1947–1954*. Amherst: University of Massachusetts Press, 1978.

McCormick, Thomas J. *America's Half-Century: United States Foreign Policy in the Cold War*. Baltimore: Johns Hopkins University Press, 1989.

McDougall, Walter A. *Promised Land, Crusader State: The American Encounter with the World since 1776*. New York: Houghton Mifflin Co., 1997.

McMahon, Robert J. *Colonialism and the Cold War: The United States and the Struggle for Indonesian Independence, 1945–1949.* Ithaca, NY: Cornell University Press, 1981.

McNeal, Patricia. *Harder than War: Catholic Peacemaking in Twentieth-Century America.* New Brunswick, NJ: Rutgers University Press, 1992.

Melanson, Richard. *Reconstructing Consensus: American Foreign Policy since the Vietnam War.* New York: St. Martin's Press, 1991.

Miller, James. *"Democracy Is in the Streets": From Port Huron to the Siege of Chicago.* New York: Touchstone, 1987.

Miller, William D. *A Harsh and Dreadful Love: Dorothy Day and the Catholic Worker Movement.* New York: Liveright, 1973.

Nadel, Alan. *Containment Culture: American Narratives, Postmodernism, and the Atomic Age.* Durham, NC: Duke University Press, 1995.

Nathan, James and James Oliver. *The United States Foreign Policy and World Order.* Boston: Little, Brown and Co., 1976–81.

Noer, Thomas J. *Cold War and Black Liberation: The United States and White Rule in Africa, 1948–1968.* Columbia: University of Missouri Press, 1985.

Paterson, Thomas G. *Meeting the Communist Threat: Truman to Reagan.* New York: Oxford University Press, 1984.

———. *On Every Front: The Making of the Cold War.* New York: W. W. Norton, 1979.

———. *Soviet-American Confrontation: Postwar Reconstruction and the Origins of the Cold War.* Baltimore, MD: Johns Hopkins University Press, 1973.

Peterson, F. Ross. *Prophet without Honor: Glen H. Taylor and the Fight for American Liberalism.* Lexington: University of Kentucky Press, 1974.

Plummer, Brenda Gayle. *Rising Wind: Black Americans and U.S. Foreign Affairs, 1935–1960.* Chapel Hill: University of North Carolina Press, 1996.

Radosh, Ronald. *Prophets on the Right: Profiles of Conservative Critics of American Globalism.* New York: Simon and Schuster, 1975.

Roberts, Nancy L. *Dorothy Day and the Catholic Worker.* Albany: State University of New York Press, 1984.

Robinson, Jo Ann. *Abraham Went Out: A Biography of A. J. Muste.* Philadelphia: Temple University Press, 1981.

Sherry, Michael S. *In the Shadow of War: The United States since the 1930s.* New Haven, CT: Yale University Press, 1995.

Smith, E. Timothy. *The United States, Italy and NATO, 1947–52.* New York: St. Martin's Press, 1991.

Stromberg, Roland N. *Collective Security and American Foreign Policy: From the League of Nations to NATO.* New York: Frederick A. Praeger, 1963.

Swanberg, W. A. *Norman Thomas: The Last Idealist.* New York: Charles Schribner's Sons, 1976.

Swomley, John M., Jr. *American Empire: The Political Ethics of Twentieth Century Conquest.* New York: Macmillan, 1970.

Tracy, James. *Direct Action: Radical Pacifism from the Union Eight to the Chicago Seven.* Chicago: University of Chicago Press, 1996.

Walker, J. Samuel, Jr. *Henry A. Wallace and American Foreign Policy.* Contributions in American History, no. 50. Westport, CT: Greenwood Press, 1976.

White, Graham and John Maze. *Henry A. Wallace: His Search for a New World Order*. Chapel Hill: University of North Carolina Press, 1995.

Williams, Phil. *The Senate and US Troops in Europe*. New York: St. Martin's Press, 1985.

Williams, William A. *American Russian Relations 1781–1947*. New York: Rinehart and Co., 1952.

———. *The Tragedy of American Diplomacy*. New York: Delta Books, 1959.

Wittner, Lawrence S. *American Intervention in Greece 1943–1949*. New York: Columbia University Press, 1982.

———. *One World or None: A History of the World Nuclear Disarmament Movement Through 1953*, vol. 1: *The Struggle against the Bomb*. Palo Alto, CA: Stanford University Press, 1993.

———. *Rebels against War: The American Peace Movement, 1941–1960*. New York: Columbia University Press, 1969.

Wooley, Wesley T. *Alternatives to Anarchy: American Supranationalism since World War II*. Bloomington: Indiana University Press, 1988.

Yarnell, Allen. *Democrats and Progressives: The 1948 Presidential Election as a Test of Postwar Liberalism*. Berkeley: University of California Press, 1974.

Yergin, Daniel. *Shattered Peace: The Origins of the Cold War and the National Security State*, Sentry edition. Boston: Houghton Mifflin Co., 1977.

Yoder, Glee. *Passing the Gift: The Story of Dan West*. Elgin, IL: Brethren Press, 1978.

ARTICLES AND CHAPTERS IN COLLECTED WORKS

Accinelli, Robert D. "Militant Internationalists: The League of National Association, the Peace Movement, and U.S. Foreign Policy, 1934–38." *Diplomatic History* 4 (winter 1980): 19–38.

———. "Pro-U.N. Internationalists and the Early Cold War: The American Association for the United Nations and U.S. Foreign Policy, 1947–52." *Diplomatic History* 9 (fall 1985): 347–62.

Alonso, Harriet Hyman. "Mayhem and Moderation: Women Peace Activists during the McCarthy Era." In *Not June Cleaver: Women and Gender in Postwar America, 1945–1960*. Edited by Joanne Meyerowitz, 128–50. Philadelphia: Temple University Press, 1994.

Anderson, Carol. "From Hope to Disillusion: African Americans, the United Natons, and the Struggle for Human Rights, 1944–1947." *Diplomatic History* 20 (fall 1996): 531–63.

"Annual Conference Resolution on Peace (1948)." *Messenger* 140 (March 1991).

Berger, Henry W. "Senator Robert A. Taft Dissents from Military Escalation." In *Cold War Critics: Alternatives to American Foreign Policy in the Truman Years*. Edited by Thomas G. Paterson, 167–204. Chicago: Quadrangle Books, 1971.

Berman, William C. "James Paul Warburg: An Establishment Maverick Challenges Truman's Policy Toward Germany." In *Cold War Critics: Alternatives to American Foreign Policy in the Truman Years*. Edited by Thomas G. Paterson, 54–75. Chicago: Quadrangle Books, 1971.

Bernstein, Barton J. "Review Essay: 'Henry A. Wallace and the Agony of American Liberalism: A Political Pariah in the Cold War.' " *Peace and Change* 2 (fall 1974): 62–67.

————. "Walter Lippmann and the Early Cold War." In *Cold War Critics: Alternatives to American Foreign Policy in the Truman Years*. Edited by Thomas G. Paterson, 18–53. Chicago: Quadrangle Books, 1971.

Bills, Scott L. "The United States, NATO and the Colonial World." In *NATO after Thirty Years*. Edited by Lawrence S. Kaplan and Robert W. Clawson, 149–64. Wilmington, DE: Scholarly Resources, 1981.

————. "The United States, NATO, and the Third World: Dominoes, Imbroglios, and Agonizing Appraisals." In *NATO after Forty Years*. Edited by Lawrence S. Kaplan, S. Victor Papacosma, Mark R. Rubin, and Ruth V. Young, 149–77. Wilmington, DE: Scholarly Resources, 1990.

Campbell, Thomas M., Jr. "NATO and the United Nations in American Foreign Policy: Building a Framework for Power." In *NATO after Thirty Years*. Edited by Lawrence S. Kaplan and Robert W. Clawson, 133–48. Wilmington, DE: Scholarly Resources, 1981.

Carlson, Allan C. "Foreign Policy, 'the American Way,' and the Passing of the Post-War Consensus." *This World* 1983 (spring/summer): 18–54.

Carpenter, Ted Galen. "United States NATO Policy at the Crossroads: The 'Great Debate' of 1950–1951." *International History Review* 8 (August 1986): 389–415.

Chatfield, Charles. "Norman Thomas: Harmony of Word and Deed." In *Peace Heroes in Twentieth-Century America*. Edited by Charles DeBenedetti, 85–121. Bloomington: Indiana University Press, 1986.

Dallek, Robert. "The Postwar World: Made in the USA." In *Estrangement: America and the World*. Edited by Sanford J. Unger, 27–49. New York: Oxford University Press, 1985.

DeBenedetti, Charles. "American Peace Activism, 1945–1985." In *Peace Movements and Political Cultures*. Edited by Charles Chatfield and Peter van den Dugen, 222–29. Knoxville: University of Tennessee Press, 1988.

————. "The American Peace Movement and the National Security State, 1941–1971." *World Affairs* 141, no. 2 (1978): 118–29.

————. "Introduction." In *Peace Heroes in Twentieth-Century America*. Edited by Charles DeBenedetti, 1–27. Bloomington: Indiana University Press, 1986.

DeConde, Alexander. "On Twentieth-Century Isolationism." In *Isolation and Security: Ideas and Interests in Twentieth-Century American Forign Policy*. Edited by Alexander DeConde, 3–32. Durham, NC: Duke University Press, 1957.

Divine, Robert and Sandra Herman. "Internationalism as a Current in the Peace Movement: A Symposium." In *Peace Movements in America*. Edited by Charles Chatfield, 171–91. New York: Schocken Books, 1973.

Doenecke, Justus D. "The Strange Career of American Isolationism, 1944–1954." *Peace and Change* 3 (summer/fall 1975): 79–83.

Falk, Richard. "Lifting the Curse of Bipartisanship." *World Policy Journal* 1 (winter 1986): 127–57.

Gaddis, John Lewis. "The Tragedy of Cold War History." *Diplomatic History* 17 (winter 1993): 1–16.

Good, Robert C. "The United States and the Colonial Debate." In *Alliance Policy in the Cold War*. Edited by Arnold Wolfers, 224–70. Baltimore, MD: Johns Hopkins University Press, 1959.

Hamby, Alonzo L. "Henry A. Wallace, the Liberals, and Soviet-American Relations." *Review of Politics* 30 (April 1968): 153–69.

Henrikson, Alan K. "The North Atlantic Alliance as a Form of World Order." In *Negotiating World Order: The Artisanship and Architecture of Global Diplomacy*. Edited by Alan K. Henrikson, 111–35. Wilmington, DE: Scholarly Resources, 1986.

Hero, Alfred O., Jr. "American Negroes and U.S. Foreign Policy: 1937–1967." *Journal of Conflict Resolution* 13, no. 2 (1969): 220–51.

Hodgson, Godfrey. "Disorder within, Disorder without." In *Estrangement: America and the World*. Edited by Sanford Unger, 129–55. New York: Oxford University Press, 1985.

Ingle, H. Larry. "The American Friends Service Committee, 1947–1949: The Cold War's Effect." *Peace and Change* 23 (January 1998): 27–48.

Josephson, Harold. "The Search for Lasting Peace: Internationalism and American Foreign Policy, 1920–1950." In *Peace Movements and Political Cultures*. Edited by Charles Chatfield and Peter van den Dugen, 204–11. Knoxville: University of Tennessee Press, 1988.

Kaner, Norman. "I. F. Stone and the Korean War." In *Cold War Critics: Alternatives to American Foreign Policy in the Truman Years*. Edited by Thomas G. Paterson, 240–65. Chicago: Quadrangle Books, 1971.

Kaplan, Lawrence S. "After Forty Years: Reflections on NATO as a Research Field." In *NATO: The Founding of the Atlantic Alliance and the Integration of Europe*. Edited by Francis H. Heller and John R. Gillingham, 15–23. New York: St. Martin's Press, 1992.

———. "Collective Security and the Case of NATO." In *The Origins of NATO*, Exeter Studies in History, no. 28. Edited by Joseph Smith, 95–109. Exeter, UK: University of Exeter Press, 1990.

Kepley, David R. "The Senate and the Great Debate of 1951." *Prologue* 14 (winter 1982): 213–26.

Kuehl, Warren F. "Concepts of Internationalism in History." *Peace and Change* 11, no. 2 (1986): 1–10.

———. "Internationalism." In *Encyclopedia of American Foreign Policy*. Edited by Alexander DeConde, II:443–54. New York: Charles Scribner's Sons, 1978.

Laville, Helen and Scott Lucas. "The American Way: Edith Sampson, the NAACP, and African American Identity in the Cold War." *Diplomatic History* 20 (fall 1996): 565–90.

Lieberman, Robbie. " 'Does That Make Peace a Bad Word?': American Responses to the Communist Peace Offensive, 1949–1950." *Peace and Change* 17 (April 1992): 198–228.

Louis, William Roger and Ronald Robinson. "The United States and the Liquidation of the British Empire in Tropical Africa, 1941–1951." In *The Transfer of Power in Africa: Decolonization 1940–1960*. Edited by Prosser Gifford and William Roger Louis, 31–55. New Haven, CT: Yale University Press, 1982.

Morley, Margaret. "Freda Kirchwey: Cold War Critic." In *Redefining the Past: Essays in Diplomatic History in Honor of William Appleman Williams*. Edited by Lloyd C. Gardner, 157–68. Corvalles: Oregon State University Press, 1986.

Paterson, Thomas G. "The Dissent of Senator Claude Pepper." In *Cold War Critics: Alternatives to American Foreign Policy in the Truman Years*. Edited by Thomas G. Paterson, 114–39. Chicago: Quadrangle Books, 1971.

———. "Introduction: American Critics of the Cold War and Their Alternatives." In *Cold War Critics: Alternatives to American Foreign Policy in the Truman Years*. Edited by Thomas G. Paterson, 3–17. Chicago: Quadrangle Books, 1971.

Peterson, F. Ross. "Fighting the Drive toward War: Glen H. Taylor, the 1948 Progressives, and the Draft." *Pacific Northwest Quarterly* (January 1970): 41–45.

Pollard, Robert A. "Economic Security and the Origins of the Cold War; Bretton Woods, the Marshall Plan, and American Rearmament, 1944–50." *Diplomatic History* 9 (summer 1985): 271–89.

Pratt, William C. "Senator Glen H. Taylor: Questioning American Unilateralism." In *Cold War Critics: Alternatives to American Foreign Policy in the Truman Years*. Edited by Thomas G. Paterson, 140–66. Chicago: Quadrangle Books, 1971.

Radosh, Ronald and Leonard P. Liggio. "Henry A. Wallace and the Open Door." In *Cold War Critics: Alternatives to American Foreign Policy in the Truman Years*. Edited by Thomas G. Paterson, 76–113. Chicago: Quadrangle Books, 1971.

Roark, James L. "American Black Leaders: The Response to Colonialism and the Cold War." *African Historical Studies* 4 (1971): 253–70.

Robinson, Jo Ann. "A. J. Muste: Prophet in the Wilderness of the of the Modern World." In *Peace Heroes in Twentieth-Century America*. Edited by Charles DeBenedetti, 145–67. Bloomington: Indiana University Press, 1986.

Smith, E. Timothy. "Beyond the Water's Edge." In *The Romance of History: Essays in Honor of Lawrence S. Kaplan*. Edited by Scott L. Bills and E. Timothy Smith. Kent, OH: Kent State University Press, 1997.

Soloman, Mark. "Black Critics of Colonialism and the Cold War." In *Cold War Critics: Alternatives to American Foreign Policy in the Truman Years*. Edited by Thomas G. Paterson, 205–39. Chicago: Quadrangle Books, 1971.

Thompson, Kenneth W. "Isolation and Collective Security: The Uses and Limits of Two Theories of International Relations." In *Isolation and Security: Ideas and Interests in Twentieth-Century American Foreign Policy*. Edited by Alexander DeConde, 159–83. Durham, NC: Duke University Press, 1957.

Von Eschen, Penny M. "Challenging Cold War Habits: African Americans, Race, and Foreign Policy." *Diplomatic History* 20 (fall 1996): 627–38.

Yoder, John Howard. "The Unique Role of the Historic Peace Churches." *Brethren Life and Thought* 14 (summer 1969): 132–49.

NEWSPAPERS AND MAGAZINES

Christian Century, 1947–49.
New York Times, 1946.

DISSERTATIONS

Bryniarski, Joan Lee. "Against the Tide: Senate Opposition to the Internationalist Foreign Policy of Presidents Franklin D. Roosevelt and Harry S. Truman, 1943–1949." Ph.D. diss., University of Maryland, 1972.

Carpenter, Ted Galen. "The Dissenters: American Isolationists and Foreign Policy, 1945–1954." Ph.D. diss., University of Texas at Austin, 1980.

Gill, Gerald Robert. "Afro-American Opposition to the United States' Wars of the Twentieth Century: Dissent, Discontent and Disinterest." Ph.D. diss., Howard University, 1985.

Goldman, Steven Charles. "The Conservative Critique of Containment: An Isolationist Alternative to Cold War Diplomacy." Ph.D. diss., Johns Hopkins University, 1974.

Gordon, Morton. "American Opposition to ERP and the North Atlantic Treaty: A Study of Anti-Administration Opinion." Ph.D. diss., University of Chicago, 1953.

Mantell, Matthew Edwin. "Opposition to the Korean War: A Study in American Dissent." Ph.D. diss., New York University, 1973.

INDEX

About the Author

E. TIMOTHY SMITH is Professor of History and Chair of the Department of History and Political Science at Barry University in Miami, Florida. In addition to writing numerous articles and book reviews, he is the author of *The United States, Italy and NATO, 1947–1952* (1991) and the co-editor of *The Romance of History: Essays in Honor of Lawrence S. Kaplan* (1997).

ISBN 0-313-30777-6

HARDCOVER BAR CODE